The Journalist
in Plato's Cave

The Journalist
in Plato's Cave

Jay Newman

Rutherford • Madison • Teaneck
Fairleigh Dickinson University Press
London and Toronto: Associated University Presses

Associated University Presses
440 Forsgate Drive
Cranbury, NJ 08512

Associated University Presses
25 Sicilian Avenue
London WC1A 2QH, England

Associated University Presses
P.O. Box 488, Port Credit
Mississauga, Ontario
Canada L5G 4M2

The paper used in this publication meets the requirements
of the American National Standard for Permanence of Paper
for Printed Library Materials Z39.48-1984.

Library of Congress Cataloging-in-Publication Data

Newman, Jay, 1948–
    The journalist in Plato's cave/Jay Newman.
        p.   cm.
    Bibliography: p.
    Includes index.
    ISBN 0-8386-3349-8 (alk. paper)
    1. Journalism—Philosophy. 2. Journalism—Objectivity.
3. Freedom of the press. 4. Press—United States—Evaluation.
5. Journalism—United States—Social aspects. I. Title.
PN4731.N46   1989
070'.01—dc 19   88-48022
                                                            CIP

PRINTED IN THE UNITED STATES OF AMERICA

To my mother, Kate Newman

Contents

Acknowledgments

I am grateful to the following publishers for permitting me to quote from copyrighted material: Oxford University Press, for material from the *Oxford English Dictionary* (1933); Princeton University Press, for a lengthy extract from José Ortega y Gasset, *Mission of the University*, trans. with an introduction by Howard Lee Nostrand. Copyright 1944, © 1972 renewed by Princeton University Press. Reprinted by permission of Princeton University Press; Macmillan Publishing Company, for excerpts from *Public Opinion* by Walter Lippmann. Copyright © 1922 by Walter Lippmann, renewed 1950 by Walter Lippmann; and Facts on File, Inc., for material from *Media Controversies*, edited by Lester A. Sobel. © 1981. Reprinted with permission of Facts on File, Inc., New York. Excerpts from *Walter Lippmann and His Times*, edited by Marquis Childs and James Reston, copyright © 1959 by Marquis Childs and James Reston, copyright renewed © 1987 by Marquis Childs and James Reston, are reprinted by permission of Brandt & Brandt Literary Agents, Inc. Chapter 4 incorporates a revised version of part of my article, "Some Reservations About Multiperspectival News," which appeared in *(International Journal of) Applied Philosophy* 1, no. 2 (Fall 1982); and I thank the editor of the journal for allowing me to make use of the material here.

I have received considerable encouragement and support from my parents, Kate and Louis Newman, my teacher, Elmer Sprague, and many of my students at the University of Guelph; and I have profited greatly from numerous conversations with my academic colleagues, Jakob Amstutz, Brian Calvert, Michael Ruse, and T. C. Williams. Finally, I am grateful to Harry Keyishian of Fairleigh Dickinson University Press, and to Julien Yoseloff, Lauren Lepow, and Nancy Kennedy of Associated University Presses, for their generous attention to the manuscript and their kindness to the author.

The Journalist
in Plato's Cave

1

Journalist and Philosopher on the Ship of State

When one reflects on the profound influence that journalism—or its absence—normally has on a given society and its members, the global community, future societies, and our perceptions of past societies, then the traditional paucity of philosophical studies of journalism might strike one as anomalous. In his famous 1922 study, *Public Opinion*, Walter Lippmann noted that it was curious that the study of the periodical press and of the sources of public information had not yet found a firm place in the social sciences: "To anyone not immersed in the routine interests of political science, it is almost inexplicable that no American student of government, no American sociologist, has ever written a book on news-gathering."[1] When Lippmann wrote these lines, he was impressed by what he took to be the great potential of social scientists to contribute to the improvement of journalism; and not long after he wrote them came a deluge of social-scientific studies of journalism that has continued unabated to this day. One thing the young Lippmann admired about social-scientific experts was what he saw as their capacity for a neutral, disinterested organization of intelligence. Whatever his later view of social scientists came to be, an older and sager Lippmann came to develop a renewed respect for the discipline that had most excited him in his student years, philosophy. Having been a witness to the Great Depression, World War II, the Holocaust, and the Cold War, a mature Lippmann was moved to speak out about the need for a "public philosophy" that would save his society from the effects of a rising tide of subjectivism and would enable it to make vital contact with the lost traditions of civility.[2] When he spoke in this way, this man who had been intellectually nursed, as an undergraduate at Harvard, with the wisdom of William James and George Santayana, must have been moved to contemplate the curious fact that unlike social scientists, philos-

13

ophers, for all their political concerns, never quite got around to making journalism a subject of sustained investigation.

But perhaps the philosophers' neglect of journalism is not as mysterious as it might initially appear. Consider an argument along the following lines: Philosophy, as its etymology tells us, is the love of wisdom, a passionate pursuit of that knowledge which is most fundamental and most important. Such knowledge inevitably involves contemplation and understanding of what is very abstract. The philosopher seeks to behold those realities that pure thought alone can apprehend;[3] thus, the moral philosopher is concerned with goodness, the metaphysician with reality, the epistemologist with knowledge and truth, the logician with rationality, the aesthetician with beauty, and so forth. Even the political philosopher, for all his practical concerns, is essentially a student of principles, the principles of social justice. But journalism as a subject matter cannot possibly be abstract in this way. Journalism is a concrete phenomenon that needs to be approached empirically, through the methods of the social sciences. And though the practice of journalism sometimes leads us to reflect on certain broad ethical and epistemological issues, journalism is nothing unique in this regard. Philosophical principles are relevant at some time or other to everything under the sun (and beyond), and certainly to all human practices, however mundane. If one so chooses, one can philosophize about journalism or cooking or stamp collecting. But such philosophizing represents a departure from the main path of philosophical thinking, which is primarily a pursuit of knowledge of the highest things.

Despite any plausibility it might initially seem to have, such an argument presumes too much. Philosophers have long regarded as one of their main responsibilities the explanation of the essential nature of the various forms of human experience. Even the most abstruse and otherworldly of metaphysical thinkers would not begrudge his fellow inquirers their right to characterize as philosophy their studies of the foundations of science, religion, history, and art. Moreover, in recent years an extensive body of literature has appeared in such areas as philosophy of law, philosophy of medicine, philosophy of education, philosophy of sport, and professional ethics; philosophers have been increasingly mindful of their obligation to shed light on practices or disciplines that are rather more central to social life than stamp collecting.

Of greater importance is the fact that as far back as the age of the Sophists and Socrates, the great philosophers have always been concerned with concretely practical matters, and particularly with concrete social and political problems. To neglect this historical fact is not only to accept a crude caricature of their enterprise but also to misunderstand the significance of even some of their most recondite metaphysical speculations. The Sophists are remembered today mainly for their radical relativism and their rhetorical trickery, but they were perhaps above all else political thinkers. Some of them, such as the great Protagoras, were heavily involved in political activity. Socrates preferred his private station to that of the statesman, but all available evidence suggests that his behavior in public was motivated largely by a desire to promote social reform. Plato is often represented as an aloof intellectual who retreated to the ivory tower of the Academy in order to contemplate timeless, transcendent essences, but some of his major works abound with detailed theories and recommendations about military, medical, economic, and even domestic matters. At the end of the *Nicomachean Ethics*, Aristotle identifies as the best life for a human being that of the contemplation of divine things, but he explicitly characterizes this book as a preface to his *Politics*, a work filled with detailed empirical political studies. Hobbes, Locke, Rousseau, Hegel, Mill, Marx, Sartre—how can we understand the metaphysical and epistemological ideas of such thinkers if we artificially divorce them from the political context in which their proponents more or less consciously embedded them? Consider finally the case of poor, misunderstood Spinoza. Spinoza is customarily portrayed in university courses as a semimystical recluse, the purveyor of a strange and opaque metaphysical system. Yet the real Spinoza was a brilliant social critic and a defender and promoter of liberty and of effective, responsible government.

In the course of their teaching, most of the great philosophers periodically touched upon subjects as concrete, as practical, and as prosaic as the subject of journalism. And yet, journalism as such rarely received direct attention from those among them who were familiar with it, and the tradition of neglecting journalism has been carried on by most of their contemporary successors.

A fruitful approach to this anomaly would be one that drew attention to the various indirect ways in which philosophers have provided us with insights relevant to an understanding of journalism. If successful, such an approach would to some extent free philosophers from the burden of appearing totally irresponsible in their lack of concern with an important social institution. Philosophers indeed have traditionally had much to say about certain matters relevant to journalism: the formation of public opinion, socialization, freedom of expression, and the aims of education, for example. Journalism as we now conceive it is a relatively modern phenomenon—we can hardly fault a Plato or an Aquinas for having failed to discuss forms of communication that did not exist in his age. But it does not take much imagination to realize that much of what Plato says about poets and sophists applies, by extension, to modern journalists, or that Spinoza's defense of freedom of speech is to some extent applicable to a modern understanding of the value of journalistic freedom.

One should also remember that newspapers and other public journals did not achieve anything approaching the influence they have today until after social philosophy had come to be seen by the general public as largely supplanted as a mode of intellectual inquiry by less abstract and more positive social and behavioral sciences. This historical fact alone, however, does not wholly explain the willingness of contemporary philosophers to leave exclusively to social scientists the task of providing society with authoritative explanations of the phenomenon of journalism. Unlike their predecessors, recent generations of philosophers have been in a position to reflect directly upon journalism and its influence; even without a historical tradition of philosophy of journalism on which to draw, they ought to have been mindful of the indirect relevance to journalism of certain traditional philosophical issues as well as of the historic capacity of philosophy to extend itself into new areas of inquiry and to keep up with the times. Now, more than ever, philosophers have been attempting to convince an often skeptical world that they still have much to offer in the way of fresh, relevant humanistic insight. Yet, a substantial body of philosophical literature on something as important as journalism has not even begun to emerge.

Here it is useful to note that despite their profession that theirs is the most synoptic, comprehensive, and integrative of intellectual disciplines, philosophers have allowed the content of philosophical discussion to be shaped largely by the whims of an academic elite. Their willingness to acquiesce in this regard has imparted to philosophy a faddishness not unlike that which one encounters in the fine arts—or in journalism. Philosophers are fond of referring to the "eternal questions," but they are all too often swept along with the latest ideological craze or methodological fashion, while topics of philosophical discussion pass in and out of favor. In our own age, we often hear intelligent general readers complain, and rightly so, that philosophy has come to be dominated by overspecialized academics who take unwarranted pride in the narrowness of their philosophical interests. Philosophers may only get around to taking journalism seriously as a subject for philosophical investigation when highly visible academics at the universities of Cambridge, Paris, and Chicago let them know that the time has finally come for them to do so. But by focusing their attention on a small number of relatively narrow issues and neglecting subjects like journalism, philosophers indicate to the intelligent general reader that they are not completely sincere when they profess to be able to offer their fellow citizens fresh, relevant humanistic insight.

The apparent anomaly of the philosophers' neglect of journalism can be approached from a wholly different perspective, one that concentrates on the philosophers' disdain for journalism. Philosophers, of course, are not the only people in our society who have grave doubts about the competence and integrity of leading journalists. The butcher and the baker complain just as often as philosophers do about journalists, perhaps even more often. But there is a difference in the character of their disdain. The ordinary person's criticism of journalists is generally diffuse, often unreasoned, and largely a function of his disagreement with the content of a particular journal. Hence, his attitude toward journalism is rather more ambivalent than the philosopher's. Although he overstates the point, Robert R. McCormick is perceptive when he observes that, "Individually, most people rail at the newspapers of today. Collectively, they will not tolerate any other kind."[4] But perhaps the philosopher's disdain for journalism is, as it ought to be, properly philosophical, and determined mainly by a conception of the journalistic enterprise as a whole. The philosopher may read newspapers and other public journals, may enjoy them, and may learn from them, but he can hardly avoid being uncomfortable with the recognition that unlike the physician, pilot, soldier, or carpenter, the journalist is one of the philosopher's greatest rivals.

The journalist has much in common with the philosopher, and on first reflection, one might suspect that this commonality would incline the philosopher favorably toward the journalistic enterprise. Philosopher and journalist are both inquirers, both do research and seek knowledge, and both interpret data and impart information. Leading journalists, like philosophers, advance positions on ethical and political issues and seek to participate in the shaping of public opinion. And, like philosophers, reflective journalists are ever mindful of the important role that they play in what is essentially a civilizing process. But it is, in fact, partly because the journalist has so much in common that the philosopher inevitably comes to perceive the journalist as a rival. The philosopher of our day recognizes that the journalist, like the poet and sophist of Plato's day, can all too easily be taken by the public to be the most authoritative of society's secular sages, and journalists are often all too willing to be viewed in this way. But the journalist is not, as such, a philosopher, and the philosopher may thus see the journalist as a usurper and interloper who has drawn away some of the attention that ought to be directed instead to the truly wise. A noted journalism professor, John Hohenberg, has written that, "If the nineteenth century was the era of the novelist who dominated mankind's literary horizon, then surely the twentieth century belongs to the journalist. . . . The journalist—when he is bold and unafraid—speaks for man."[5] Even the philosopher's traditional rival, the creative writer, now has trouble competing with the journalist. For the philosopher himself, as neglected as ever, there is simply no contest. No wonder then that, reading the columns of journalists whose casual opinions reach an audience of thousands or millions, the philosopher is sometimes filled with a *ressentiment* that leads to disdain.

This disdain is heightened by the philosopher's awareness of the journalist's customary lack of interest in what the philosopher has to offer. For every Lippmann who takes philosophy seriously, there are a hundred journalists who could not care less about the insights of classical or contemporary philosophers. The contemporary philosopher is, to be sure, partly responsible for this state of affairs; if he would talk directly about journalism, more journalists would lend him an ear. But the philosopher will rightly argue that journalists have generally shown little interest in philosophical discussions of subjects that ought to concern journalists—ethical, political, educational, subjects, amongst others—and that even if recent philosophy has been somewhat sterile and overspecialized, journalists have not shown a compensatory interest in the rich insights of the classical philosophers.

The journalists' lack of interest in philosophy manifests itself on at least three levels. Journalism professor John C. Merrill has lamented that journalism may be more than aphilosophical, and may actually be antiphilosophical: "Philosophy is widely viewed as irrelevant, a kind of pastime for ivory-tower dwellers, of little value to the hard and real world of journalism."[6] Merrill regrets this view, since he believes that philosophizing can help journalists in their work by giving them a better understanding of the essential nature of the journalistic enterprise. However, journalists have been said to operate on the bases of conventions of their trade and of trial and error.[7] The leading historian of American journalism, Frank Luther Mott, also has observed that, "The great danger in such a process is that there should be too little sound and philosophical thinking about the aims and responsibilities of journalism by the men who are making it. The reporter has too often taken over from his teachers in the newsroom the idea that certain elements of interest . . . form an informal code—the unwritten but accepted rules of the 'newspaper game,' without much thinking or much wise guidance."[8]

Journalists are understandably sensitive to philosophical criticisms of their work. A good example of this sensitivity can be found in the hostile reaction of the larger part of the American periodical press to the 1947 report of the Hutchins Commission on the responsibilities of a free press. The report was distinguished by a significant amount of philosophical content—as several members of the commission were intellectuals with a philosophical inclination—and the philosophical aspect of the document was a convenient target of ridicule for journalists and editors resentful of the report's criticisms. Thus, as Margaret A. Blanchard has observed, while a significant number of editors saw much value in the report's philosophical framework for journalistic reform, critics of the report often dismissed it as "scholarly and abstractional."[9]

A second level on which the journalists' lack of interest in philosophy manifests itself is in the lack of philosophical sophistication that journalists bring to their discussion of moral and political issues. Of course, if the journalists' analyses of social issues are often rather shallow and one-dimensional, that is partly because of specific professional constraints on their work; the journalist obviously is much more concerned than the philosopher with meeting deadlines, keeping articles concise, and making his writing comprehensible and interesting to a wide audience. But journalists also often reveal an ignorance of their subject matter that is rooted in their refusal to learn from the most thoughtful and disciplined writers on moral and political subjects.

Finally, and perhaps most importantly, journalists, particularly in North America, do not, as a general rule, think that philosophy is much worth writing about. Thus they convey to the readers of public journals the message that philosophy is not something that readers themselves should take very seriously. Whatever its weaknesses and limitations, the philosophy of any age deserves a degree of attention that journalists have consistently failed to give it. Even in the finest and most respected public journals, philosophy receives only a small fraction of the attention that is given to sports, cinema, and high society. (Note that I am speaking here not of sensationalistic tabloids but of the most serious public journals.) The astute Canadian journalist, Robert Fulford, observed a generation ago that, "In the 1950's the Canadian newspaper reader was told just what happened every time a government fell in France—because that was politics, and obviously important; but in the same period he was not told what Jean-Paul Sartre was saying and doing—because that was philosophy, and not interesting. Yet in the long run, or maybe even the short, the ramifications of Sartre's activities might be more important than those of a cabinet shuffle."[10] What Fulford said about the Canadian papers of the 1950s applies as well to the leading public journals of our own time, particularly in North America but also in other parts of the world.

I suggest that the philosopher's disdain for the journalist is one of the factors that contributes to his neglect of journalism. There is little value to him in unseemly whining; but if the usurper will not take the philosopher seriously, the philosopher may respond in kind. The philosopher's strategy of response is not calculated or premeditated, but rather a natural, spontaneous one, for the philosopher is not so much seeking revenge as consolation and a renewed sense of the social value of his own work. It is easy enough in any case for the philosopher to dismiss journalism, for the arguments of intellectuals against journalism are as numerous and accessible as the arguments of unreasonable people against philosophy. Thus the philosopher may reflect, "Journalism is but one more of many modern forms of sophistry. The journalist has certain research and writing skills, but he is not a true professional or craftsman like the physician, jurist, statesman, scientist, educator, or artist. He writes about all sorts of things, but unlike the scholar, he knows relatively little about the subjects he discusses. He is merely involved in a business, the selling of news and opinions; and like the sophists of old, his success is largely a function of his ability to tell his readers in the general public more or less whatever they want to hear. The journalist may mistakenly believe that he creatively exercises an influence on public opinion, but except on rare occasions, whatever judgments the journalist advances, and whatever influence they exert, have already been determined by factors outside of his control. And in any case, the journalist's influence is ephemeral; public journals do not have the lasting importance that great books do, and ordinary opinions do not have the lasting importance of those ideas that result from the free, patiently nurtured, disciplined inquiry of the genuine thinker who takes a wide view of all things." Consoled by these not altogether satisfactory assumptions, the philosopher proceeds to turn over the matter of journalism to the positivistic social scientist who specializes in causal explanations of human behavior.

This last explanation of the philosopher's neglect of journalism as a subject for investigation may well strike one as somewhat contrived, and perhaps it is, for such is often the case with explanations of apparent historical anomalies. Still, one should not underestimate the significance of the philosopher's traditional *ressentiment*. Certainly it is one of the central themes of the history of philosophy that if only the naive, ignorant masses would start listening to the noble, high-minded intellectual instead of the slick, self-serving manipulator of public opinion, huge leaps on the scale of civilization would be possible. It is not to the credit of the philosopher that his disdain for something such as journalism should be so much a function of his resentment. The philosopher, one could rightly argue, ought to be above resentment; but even the greatest of philosophers have been human, all too human. The philosopher's negative estimation of the journalist involves a properly philosophical, if flawed, view of the essential nature of journalism. The philosopher takes both the journalist's popularity with the masses of ignorant readers and the journalist's neglect of philosophers and philosophy as evidence that the journalist lacks moral earnestness. It is interesting to note that while the philosopher is ordinarily willing to regard a politician's lack of moral earnestness as a defect on the part of the particular politician, not on the part of statesmanship in general, the philosopher is more inclined to see a journalist's lack of moral earnestness as a defect in the journalistic enterprise itself, even if he is prepared to grant that some journalists are decent souls. Surely this in itself indicates that the philosopher recognizes the journalist as a rival; the idea of a philosophical statesman is not inconceivable for him, but the philosopher ordinarily cannot see much point in trying to turn a journalist into a philosopher. The best that the typical philosopher thinks he can do in this regard is to attempt to interest the journalist in learning a few things from him, or perhaps better yet, to get the journalist to share his power with him. But recognizing the likely difficulties involved in achieving such ends, the philosopher customarily retreats to the academy in the hopes of influencing impressionable minds on a wholly different front.

Lippmann, obviously influenced by his philosophical education, decided to conclude *Public Opinion* with a chapter entitled, "The Appeal to Reason."[11] Here he reiterates his position that journalism would benefit greatly from the "intelligence work" of social-scientific experts. What is most striking about this final chapter, however, is Lippmann's observation that humanity has paid a great price for the philosopher's resentment. Lippmann appropriately focuses his attention on the famous ship parable in Plato's *Republic*, though his interpretation of it is misleading.

The ship parable is a device employed by Plato to explain why the philosopher is useless in existing societies. Plato invites us to consider a certain state of affairs aboard a ship (the ship of state) in which the master (the public), though stronger than the others (individuals) on the ship, cannot hear or see very well and is not too adept at navigational skills. Sailors (politicians) are quarreling with each other over who among them should be given control of the helm (political power), but none of them has ever studied the art of navigation (political philosophy) or is even willing to acknowledge that such an art can be taught. The sailors try to induce the master to give them control of the helm. They dispose in various ways of their rivals, and finally, when all other inducements have failed, they drug the naive master, who then turns control of the ship over to them. They praise the shrewdest among them as a true navigator, a true pilot, and proceed to steer the ship into perilous waters. Such people could hardly be expected to appreciate a true navigator (a philosopher), and when they saw him looking into the sky (reflecting on philosophical principles, or more specifically, timeless essences), they would not understand that what he is doing is trying to chart a safe course for the ship but, instead, would assume him to be a mere stargazer (a useless visionary). Plato's immediate conclusion is plain enough—it is ultimately not the philosopher's fault that the ship of state is lost in perilous waters; it is more the fault of those who do not appreciate what the philosopher has to offer.[12]

What impressed Lippmann most about the ship parable is the philosopher's *ressentiment*. He tells us that Plato, speaking through the character of Socrates,

> becomes defiant and warns Adeimantus that he must "attribute the uselessness" of philosophers "to the fault of those who will not use them, and not to themselves. The pilot should not humbly beg the sailors to be commended by him—that is not the order of nature." And with this haughty gesture, he hurriedly picked up the tools of reason, and disappeared into the Academy, leaving the world to Machiavelli.
>
> Thus, in the first great encounter between reason and politics, the strategy of reason was to retire in anger. But meanwhile, as Plato tells us, the ship is at sea.[13]

What Lippmann fails to see here is that for all his resentment, Plato was neither a fatalist nor an irredeemable cynic. On the contrary, he goes on in the *Republic* to elaborate a two-dimensional strategy for dealing with the situation on board the ship of state. First, as Lippmann himself acknowledges, Plato points to the value of education, so that those with a philosophical nature will not become corrupt, ambitious sailors but true navigators who have founded an ideal republic in their own souls. This move is all but pooh-poohed by Lippmann, who, in the self-applauding tones of one who had abandoned the academy for the world of professional journalism, reflects, "For education is a matter of years, the emergency a matter of hours. It would be altogether academic, then, to tell the pilot that the true remedy is, for example, an education that will endow sailors with a better sense of evidence. You can tell that only to shipmasters on dry land."[14] Clearly one implication of Lippmann's observation is that the kind of enlightenment that journalists can provide is very important because the philosopher's remedy for pressing social problems is too time-consuming to be of immediate value.

But there is, in fact, a second dimension to Plato's strategy. In important but too often neglected lines of the *Republic*, Socrates urges Adeimantus not to condemn the masses but rather to learn to explain to them, in a gentle, unpretentious way, what it is that the true philosopher has to offer his society. Plato has Socrates suggest here, in effect, that the public will "come around" if only the philosopher masters the art of public relations.[15] Lippmann says that, "It will help us to cherish Plato's ideals, without sharing his hasty conclusion about the perversity of those who do not listen to reason."[16] But despite his resentment, Plato does not see the public as wholly perverse and believes that the public can be swayed by an intellectual's uncontentious appeal. Thus, Plato does not merely blame the public for its neglect of the intellectual; he also blames the philosopher himself for not having worked at communicating with the public and explaining to the "master" of the ship that the true navigator is not a sophistical manipulator who has been drugging him and creating chaos but someone quite different. Here Plato is not talking about the education of future leaders but about the art of public relations.

Who in Plato's parable are the corrupt, ambitious sailors on the ship administering drugs to the master? Obviously Plato is thinking here of those in society who seek a political power that they are incapable of properly exercising. These are not ordinary people but bright, ambitious people who through poor education have become self-serving, manipulative materialists. These people who have gained control of the helm are not just politicians in the narrow sense of the word. Following the ship parable, Plato has rather little to say about statesmen, though it is clearly the statesman that he has in mind when he speaks of that particular sailor who has improperly been held up by his fellow sailors to be a genuine navigator. Plato goes on to condemn other corrupt sailors, the agents of the incompetent statesmen. These, for Plato, are sophists, talented pseudo-intellectuals who, having passed themselves off as wise men, have given genuine intellectuals a bad reputation.[17] Yet, Plato observes, it is ironic that these corrupt opinion-makers who drug the public are in the last analysis the creatures of the public itself, the Great Sophist, which by the praise and favors it distributes, leads the sophists to serve up to it what it wants to hear, a polished and somewhat intellectualized version of the opinions it already holds. What the sophist provides the public with is a slightly distorted image of what on some level of consciousness it already takes to be true. So while the sophist successfully manipulates the public in such a way as to obtain for himself fame, material benefits, and a feeling of power, the influence that he has is largely illusory. Only the true philosopher who actually educates the public has the real power of transforming public opinion.

Here, the journalist enters the picture. First, it may be observed that many a modern journalist has much in common with Plato's sophists. (I speak of Plato's sophists because Plato's characterization of the real Sophists was not altogether accurate or fair.) In his pursuit of various conventionally desired benefits, the journalist may well be prepared to pander to the public, to serve as an agent of the established order or of the Great Sophist itself, to scoff at the true intellectual and undermine his chances of ascension, and to pride himself in his illusory power over public opinion. However, the journalist does not have to be a sophist; other vocations are open to him. He may be bright enough to become a true navigator himself, but if the spirit does not move him to do so, or circumstances do not permit him to do so, then he can at least serve as an agent of the true navigator, the wise and just sage. With his special gift for agreeable and uncontentious expression, he can urge his fellow sailors to follow a higher road than that on which they are now embarked; he can urge the somewhat isolated and dispirited navigator to play his proper role on this ship of state; and he can approach the master himself, feeding him nutritious fare rather than mind-unsettling narcotics.

This brings me to the third implication of Plato's analysis. The intellectual must not write the journalist off, but must take him seriously. He must help the journalist to avoid turning into a selfish, sycophantic poseur. Mindful of the journalist's special gifts, the philosopher must help him to cultivate those gifts in an intelligent, disciplined, socially constructive way. If the journalist will not become an intellectual himself, then the intellectual must at least learn to make use of him, not for narrow ends but for the greater good of the community. The philosopher may need the journalist to speak to the master on his behalf; or he may need the journalist to show him how to communicate with the master. If he studies the journalist closely, he may come to understand more clearly his own proper role on the ship of state. The philosopher must overcome his resentment on all levels (with respect to the public, the politicians, and the journalists) and must, in the words of one of Plato's most famous images, "return to the cave." Plato himself saw that the philosopher indeed can and must do so.

To be sure, all this talk about what the philosopher ought to do should be taken with a grain of salt. No one has ever been better than the philosopher at coining slogans to justify his flight from social responsibility: "the contemplative life," "knowledge for its own sake," "the disinterested pursuit of wisdom." If philosophers have one mission, then they have a thousand, and who can blame them if, like Socrates, they sincerely believe that they have opted not to go where they cannot do themselves or their fellow citizens any good?[18] So keenly did Plato understand the philosophers' escapist tendencies, as well as the pleasures of pure reflection, that he was prepared to argue that philosophers, despite their understanding of moral and political matters, would often have to be compelled to return to the cave to play their proper part in a world dominated by the unenlightened.[19] The philosopher can put his knowledge to any number of uses, but if he is going to take seriously the idea that he has a social responsibility, then he cannot cut himself off from the world of ordinary people, nor can he afford to ignore that particular institution which perhaps more than any other has the dual capacity to reveal and to shape public opinion.

But why should the journalist have any interest in what the philosopher has to say about journalism? If, as critics of the Hutchins Commission suggested, philosophical discussion of journalism is too "scholarly and abstractional," then of what use is it to someone whose beat—as journalists say—is out there in the real world of flesh-and-blood human beings and not in a world of eternal principles and timeless essences? Why should the journalist take what philosophers have to say any more seriously than what the butcher, baker, or politician has to say? Several answers could be given to these questions, but they all amount in the end to the same basic answer: if the journalist would listen to what the philosopher has to say about journalism, then he might well become a better journalist as well as a better person. And yet, the journalist already seems to get on well enough in his trade, does he not? And when he needs hard information about his vocation, the social-scientific experts will readily provide him with it. So what exactly is it that the philosopher alone can do for him to help him to be better at his craft? And is it not the scandal of philosophy that philosophers themselves, after twenty-five centuries of philosophizing, have not been able to agree among themselves as to precisely what it is that they are doing?

Philosophers have, over the centuries, performed conceptual analysis, though they have only lately called it by this name. From the days when old Socrates walked through the streets of Athens asking prominent pseudo-authorities questions like, "What is piety?" and "What is courage?," philosophers have regarded it as important to work at the clarification of very basic concepts. Sometimes it is enough for them to show, as Socrates did, that people customarily use important words in a dangerously casual way and that they need to do a good deal more careful thinking about how they use such words. Sometimes philosophers think that their conceptual analyses will actually lead them to an understanding of the essential nature of the realities under investigation. It is not inconceivable that philosophical analysis could help the journalist to understand better what, for example, journalism or news or freedom of the press is. For questions about what a thing *is*, about what a thing's essential nature is, are not ordinary social-scientific questions but questions of a more abstract order. Hence, as J. C. Merrill has pointed out to budding journalists, "Philosophizing in journalism helps us design meaningful definitions for ourselves which can help us in our work. . . ."[20]

More importantly, philosophy, at its best the most synoptic of intellectual disciplines, can help to place journalism in a broad context. It can help people, if they are sufficiently intellectually ambitious, to view journalism and its various aspects as Spinoza wished them to view things, *sub specie aeternitatis*, "under the aspect of eternity." The journalist, as will be seen many times in the course of this inquiry, is forced, by the very nature of his craft, to take a narrow perspective of the matters that he reports and discusses. At times, however, he needs to have in the back of his mind a wider view of things, and particularly of the relation of his own craft to other things, and here the philosopher might well be able to offer him some assistance.

Again, the philosopher can help the social scientist in explaining to the journalist what it is that the journalist does. Of course, the typical journalist is intelligent and responsible enough to have formed a working concept for himself of what his job is all about. But sometimes a scholar—or even a casual observer—can point out to a journalist certain features of the journalistic enterprise of which he was not consciously aware, or uncover certain latent effects of the journalistic process.

Most importantly of all, it is philosophy more than any other intellectual discipline (with the possible exception of theology) that is prepared, indeed required, to address, in the most direct way possible, the most basic normative questions—questions of value, and particularly moral or ethical questions. As Merrill suggests, "One of the most important branches of philosophy is ethics, the theory of right conduct. The journalist faces ethical decisions every day; he can better make them if he has a moral philosophy based on a consistent and individually meaningful set of principles."[21] The philosopher is hardly in a position to tell a journalist what to do when faced with a complicated moral dilemma stemming from his journalistic work; the philosopher does not know enough about the day-to-day work of the journalist to make an authoritative judgment, nor is it the business of the philosopher to usurp the right and responsibility of another human being to make moral decisions. But the philosopher can do various things to help the journalist make more reasonable moral decisions. As a critical historian of moral ideas, the philosopher can draw the journalist's attention to the strengths and weaknesses of the various principles, criteria, standards, and methods that reflective people have always employed in arriving at solutions to concrete moral problems. He can provide the journalist with a whole chest of analytical tools for rationally handling specific moral problems. At the same time, by helping the journalist to envision what a journalist ideally might be, he enables the journalist to act on the basis of a "total journalistic *Weltanschauung*" rather than on the basis of arbitrary conventions and traditions or a haphazard trial-and-error method.[22] In doing so, he helps the journalist to avoid traditional journalistic abuses, and to see why certain actions constitute abuses.

The philosopher thus can give the journalist a new and appropriate sense of freedom and dignity. As a social-scientific student of public opinion has observed, "That American newspapers have a high and exaggerated notion of their own importance is beyond doubt."[23] Still, I suspect that for all of the arrogance and posturing of a few highly visible journalists and media celebrities, many journalistic journeymen, and the more thoughtful and responsible well-placed journalists and editors, have worried not a little about the extent to which they have become cogs in a monolithic, overinstitutionalized entertainment-cum-propaganda machine. A troubled Merrill complains that, "Journalism is becoming a depersonalized, mechanistic monster increasingly controlled by outside forces and most journalists appear not to know it or to care about it."[24] Merrill has almost surely underestimated the sensitivity of his colleagues; but in any case, philosophy can help to give the troubled journalist a new lease on his professional life, a heightened understanding of the nature, value, and potentialities of his work, and an elevated ability to give polished, reasonable responses to the ever present critics and detractors of a free press, critics who are usually even less philosophically sophisticated than journalists themselves.

However, in the last analysis, the main service that a philosophical investigation of journalism should perform is not simply one for philosophers or journalists or any other group within society, but for the commonwealth itself. Disturbed by the power of journalists in liberal democracies who "wield such great power virtually unchecked by law,"[25] Jean-Louis Servan-Schreiber warns that "journalists commit the sin of pride when they claim privileged status for themselves."[26] The investigative journalist is probably sincere when he insists that his investigations are for the good of the commonwealth and not simply for his own professional advancement. And journalists have often done a commendable job, all things considered, of checking the abuses perpetrated by their own colleagues. But time has shown that of all those who could carry on a useful public investigation of the aims, practices, and possibilities of journalism, few are as likely to be as judicious, sensible, and magnanimous as those Socratic inquirers who, having been able to transcend any spirit of resentment, will see it as their dual responsibility to ask the most probing of basic questions and to exhort all around them to pursue virtue above all things.[27]

Philosophy and journalism, at their best, have both been great forces for the advancement of civilization and the checking of barbarism; but both could be greater forces. It would not hurt philosophers and journalists to take one another—and their relation to one another—more seriously as subjects for reflection. In this century, there has been unprecedented violence, genocide, torture, exploitation, and callousness—enough to make the most heinous of ancient barbarians wince in horror. The typical philosopher and journalist both seem to believe that, for the most part, they are doing their jobs properly and are serving the needs of humanity as effectively as they can, at least given the circumstances under which they find themselves functioning. Yet their critics have been heard to contend that too many philosophers and journalists have become lost in their respective professional games. The philosopher, it has been argued, has become too comfortable in the sheltered environment of the academy, preoccupied with the preparation of shallow lectures for prematurely jaded youths and with narrow, technical scholarly articles and conference papers for a self-impressed intellectual elite. The journalist, it has been argued, is out there in the real world, asking loaded, imprecise questions to all the wrong people, writing shallow or sensational copy, exchanging gossip with politicians and celebrities whose importance he has promoted, and concocting hasty, half-baked interpretations of the supposedly significant events of the day. At the same time, interest groups rant on, yet even with shrewd press agents, rarely manage to shake the Great Sophist out of its narcosis for long. But meanwhile the ship is at sea.

2

The Essential Nature of Journalism

Even people who neither know nor care much about classical philosophy are familiar with the historical image of Socrates going about the streets of Athens asking "Socratic" questions of prominent pretenders to wisdom. It is not easy to explain precisely how Socrates understood his philosophical mission, for his understanding of his mission was rather more personal than that of most later philosophers. It will suffice for us to note here that Socrates believed that he had a religious obligation to show that those people in his society who were widely accepted as authorities on high matters were unable to give satisfactory answers to the most abstract and yet most fundamental questions about the particular subject matter on which they professed (and were generally taken) to be knowledgeable. The real Socrates (as opposed to the character named Socrates that we meet in Plato's middle dialogues) never seemed to get around to attempting to provide satisfactory answers to his own questions. While his student, Plato, and all subsequent philosophers have been ready with answers, Socrates himself was content with indicating to his audiences the need for critical inquiry with respect to the most basic and, hence, highest matters, and particularly those related to virtue.

The questions that Socrates asked took various forms, but the Socratic questions that are most famous are those of the form, "What is X?"—as for example, "What is piety?" The supposed authorities Socrates questioned would normally answer first by giving various examples of the X in question. Socrates would then demand that they give some account of what it was that the things they had enumerated had in common by virtue of which they were to be regarded as genuine instances of X. The experts would make several attempts to fulfill this demand, while Socrates would proceed to show them that all their analyses were inadequate. This public demonstration of their ignorance was, of course, rather embarrassing to them, and it is not surprising that Socrates made himself many enemies in high places.[1]

If Socrates were alive today, he might well have been interested both in what journalists are doing and in what they think they are doing, and he might have sought out opportunities to confront the most celebrated of our journalists with a question like, "What is journalism?" Unfortunately, our leading journalists do not make themselves as available for questioning as the celebrities of Socrates's society did, or for that matter, as most modern politicians do. And, in their disinclination to be questioned themselves, and in their preference to ask other people questions, journalists have something important in common with Socrates. It may be that if philosophers expressed a desire to ask journalists questions, some journalists might be happy to oblige. Still, I suspect that someone like Socrates would not have had an easy time in our society in getting prominent people—journalists or politicians or even entertainers—to answer his peculiar questions in public. Difficult as it may be to believe, the celebrities of Socrates's age were generally more accessible than those of our own, partly because journalists and press agents did not stand between celebrities and the public.

However, if Socrates did manage to get a well-known syndicated columnist to answer his question about the nature of journalism, it is not unlikely that his respondent would do something that none of Socrates's ancient respondents could do: he would reach into his brief case, pull out a small paperbound dictionary, and read out for Socrates's benefit the definition of *journalism*. Such behavior would disturb Socrates, and rightly so, for any number of reasons, and he could have had a fine old time poking fun at the dictionary's superficial analysis. Still, a sad fact for modern defenders of classical humanism is that an impressive and reasonably reliable lexicographical source like, say, the *Oxford English Dictionary*, would indeed make a large part of Socratic inquiry unnecessary. Certain British linguistic philosophers of the 1950s and 1960s overstated the relevant point when they argued that the traditional problems of philosophy are pseudo-problems that arise from a distortion of ordinary, everyday language. If something like the *O.E.D.* had existed in Socrates's time, however, Plato would have had a much harder time establishing that the knowledge of "timeless, transcendent essences" is so terribly esoteric.

The *O.E.D.* (1933) tells us that *journalism* corresponds to the French *journalisme* and involves, first, "The occupation or profession of a journalist; journalistic writing; the public journals collectively," or second, "The keeping of a journal; the practice of journalizing." It is the first kind of journalism that concerns us here, and we should consider in relation to it certain other definitions in the *O.E.D.* With respect to the kind of journalism that interests us, the journalist is, "One who earns his living by editing or writing for a public journal or journals"; and a public journal—as opposed to one of the various kinds of *private* journals that so many of us keep—is, "A daily newspaper or other publication; hence, by extension, any periodical publication containing news or dealing with matters of current interest in any particular sphere." Although that is obviously the kind of journal that concerns us in this study, we may briefly take note of certain other kinds of journal that have a public dimension, such as, "A daily record of commercial transactions, entered as they occur, in order to [*sic*] the keeping of accounts," "A daily record of events or occurrences kept for private or official use," and, "A register of daily transactions kept by a public body or an association." The recurrence of the word *daily* in the above lines reminds us that the *jour* at the beginning of the French words, *journalisme*, *journaliste*, and *journal*, and their English equivalents, is, of course, the French term for *day*.

One must not expect too much enlightenment from dictionary definitions, for no matter how careful their research and expression are, lexicographers can never capture all the nuances that a term can have in ordinary, everyday language or in various technical and semi-technical languages. Also, the biases of lexicographers, as of all people, affect their perceptions and judgments in subtle ways. Moreover, language is a changing, evolving phenomenon, and words, as the *O.E.D.* says, have a way of becoming extended. And most importantly, the understanding of a thing that a dictionary aims at giving us is of a relatively minimal degree; the lexicographer does not pretend to be a theorist or theoretician. Thus, Socrates and Plato would still have questions left to ask the syndicated columnist about the essential nature of journalism. But to arrive at a sound working understanding of the essential nature of journalism, a good place to begin is to consider what a respected dictionary says that journalism is, and to relate that definition to one's own intuitive, pre-theoretical understanding of what journalism is. I suspect that to most of us, the relevant definitions in the *O.E.D.* sound accurate enough, and perhaps it would be unreasonable to expect much more accuracy from such a work. The definitions are necessarily quite indeterminate in places, and they appropriately indicate that something can be journalism in one sense but not in another. Nevertheless, it would be a mistake to assume that they are beyond criticism.

When one reflects on the *O.E.D.* definitions, one is apt to be struck first by the analysis of journalism as a kind of writing, journalistic writing. Journalism can be understood as a kind of writing on several levels: it can be the activity of journalistic writing, an activity that constitutes the occupation or profession of the journalist, the person who ordinarily earns his living by writing (or editing) for a public journal or journals; it can be a product, whatever published writing (or writing prepared for publication) that is the result of the activity of journalistic writing; or it can be the totality of all the writing that has appeared or will appear in public journals. If journalism is essentially a kind of writing, then it follows that it is not entirely appropriate to regard as journalism anything that is not writing (or editing). Consider now some interesting implications.

First, if a particular activity is involved in the publication of a public journal but is not the specific activity of writing (or editing), then the person who is engaged in that activity, important though he may be to the publication process, is not, strictly speaking, a journalist. A typesetter or financial manager is only producing journalism in a secondary sense at most. What is perhaps not always so obvious is that a publisher as such is not a journalist and is only producing journalism insofar as he is making it economically possible for journalists and other writers to publish their journalistic writing. We often hear it said that journalism is a business, but a publisher—money-conscious or not—is no more a journalist than the owner of an art gallery is an artist. Journalist and artist alike normally hope to receive financial recompense for their work, as do the publisher and gallery owner. But as Plato points out early in the *Republic*, a clear and useful distinction can be drawn between the practice of a craft as such and the earning of income, by the craftsman himself or his employer, through that practice.[2] Indeed, we know that there are certain inspired, high-minded journalists and publishers who, like inspired artists and their patrons, have all but lost sight of economic necessities and pursue lofty objectives at the expense of personal economic deprivation. Moreover, there are independently wealthy journalists and publishers who can afford to do what they like, even if it does not produce income. In any case, as venal as a particular journalist and his publisher might be, or whatever their ulterior motives might be, the publisher always depends for his material on the journalist's practice of his craft, a writing craft, and it is the practice of that craft, or the writing that results from it, that constitutes journalism in a primary sense.

Several special cases merit consideration here. The first is that of the non-professional contributor to public journals, the individual who does not see it as his occupation to write for public journals but rather conceives of his writing as a side line, a hobby, an extension of his primary line of work, or the fulfillment of his social responsibility as a particularly knowledgeable or thoughtful citizen. If such a person writes material for public journals that is comparable to the material written by the typical professional journalist, and if he finds a place for his writing in a public journal, then it would seem proper to say that he is producing journalism or journalistic writing, and that to some extent he is engaged in the activity of journalism. However, as the *O.E.D* definitions indicate, it might not be appropriate to characterize him as a journalist, even if he is as competent at the craft of journalistic writing as the person who earns his living by that craft. Now, dictionary definitions are not entirely helpful here, for as already observed, even a full-fledged journalist does not necessarily earn a living through his work, or even aspire to do so; and he might even earn less through his journalistic writing than does the expert from another field who contributes to public journals as a side line. But the full-fledged journalist conceives of journalistic writing as his occupation; whether or not he makes a living from it, his journalistic writing is what occupies the major part of his attention as a productive human being. Sometimes common sense requires faithfulness to the spirit rather than the letter of the lexical definitions, and it seems appropriate to conclude that just as there are journalists who do not literally earn a living through their journalistic writing, there are non-journalists who produce genuine and often important journalism in a primary sense of the term and who are very much involved in the actual activity of journalism.

Another special case is that of the editor, who is singled out for special mention in one of the *O.E.D.* definitions. The concept of an editor is a notoriously ambiguous one: there are editors who work directly on copy and there are others who do not, but instead make judgments about such matters as what kinds of articles should be published or what particular political orientation should be adopted in the journal's opinion pages. Still other editors are primarily administrators or managers. The editor who works on copy is quite directly involved in the writing process, and it is not hard to see why it is often deemed appropriate to characterize him as a journalist. The editor who makes judgments about what will be published in his journal is involved less directly in the writing process as such, but even here he can be seen as involved in determining how the writing in a journal will look. The administrative editor's situation is somewhat more problematic—he seems to be much more like a publisher than a journalist. Yet if satisfactory performance of his work requires him to have had extensive past experience at journalistic writing, or at least in-depth understanding of what is involved in the journalistic writer's craft, then perhaps he is close enough to the writing process to qualify as a participant in it.

A third special case is that of the individual who contributes to public journals what some would characterize as non-journalistic writing, items such as crossword puzzles or comics. Such a person might well earn his living by writing for a public journal, but is he producing journalism and engaged in the activity of journalism? Since his contribution is peripheral to the main content of a public journal ("news or . . . matters of current interest in any particular sphere"), it appears somewhat inappropriate to characterize his work as journalism. Yet the lexical definitions do not in themselves give us much guidance about how to view such a case.

Upon considering these three special cases, one realizes that the concept of journalistic writing is a rather ambiguous one. Journalistic writing can be thought of as an activity or as the product of that activity; it can be what journalists do or something that even some non-journalists do; it can be thought of as writing in a strict sense of the word or as a participation in the writing process; and it can be viewed as whatever writing appears in public journals, or as only the writing that constitutes the main content of those journals.

A second implication of the idea that journalism is essentially a kind of writing is that the research and investigation associated with journalism are secondary aspects of journalism at most and perhaps even conceptually irrelevant to journalism. How can this be? A popular image of the journalist is that of the observer and inquirer out there in the field where the action is, the hearty soul collecting information under difficult and sometimes dangerous circumstances so that he can file the report that will let the public know what is really happening. It is an image of the correspondent, notebook in hand, asking the penetrating questions, an image of the tough-minded character breaking down the wall of illusion and digging out the hard facts. A public journal can only inform if it has information to pass on to its readers, and as this is the case, it might well seem that research and investigation are as central to the activity of journalism as writing is. However, a dictionary like the *O.E.D.* provides us with definitions, not popular images; and it is not a lexicographical error that has led to the *O.E.D.*'s apparent undervaluation of the investigative aspect of journalism. When we hear the word *bird*, we may well think of a creature in flight, and it is only on reflection that we remember that not all of our feathered friends can fly. So it is with the word *journalism*. Whatever images it immediately brings to mind, the fact is that it is properly and commonly applied to activities other than reporting from the field. There are journalists who never venture out into the field but instead explain, interpret, theorize, predict, assess, praise, blame, signalize, and in a word, communicate.[3] The "communicator," Servan-Schreiber points out, often "finds on his desk all the information supplied by the news agency supermarkets";[4] and it may actually be that "one of the greatest weaknesses of the press is that its ability to investigate is used too little."[5] Writing is the sine qua non of journalism; information gathered but not published is not journalism, but a public journal can and often does rely on information provided to it by eyewitnesses, informers, anonymous sources, experts, and agencies. Now, perhaps most journalists are inquirers in the sense of being investigators, just as most birds fly. The journalist needs something to write, and reporting from the field is certainly a principal form of journalistic writing, perhaps the most important form of all. It is no wonder then that the journalist's inquiry and reporting often appear to be seamlessly fused. The reports of correspondents have a significance, impact, and prima facie trustworthiness that most second-hand accounts do not. It is the reporting of its field correspondents that gives a public journal much of its glamour and vitality. But the question here is not whether, or to what extent, research and investigation ought to proceed journalistic writing; the question before us is whether investigative inquiry is a necessary condition of journalism in the way that writing is. And this is a question that the O.E.D. definitions have clearly and instructively answered for us.

A related implication of the idea that journalism is essentially a kind of writing is that journalism is a branch of literature. If literature is associated with belles-lettres, this may be a hard notion to swallow, for journalistic writing rarely has the qualities that we admire most in poetry, drama, fiction, philosophical writing, or even the better nonfiction published in books directed at a general audience. If journalistic writing lacks the high literary qualities that characterize these other forms of literature, it is not necessarily because journalists are, as a general rule, inferior writers. Of journalism, it is literally true that time is of the essence. News and matters of current interest are normally at the heart of a public journal, and the journalist, who must meet deadlines and get his material to press while it is still fresh and timely, cannot afford the luxury of patiently revising his material over and over again. Moreover, the general readers for whom he is writing do not, for the most part, have either the time or inclination to appreciate profound stylistic subtleties in journalistic writing, and many of them do not even have the ability; they expect something of a different order than belles-lettres from the periodical press. Journalistic writing that appears to them to be even slightly stylistically mannered strikes them as pretentious. (The exception to this rule, of course, is the literary quarterly or monthly that is known for its special emphasis on stylish writing.) Nevertheless, good journalism is good writing of a particular kind, and like all good writing, it has something to say and says it well. Like respectable standard nonfiction, it is clear, concise, vivid, grammatically and syntactically correct, and generally readable. It imparts information and proposes ideas as precisely and accurately as can reasonably be expected, and it does not distract the reader's attention by treating its content as a vehicle for formal, stylistic, or rhetorical flourishes and experiments. It effectively performs its particular functions, whatever they may be.

It is somewhat misleading to speak of a journalistic style of writing. All journalistic writing is partly shaped by the traditional content of public journals and by the temporal and other pressures that encroach upon the freedom of all journalists. Journalists are generally respectful of certain stylistic traditions and conventions that they see as having evolved in the writing of respected predecessors and colleagues. But one must be careful not to overestimate the stylistic sameness of journalistic writing. There is a high degree of uniformity within particular public journals that is largely a function of editorial policy. However, it does not take much skill to distinguish, for example, between an article that comes from a tabloid and one that comes from a journal with a more sober editorial policy. Even with regard to a particular journal, the most rigid editorial policy cannot wholly suppress the stylistic individuality of the journal's contributors.

Good writing, journalistic or otherwise, involves more than the mastery of basic writing skills. A good writer has something significant to say, and having something significant to say requires a variety of intellectual abilities. Research and investigation give a journalist something to report, and a good inquirer has more to report than a mediocre one; moreover, he has a better understanding of what is worth reporting and what is not. A good journalistic commentator is thoughtful, reasonable, and knowledgeable. He is able to frame whatever he is commenting upon in a broad context and to draw on relevant facts and ideas from the various intellectual disciplines when doing his interpreting and assessing. He has critical skills, a respect for the canons of logic, and an open mind.[6] He has the ability to organize and systematize his thoughts on a given subject, and an appreciation of the interests, abilities, and knowledge of those in the audience for which he is writing. Like an Erasmus, Milton, Lessing, or Emerson, he not only gives careful thought to what subjects merit consideration but is as profound as possible, given his circumstances, in dealing with his subjects.

A fourth implication of characterizing journalism as a form of writing is that journalism should in theory be distinguished from media of communication that, while resembling it in important ways, do not involve the written word. I am on shaky ground here, for in recent years, it has become quite acceptable to speak about, for example, broadcast journalism. Words written and words spoken are, of course, in an obvious sense the same words, and a written news report that is published in a journal is in an obvious sense the same report when it is read over the airwaves, so it is not surprising that news reports and analyses on radio and television, even when they do not involve the actual reading of something written, are widely and increasingly regarded as journalism in an extended sense of the word. Respecting the natural evolution of linguistic usage, as will the dictionaries of the future, it is still useful to remember that something like broadcast journalism is journalism in an extended and, perhaps, secondary sense of the word. This point also applies to what is often called now photojournalism or news photography. Photographs can often perform some of the functions that journalistic writing is meant to perform, and sometimes they can even convey information or a message to a degree that words cannot. But though their place in public journals has been consecrated by tradition— they are essentially a supplement to journalistic writing. The inverse of the ancient Oriental proverb is more relevant here than the original: one word is worth ten thousand pictures. (Consider, for example, such words as *I*, *infinity*, *peace*, *integrity*, and *redemption*.) I shall return to this point in a moment.

It is not my intention to detract in any way from the value and importance of such media as broadcast journalism and photojournalism, or even to deny them their widely acknowledged status as journalism. However, it is of more than historical significance that journalism in its primary sense is associated with written communication. Indeed, since much that can be said about the periodical press does not apply to other media of mass communication, I am obliged to indicate here that I take the work of the periodical press to be my paradigm of journalism. While acknowledging that much that can be said about this paradigm also applies to the other media, I am particularly sensitive to the fact that the printed media, as Fred Siebert suggests, "have gathered about them more of the theory and philosophy of mass communication."[7]

Since in recent years there has been much social-scientific discussion of the differing impact of the printed media and alternative media of communication, I shall confine myself to a few rudimentary observations. First, while journalistic writing, given its usual content, tends to have a relative transience in comparison with belles-lettres and philosophical and scientific literature, and is normally read rather more cursorily, it can ordinarily be scrutinized more closely than the spoken report or analysis, and hence, it tends to partake more of the essence of permanence than the other forms of mass communication now characterized as journalistic. When we read an article in a public journal, some statement or passage may well lead us to pause, read it over a few times, reflect on it, and perhaps cut it out and put it in a desk drawer. As a physical object, journalistic writing is recorded in a way and to an extent that the spoken word is not. Of course, broadcast journalism can be recorded, too, and a radio or television newscaster knows that his audience can obtain access to exactly what was said. But the typical audience member does not make a habit of taping radio and television news programs, and fascinated or outraged though a listener may occasionally be by what he has heard, he generally puts it out of his mind as he listens to the remainder of the broadcast.

Secondly, as Plato observes, visual imagery generally does not invite reflection in the way or to the extent that language does, and in many cases seems to turn off the reflective mind.[8] Reading normally requires, or at least elicits, more interpretive and analytical activity than listening to speech does, and the latter, in turn, ordinarily occasions more of such activity than looking at an image does. This is not the place for a psychological analysis of a complex phenomenon, but it may be noted, following Plato, that language brings us in touch with abstractions in a way and to an extent that visual imagery, which objectifies the concrete, cannot. One is thus left to ponder the mighty power of the *logos*, which so awed the ancients.

Thirdly, given the present state of communications technology, we can see why broadcast journalists are not allowed the latitude to express themselves as freely as print journalists. Broadcasters themselves appreciate the fact that most communicators do not have the same degree of access to the airwaves that they have to printed media. Hence, it is hardly coincidental that, as Bernard Hennessey has observed, "The printed media are relatively unregulated by goverments and are jealous of their freedom from regulation. The electronic media have a different history and posture in relation to governments. . . ."[9] The point here is not, as it is often taken to be, that broadcast journalism is intrinsically more influential than journalistic writing—though it may well have more influence on less reflective audiences—but rather that the technology of print itself allows for more freedom of expression than the technology of broadcasting presently allows. Hence, in totalitarian states, broadcast journalism is almost inevitably reduced to an instrument for the dissemination of government-approved propaganda, while in more democratic societies, broadcast journalists generally acquiesce to public and governmental demands that they lean in the direction of blandness rather than contentiousness.

Finally, the obvious fact that journalistic writing is addressed to an audience of people who are literate should not be ignored. Though we sometimes take literacy for granted in our advanced society, it should be remembered that a functionally literate audience is, by one important criterion, a relatively highly civilized one, and that a journalistic writer can presume a certain intellectual competence on the part of his audience that many other communicators cannot.

I realize that the four points that I have just made make print journalism look rather more useful, serious, and important than its rivals. Much print journalism, however, is quite insignificant; sensationalist yellow journalism at its worst has plumbed depths that none of its rivals has yet been able to fathom. Broadcast journalism, when it manages to do completely without the written word, is the heir to the oldest and perhaps most honorable tradition in communications, the oral-aural tradition. It is worth noting that the most erudite of all students of communication, Harold Innis, was moved not long ago to make a "plea for consideration of the role of the oral tradition."[10] At its best, broadcast journalism is more faithful to the spirit of Socratic dialogue than a book of philosophy is. News photography too is an heir to an old and often honorable tradition in communications, that of visual representation. The tradition to which journalism in its primary sense is heir is that of the written word, but more specifically, that of the printed word. Thus, McCormick spoke well when he remarked that the newspaper "is not a new monster created by a few men in the newspaper profession but the heir to most of the explosive phenomena of the printing press."[11] Journalism and journalists are, of course, commonly referred to as the press. This fact in itself not only reminds us of the tradition to which journalism in its primary sense belongs but of how central to that tradition it has become. When we talk about the press, we sometimes forget that the periodical press is only a part of the publishing world, and indeed the earliest defenders of freedom of the press were not defending journalistic freedom but rather freedom of written expression for authors of philosophical, theological, and scientific books and tracts.

I have considered several implications of the idea that journalism is essentially a kind of writing, and while in certain extended and secondary senses of the term, journalism does not refer directly to writing, I think there is wisdom in beginning an analysis of what journalism is by placing it in the category of writing. Now that I have considered the genus to which it belongs, I will consider its differentia. I have already noted that to some extent the concept of journalistic writing is ambiguous, but we have not as yet considered directly that feature which the *O.E.D.* definitions explicitly indicate as distinguishing journalism from other kinds of writing. We turn then to the dictionary's characterization of a public journal as a daily publication, or, by extension, a periodical publication.

That little French word, *jour*, is central to the family of words that we have been considering. The public journal is in its primary sense a daily publication and in an extended sense a periodical one. The journalist, if he does not actually have a daily or periodical quota of words to write, always carries out his occupational task with the realization that the publication in which his work will appear comes out on a regular basis. It is the periodicity of the public journal that imparts to journalism its distinguishing features as a particular form of writing, although not all of those features are unique to journalistic writing. A public journal appears regularly, or at least more or less so; a publication that appears at highly irregular intervals does not qualify as a public journal. The regularity of the public journal's appearance is significant for many reasons, not the least of which is that readers regularly expect and await its forthcoming editions. Now, a public journal has an identity as a particular object that is continuous in time; we do not give the name of public journal to a set of things that simply have a great deal in common but rather to an object that, in spite of the vast number of changes it undergoes from edition to edition, maintains its identity as a discernible, unified, integrated particular. The specific content of the *Times* or *Daily Mercury* changes from edition to edition, and the journalists, editors, and supporting workers who produced the journal a century ago are all gone now and have been replaced by a completely different group of people. Yet any of a number of factors, in conjunction with others if not individually, can provide the journal with enough in the way of continuity to endow it with its identity as a particular object. Some of these factors tend to be more impressive than others, so that often legitimate questions arise as to whether a particular journal is the same journal that we read last month or that our great-grandparents read a century ago. The diversity of factors that may be seen as contributing to the journal's continuity and identity is itself quite remarkable; consider, for example, such factors as the journal's name, its publishers, its editors, its columnists, its editorial policy, and its producers' sense of professional kinship with those they take to be their corporate predecessors. Questions about identity are often notoriously metaphysical, but the questions that arise with respect to the identity or sameness of a particular journal arise mainly because ordinary speakers of our language have not been sufficiently troubled about the relevant ambiguities to work toward establishing precise criteria. In setting this problem aside, I am working on the assumption that there are enough paradigms available to carry on with an investigation.

However, the essential connection between a journal's identity and its periodicity must be noted. It is a particular journal, not just journalistic writing as such, that periodically appears; it is that journal that recurs and whose appearance is awaited by its regular readers. (An individual issue of a journal is the way it is—at least partly, if not largely, because of the nature of the reappearing object that it instantiates.) That number is one of a series, and the character of earlier numbers in that series is a primary determinant of the journalistic writing that has gone into the latest issue and will go into future issues.

The periodicity that imparts to a journal its periodical character is also somewhat ambiguous, and again legitimate questions may arise as to whether a particular publication appears regularly enough and frequently enough to qualify as a public journal. Though we do not reserve the title of journal for only those publications that appear literally on a daily basis, we might well be reluctant to apply that title to a publication that reappeared only every eighteen years, or to a publication that reappeared at highly irregular intervals. Again, ordinary speakers of our language have not been sufficiently bothered by the relevant ambiguities to work toward establishing precise criteria, and some people are inclined to characterize as a public journal a particular publication that other people will believe appears too rarely or too irregularly to qualify as a genuine public journal.

Consider now some of the implications or consequences of the public journal's periodicity, a periodicity that, as we have seen, involves its identity and continuity. The first is that a public journal regularly requires material to be written for it; it requires writing on a periodical basis. A general book publisher also requires manuscripts, for without manuscripts to publish, the typical publishing house will not only fail financially but will not be fulfilling the condition that is the sine qua non of general book publishing; but the publisher of a public journal requires material more urgently than a general book publisher. A book publisher may well find it necessary at certain times to encourage gifted or popular authors to submit manuscripts to his house, but for various reasons he is normally not under the same pressure to obtain material as the journal publisher is. The book publisher can often afford to wait for the manuscripts of authors who write at the pace and frequency they find appropriate for themselves; and he often finds himself having to reject many manuscripts that he regards as in some sense worthy of publication. If he earns a particularly large profit from a handful of publications, he may be willing to reduce significantly the number of his offerings for a given season. When all else fails, he can fall back on the imaginative publication of reprints, classics, or reference works. But the journal publisher does not have these options. His audience expects and awaits the latest issue of his journal. He cannot afford to skip numbers, for regular readers will rightly see the journal publisher who is unreliable in this way as having failed to live up to his obligation and commitment as a journal publisher. Furthermore, the readers of a journal expect new, fresh material; they will ordinarily not tolerate a public journal that simply reprints old material, no matter how good that old material may be. Although there is a market for a limited number of journals that specialize in the anthologizing of previously published material, people who want to read such material customarily go elsewhere for it. The journal publisher thus cannot normally afford to wait for contributors who work at their own preferred pace and frequency; he has deadlines to meet, and he is obliged to pass those deadlines on to at least some of the writers who contribute to his journal. This practical consideration, among others, virtually forces him to employ a staff of regular professional writers who can produce material promptly, continuously, and on demand. He may welcome occasional pieces by academics and other writers who have been inspired to comment on an issue of special interest to them; but he cannot rely on material produced by occasional contributors if he is to get issues of his journal out regularly and frequently. Of course, the more frequently a periodical appears, the more its publisher is disposed to rely on a regular staff of full-time professional contributors. The publisher of a respected quarterly may indeed find himself able to rely primarily on pieces by occasional contributors, but the publisher of a daily newspaper cannot. But even the publisher of a respected quarterly does not have the option of skipping numbers, and moreover, his publication, if it relies exclusively on the pieces of occasional contributors, may be sufficiently different from the pure type of public journal to qualify more as a scholarly or creative arts journal.

The professional journalist, the individual whose occupation it is to write for public journals, is necessarily sensitive to the journal publishers' need for a constant and regular supply of written material. He knows that it is his job to supply that material on a regular basis. He knows that he cannot afford the luxury of only writing on the basis of inspiration. Now, the academic who seeks tenure and promotion, and the writer of fiction who needs to put bread on his table, both know that they must turn out a certain amount of written material in a somewhat perfunctory manner, and interestingly, when they write in this uninspired, almost mechanical way, they sometimes self-disparagingly describe themselves as "doing journalism." What they recognize is that the journalist is the classic paradigm of the writer who is required, by the nature of his occupation, to produce most of his material by routine and under the pressure of having to meet strict deadlines. The journalist may dream, as the academic and novelist do, of producing an inspired magnum opus, but unlike these other writers, he cannot sincerely regard the material that he turns out on a regular basis as being just a means to a higher vocational end and merely secondary or even tangential to his professional mission in life.

One consequence of the periodicity of the public journal is that it deprives the journalist of the opportunity to write with the same degree of inspiration (and the same degree of care) available, at least, to those writers traditionally conceived as authors, or at least the less venal and materialistic of these. The periodicity of the public journal also limits the creativity of the journalist in a quite different but equally important way. Journalistic writing must fit neatly into the public journal in which it will appear. Every public journal has a certain character determined by various of the factors that go into giving it its identity and continuity, and particularly by its editorial policy. The typical journalist knows that he must respect certain wishes not only of a public journal's publishers and editors but of its regular readers, who have come to expect certain traditions and conventions in style and content to be observed in the pages of each and every issue of that journal. Readers expect the latest issue of the journal to look more or less like earlier ones, or at least the more recent of earlier ones. Of course, editorial policy changes, and readers will look favorably on what they take to be improvements in the journal. They may even welcome with open arms the new columnist with a highly innovative approach to his craft or subject matter. But neither readers nor editors of the *Times* and *Daily Mercury* will take kindly to reporters who want to write in the way that Søren Kierkegaard or James Joyce does. Again, the Englishman who regularly reads the *Sun* on his way to work does not want the *Sun* to start looking like the *Times*, and his neighbor who is accustomed to reading the *Times* does not want the *Times* to take on the principal distinguishing characteristics of the *Sun*; and neither wants his daily newspaper to read in places like Wittgenstein's *Tractatus*, the Rig-Veda, or *Mein Kampf*. In preparing his material for a particular journal (or a particular type of journal), the typical journalist is not only guided partly by his interpretation of what editors and readers demand but by his own direct understanding of what the particular journal is about, this understanding having been shaped by his own reading of earlier issues. Whatever personal touches he may want to add, or whatever reforms he may want to institute, he knows that his own contribution to the periodical must not stand out too much. Notice that I speak here of the typical journalist and not of that rare bird who is so gifted, distinguished, or well placed, that he can afford to do pretty much what he wants.

The difference here between journalists and other writers is again one of degree. If the periodicity of the journal has a limiting effect on the journalist's creativity, it does not necessarily stultify that creativity. One of the outstanding features of the leading daily newspapers of our age is their mosaic quality, and this quality also marks some other public journals. Just as a major journal aims at being rather comprehensive in subject matter, its editors will tolerate and, to some extent, encourage a variety of journalistic styles, particularly in analyses and features. Moreover, publishers are ordinarily concerned with attracting new readers as well as holding on to the ones they already have, and so they appreciate the value of a new contributor who is intelligently innovative without being disrespectful of the journal's general character. And at the same time, journalists are certainly not the only writers who have to take into consideration the demands of publishers, editors, and prospective readers. Any writer, and particularly the contributor to a series or anthology, recognizes the need to make his work fit into a publisher's publishing program and some readers' reading programs. But what is important to note here is the extent to which the periodicity of the public journal is a factor in limiting the journalist's creativity. Journalism is perhaps the most cooperative form of publication: the journalist's work stands side by side with the work of other contributors to the journal, and is perceived in a context defined partly by contributors to past issues of the journal. When readers cite the journalist's report or view, they may well pass on to their fellows the information that, "*The Daily Mercury* said . . . ," and they will then be taking as their source the object that is continuous in time and only instantiated in a given issue.

Perhaps the most important consequence of the public journal's periodicity is to be found in its content or subject matter. There is a vast amount of literature to be found in libraries, in bookstores, in dentist's offices, and on living room coffee tables, and the journal publisher is well aware that he must compete for readers' attention. The question in his mind is what he can offer readers that they cannot get—or get as conveniently—from the great and not-so-great authors of the past—poets, novelists, philosophers, and the like—and from their most recent successors. Of course, he could conceivably offer readers more of the same, and there is certainly a market today, as always, for quarterlies and monthlies that specialize in offering poetry and other literary work. There is not a necessary connection between periodical publication and news, and if Innis is right, then the emphasis of North American journalism on news is basically a result of certain historical conditions that prevailed in the early nineteenth century.[12] Certainly even a *daily* journal that specialized exclusively in the publication of literary, historical, or even scientific material is not inconceivable. But if there were a market for such a daily journal, it would surely be a very small one and not significant enough to sustain journalism at anything like its present level of popularity and importance. It is only natural that publishers and journalists should exploit the possibilities of a periodical publication, and if there is anything that a regular, continuing publication can offer that other publications cannot, it is fresh information and discussion about events that regularly, continuously occur. Every new issue can tell us about what is new in our world, the world of the readers. It can bring us the news. For all their greatness, Plato, Livy, and Thoreau cannot bring us the news; what they have to say is relevant to our lives in several important ways, but they are long gone now, and in one important sense at least, their world is not our world.

Daily newspapers came into existence at a time when they had no serious rivals in the field of news coverage. Radio and television were, at most, dreams in the minds of science fiction writers, and book publication was a relatively slow and cumbersome process. Today radio and television can bring us live coverage of the important (or the trivial) events of the day, and book publishers can put out detailed analyses of world affairs in a matter of months or even weeks. If daily newspapers have managed to survive in the presence of fierce competition from other news media, it is partly because we have become accustomed to reading them but also partly because we feel that they provide something in the way of news reporting and interpretation that we have not as yet been able to get—and perhaps never will get—from its competitors. The same holds true of monthlies, quarterlies, and other journals that we call by the name of public journals.

As one of the *O.E.D.* definitions clearly and explicitly indicates, the daily newspaper is the principal paradigm and purest type of the public journal, and other periodical publications qualify as public journals insofar as they contain news or deal with matters of current interest. Even if there is not a necessary connection between journalism and news, historical circumstances have inevitably led to our customary association of journalism with the public journal, a publication that not only is issued on a regular basis but exploits its periodicity by concentrating its attention on current events and matters relevant to them. The term *journal* still appears in the names of countless scholarly, scientific, and literary periodicals. Such publications do provide, report upon, and examine things that are new in a particular sphere; they present us with new writing on recent events or recent research, or with new insights into historical, continuing, or even timeless matters that can now be understood in a new light. But the technical matters with which they deal are of interest primarily to specialists, not to the general public, and it is not surprising that the people who write for them are usually also specialists, and not journalists. If material from such publications is likely to be of interest to a significant portion of the general public, journalists will eventually report on it in the public journals.

At this point then it is appropriate to set aside our somewhat artificial consideration of the public journal—the expression itself seems rather more stilted now than it did in 1933—and consider specifically newspapers and other news journals. We tend to distinguish newspapers from other news journals more by their physical aspect than any other factor; when the journal is made of newsprint or another inexpensive paper, and when it has no cover or binding, we normally call it a newspaper, and otherwise we call it a news magazine. Frequency of appearance is not as important a factor in distinguishing newspapers from other news journals; many newspapers, of course, do not appear daily or even weekly, and some appear less frequently than popular news magazines.

What is news, and why are people interested in reading and writing it? The term *news* is not a particularly technical one and refers basically to a report or interpretation of recent events. According to Mott, the term, which in the sixteenth century came into common use for *tidings*, refers to the report itself rather than to the event it reports: "News is always a report. The event itself is not news."[13] Journalism, of course, is not simply the passing on or dissemination of news. All of us regularly pass on news without being involved in journalism, as, for example, when in casual conversation we inform people about a mutual friend's recent activities, or when we include some gossip in personal letters. The dissemination of news becomes journalism when it is written for (or in) a newspaper or other public journal. What distinguishes news from other reports and interpretations is the recentness of the events it describes; the freshness of it is precisely that quality of it that makes the periodical publication an appropriate vehicle for it. Mott puts it this way: "The one quality of the report which is necessary in order to make it 'news' is timeliness. In other words, news must be new."[14] What is essential to the phenomenon of news is A's reporting of a recent event to B, or by extension, A's shedding new light on a recent event of which B only has limited awareness or understanding. If we try to build more into our definition of news, we risk theorizing somewhat arbitrarily, as, for example, Warren Breed does when he writes, "What is news? Most definitions contain two elements: (1) the recent event and (2) the readers."[15] This empirical claim is almost surely false, but more importantly, Breed implicitly endorses a misleading lexical analysis, for surely news is often heard rather than read. Breed is obviously looking here at news within the context of journalism; but even so, the writer is as central to the journalistic news process as the reader is.

Breed actually goes some way toward correcting his original formula, and he does so by elaborating upon it rather than simplifying it. His analysis of the elements of news, though still flawed, is instructive:

> The elements of news include: (1) the event, the idea, the fact, the thing, the happening, the speech, the statement. (2) This event must be recent or timely, or "brought up to date" by some device; (3) It must be presented in an understandable (usually interesting) fashion; (4) It must be published, broadcast, or otherwise made available to people; and (5) it must be read or heard by people; its news value depends upon the interest it arouses in people.[16]

This analysis not only corrects the original formula in places but indicates some interesting ramifications of the essential nature of news. First, the event that news reports may take any of a number of forms and is not necessarily a sudden, dramatic occurrence such as a murder, storm, election, or coup. We often contrast actions with words, but a speech or statement is, in its own way, as much an event as a murder. Again, a state of affairs that has only gradually developed, such as the inflation rate or the average age of civil servants having reached such-and-such a level, is a kind of report-able event. Even an idea that has not been articulated is an event, and having been initially formulated and maintained over time, it shapes an agent's behavior; indeed, a major part of journalism is uncovering the ideas that have animated the behavior of influential figures. Secondly, news sometimes reports events that, though not recent in themselves, are significantly relevant to recent events. Such news brings historical states of affairs up to date by showing how they have been a factor in the shaping of current events, or how current events represent a significant departure from some historical pattern. Thirdly, since news is communication, the successful re-porting of recent events requires a particular medium of com-munication. And finally, news, being a social phenomenon, has more or less value—by one criterion of value—in proportion to how receptive readers or listeners are to it.

This last point is important, so it is unfortunate that Breed's last comment obscures it somewhat by blurring a crucial distinction. People pass on news because they presume, rightly or wrongly, that it is somehow in the interest of the reader or listener to have a certain degree of awareness and understanding of certain recent events. Thus, while the passing on of news is, in various ways, in the interest of the communicator himself, the primary determinant of the value of news is normally how well it serves the needs and sat-isfies the desires of those who receive it. Another major determi-nant is the extent to which the receiver's new awareness can benefit society (or humanity) as a whole. News requires a receiver, or at least a potential receiver; it is a social phenomenon, and the com-municator not only has a need or desire to express himself but to express himself to another human being, and often, to as many other human beings as possible. He is not only concerned with his own personal interests, but even if he were, he would still have to take account of the interests of potential receivers of his report. He wants people to listen to him, and he needs to arouse their interest in what he has to say. But it is a misleading oversimplification of these matters to say, as Breed does, that the value of his report "de-pends upon the interest it arouses in people." Arousing interest in what one has to say is normally a major condition of getting people to listen attentively to one's report. But the value of news is a func-tion of much more than simply how much interest it arouses. In-formation about a movie starlet's latest romance may arouse con-siderably more interest in the general public than a revelation of mismanagement by high-ranking government officials, yet it hardly qualifies as more valuable by the most important criteria of value (even in the eyes of the reflective individual who regretfully admits a fascination with the private lives of celebrities in the entertainment world). The value of news cannot properly be located exclusively in the efficacy with which it fulfills the preliminary condition of arousing interest; and indeed, the most valuable news, for receivers themselves and for their fellow human beings, is often that in which it is most difficult to arouse interest in a substantial portion of the general public. The value of communication lies not only in the efficacy with which it has been communicated—how impressively or to what number of people—but in its content. Obviously, inability to arouse interest in what one has to say diminishes the value of one's report by one important criterion of value; but the great communicator is not simply the person who gets many people to listen attentively to his report but rather the person who gets them to listen attentively to a report that has substantial value in its own right, not only for the receivers themselves but for all people who stand to be affected by the receivers' new awareness or understanding. The ambiguity in the word *interest* itself is worth noting: valuable news not only arouses interest but is in the interest of the potential receivers and in the public interest.

Insofar as Breed is himself aware of these facts, it way be inferred that Breed did not mean to leave the impression that the normative element of news is to be understood purely in terms of the efficacy with which the report arouses interest. And one can agree with Breed that news requires from the communicator not only general communication skills but an appreciation of various factors that influence the quality and degree of receptivity of potential readers and listeners. But what is perhaps most significant about Breed's analysis is that it recognizes the whole matter of value as an essential element of news. Our raw lexical definition of news seems to be purely descriptive: A reports a recent event to B. We are not, however, describing here the movements of planets or geological phenomena; we are considering human behavior, and regardless of what certain behaviorist social scientists say to the contrary, human behavior, and particularly intentional behavior in social relations, is largely a function of human valuation. Hence, a definition of news is somewhat empty if it does not indicate what sort of motives inspire individuals to pass on news and to be receptive to it. The possible motives, and the values related to them, are, in fact, too numerous, too diverse, and at times too subtle or too personal to be packaged together into a neat definition. Nevertheless, it is important to be aware of the fact that participants in the news process rightly see news as at least potentially something of value, and it is profitable for us to have some understanding of the major forms of value that news can have.

The determination of these various forms of value is a matter that will persist to the end of this inquiry, and whatever analysis is derived at this stage will necessarily be sketchy and incomplete. Sustained reflection on questions of value ultimately leads into the realm of philosophical speculation. It is foolish to take the value of something as complex as news to be self-evident; but neither is one forced here to theorize in an intellectual vacuum. We have all had countless experiences with news—with reporting recent events, listening to such reports, reading them, and thinking about them (individually and generically). As for issues related to value and valuation, even relatively unreflective people think about these from time to time, and a steady stream of views on these issues has poured forth for centuries from not only philosophers and journalists, but also humanists, behavioral and social scientists, and even biologists. We have all formed a conception of typical news stories, not only on the basis of reading news publications and daily conversation, but on the basis of an interpretation of history and classical literature, and we have developed certain working ideas about the function of news in our lives as social beings. These working ideas are generally not very sophisticated, and we realize on deeper reflection that the matter of news value, like the general matter of value itself, gives rise to genuinely philosophical questions that, depending on our inclination, we choose to pursue or set aside.

The crudest possible approach to the question of news value is one that treats the desire to receive or impart news as virtually an irreducible, unanalyzable absolute like the desire for self-preservation, food, sex, or feelings of competence. Thus it is slightly disconcerting to find such a serious student of journalism as Mott attaching the importance that he does to what he terms *news-hunger.* "News-hunger," he writes, "is fundamental in human nature. It is characteristic of social man, whether he is conscious of it or not. The basic drives are those for food, shelter, and sex expression; after these are satisfied, other desires crowd forward—for social life, for recognition among one's fellows, for new experience and adventure. These latter desires are greatly stimulated by information, or news, about others."[17] Mott recognizes that desire for news is not of the same order as desire for food, and he recognizes that news is an instrument for the satisfaction of certain basic social desires. Yet the very term *news-hunger* has almost a depth-psychological ring to it, especially in the context of Mott's reference to the possible limitations of our consciousness of this fundamental force. It all but implies that explanations of news value are, in the final analysis, after the fact and somewhat contrived. Mott himself indirectly recognizes that the term covers a wide range of desires, for he grants that, "There are . . . degrees and gradations of news-hunger, ranging from that which is based on mere idle curiosity to that which derives from agonies of personal anxiety".[18] Clearly he is not prepared to admit, however, the possibility that the various desires that he has in mind are too different to be helpfully characterized as manifestations of a common hunger.

Breed, in contrast, takes delight in the diversity of functions that a newspaper performs:

> Among these are: (1) business, private profit for the owners; (2) news dissemination; (3) news suppression; (4) commericial: advertising; (5) entertainment and diversion; (6) escape—both by reading the paper and by not reading but by becoming lost in it for a half-hour; (7) crusading for causes; (8) watchdogging; (9) arbitrating; (10) maintaining the status quo; (11) standardizing thought and action; (12) serving as a channel for special interests; (13) providing a pleasant picture of the community: the magic mirror; (14) conferring status upon individuals in the news; (15) providing an outlet for complaints (letters to the editor); (16) serving consistently, day in and day out, as a stimulus to public opinion, through both intellectual and emotional reactions of readers; and probably many more.[19]

Breed is talking here about the functions of a newspaper, not the functions of news as such, and it is profitable to note here the various possible functions of a modern newspaper that are related only marginally, at most, to news itself. Also, Breed's list does not focus specifically on the value of news to individual readers. Nevertheless, several items on Breed's list suggest that Mott's news-hunger is being called upon to carry a very heavy—and inconsistent—conceptual burden. The reporter's hunger to inform and interpret may involve desires to profit materially, entertain, crusade, pander, pacify, stimulate, or so forth; and the receiver's hunger to be informed and enlightened may involve desires to be entertained, freed from responsibilities, clued into moral responsibilities, tranquilized, or stimulated, for example. Breed's analysis suggests that the value of news is largely instrumental and very much multi-faceted, and that many of the functions of news are essentially unrelated to one another. If this analysis is a fairly accurate one as far as it goes, as I think it is, then it follows that news is better viewed as a vehicle for the satisfaction of a wide range of independent and even inconsistent desires than as a response to a basic hunger that merely has different gradations. The desire to be tranquilized, for example, is qualitatively different from—indeed, contrary to—the desire to be stimulated.

The analyses of Mott and Breed are both descriptive rather than prescriptive; both writers have endeavored to understand news as it is, rather than as it could be. Undoubtedly, both writers have ideas about how the journalistic news process can be improved, but their general conception of news value is rooted in what they perceive as the actual motives, conscious or unconscious, that have traditionally induced journalists and newspaper readers to participate in the news process. Anyone with a more philosophical inclination will be tempted to go further and ask, "Given our highest moral ideals, what are we to take to be the noblest uses to which news could be put?" To ask this rather Platonic question aloud is to risk being regarded as an illiberal apologist for well-meant but dangerous manipulation and propagandizing. But one should not be intimidated by the critic who, while posing as a defender of freedom of thought and expression, is just a cynic and a pessimist. News value need not be determined exclusively by looking at what people have traditionally done with news in the past; surely it is worth one's while to consider here how news could be used to promote and realize the highest and most general of human values, the ideals of a civilized person and a civilized society.

Consider this example. Mott writes that, "There is also, in this news-hunger we have been discussing, often a desire for self-improvement."[20] For Mott, this desire for self-improvement is, like "mere idle curiosity," just one more of many degrees or gradations of news-hunger. But Mott's reference to the desire for self-improvement calls to mind what any historian of ideas will recognize as one of the classical moral ideals—self-realization or self-perfection. Now, if self-realization is of a higher order of moral value than satisfying idle curiosity or being entertained, then news reporter and news receiver alike are being somewhat reprehensible if they treat the promotion of self-realization as just one more of many equally important tasks that the news process can conceivably perform. This point can be put in another way: news has value not only in relation to its intrinsic properties as news but in its relation to general values, particularly those that we characterize as ideals. Only the most naive ethical subjectivist holds that values as such are to be determined solely by considering how, as a general rule, ordinary people actually behave. Once we are prepared to acknowledge that a majority can behave immorally, then we ought to be willing to acknowledge, ipso facto, that there is a very important sense in which the news to which the majority of people are ordinarily most receptive is not necessarily news of great value.

I grant, however, that when I talk about the potential or ideal value of news, I am already rather more removed from my consideration of the essential nature of news than when I talk about the perceived value of news, that is, the extent to which news satisfies the immediate desires people actually have when they opt to participate in the news process as reporters or receivers. News is not essentially a good thing any more than human beings are essentially good individuals, even if people are somehow striving, both generally and as participants in the news process, to be good and to behave in the right way. When a description of the essential nature of a thing is requested, it is normally a minimally theoretical definition that is being elicited, even if a great deal of theorizing is required to arrive at that definition. And, as noted earlier, such a definition of news is, if somewhat empty, certainly available.

Nevertheless, if one is to attain more than a shallow understanding of news and of journalism, one must be ever mindful of the fact that participants in the news process have values and that their values, which are general and abstract as well as specific and concrete, establish the framework within which determinations of news value are made. These values normally come together to form a system that, along with the agent's empirical and metaphysical judgments and emotional tendencies, goes into making up the agent's particular world view, a world view that he brings to the news process. News is a social process, indeed a social institution, and it takes the form it does because of the world views of the people who have made it what it is. Values themselves can be scrutinized on several levels. We can analyze, in a largely descriptive, empirical, or phenomenological way, the immediate desires or aims that motivate people; we can consider the ideals that a person has as an individual or as a member of a community; or we can speculate with respect to the ideals that a person or community ought to have, values in the loftiest and most profound sense of the term. The actual values of people are subject to critical analysis when we examine them from the perspective of this third level of scrutiny. And so it is with news value as with value in general.

It is the axiological or value dimension of the news process that makes journalism so philosophically interesting. The journalist brings to his work certain general values that form the framework within which he develops his conception of news value; so too does the receiver. Reporter and receiver have also arrived at certain judgments, empirical and normative, about the values of their counterpart in the news process. It is the diversity of the value systems that participants in the news process bring to their role in that process, and the diversity of their perceptions of the value system of their counterpart in the process, that make journalism much more than the simple, straightforward satisfaction of a universal hunger.

Servan-Schreiber is rather cynical when he writes that, "Every country has the media it deserves. Indeed, the media themselves provide only a slightly distorted image of the society they mirror."[21] Marshall McLuhan shows more restraint—although not enough—when he theorizes that, "As forms, as media, the book and the newspaper would seem to be as incompatible as any two media could be. The owners of media always endeavor to give the public what it wants, because they sense that their power is in the *medium* and not in the *message* or the program."[22] The authors would seem to have underestimated the complexity of human valuation, for even if one were to grant, as one most certainly should not, that the reporter, interpreter, and editor will always strive desperately to follow the tune called by the news consumer, the fact remains that, given their different world views and their partly inaccurate perceptions of each other's world view, journalist and receiver will frequently function at cross-purposes in the news process. I shall illustrate this point with a few snippets of fictional but, I believe, realistic conversation:

19 September

JOURNALIST A: I am preparing a series of articles on discrimination against bald people.

JOURNALIST B: Do you really expect there to be much reader interest in it?

JOURNALIST A: Yes, I do. It will be something of an exposé, with some interesting political ramifications. And there is a human interest angle, too. After all, there are plenty of bald people around, and everyone has a bald person or two in his circle of close friends or relatives. Anyway, if all else fails, the series should have a certain entertainment value.

21 November

READER C: The paper has been running a ridiculous series of articles on discrimination against bald people. I wonder what kind of editors think these things up. With all of the important events taking place in the world, look at what they come up with! They obviously have very little respect for their readers.

READER D: I have to confess that I thought the last article in the series was pretty clever. I think that what they are trying to show is how silly all of this civil rights activism has been getting.

28 February

JOURNALIST B: What kind of response did you get to your series on discrimination against bald people?

JOURNALIST A: A disappointing one. We received a few appreciative letters from bald people, but most readers didn't seem to get the point that I was trying to get across.

JOURNALIST B: What do you think went wrong?

JOURNALIST A: I'm not quite sure, but maybe I tend to overestimate the intelligence and good will of most of our readers. I suppose that many people did find the series interesting and informative, but we just haven't heard from them. You know how this business is. Anyway, I'm glad that I wrote those articles. Mistreatment of minorities needs to be brought to the public's attention, whether those smug bigots out there like it or not.

In these brief dialogues, various conflicts and misunderstandings come into play, although some are not as obvious as others. The writer believes that his articles are important; one reader disagrees, while the other thinks they are important for a reason that is not only different from the writer's but contrary to it. The writer may have done a bad job of getting his point across, and the readers may be somewhat obtuse; but the diversity of their value systems—both generally and with respect to news—has clearly contributed to the diversity of their interpretations and assessments of the reports. In any case, the writer and his two readers do not understand each other's values, and they begin and end with unsatisfactory, and perhaps unfair, expectations of each other. The readers disagree with each other too, and it may well be that the two journalists do as well, for B's initial question suggests that the value of his colleague's series may not be immediately obvious to him. Finally, the ambiguity of the writer's value system is worth noting. The writer seems to have conflicting views about how important it is that his articles be favorably received; initially, he does not dismiss as irrelevant his colleague's question about reader interest, and he seems to attach some importance to the aspects of his articles that are likely to elicit a lively and positive response. Yet his final remarks, while perhaps suggesting sour grapes on his part, indicate that he is capable of perceiving himself as someone whose obligation it is to rise above journalistic pandering. It is not clear to us, or perhaps even to him, how much importance he actually attaches overall to each of his roles as stimulator, entertainer, social critic, social reformer, or righteous prophet. And yet, in the last analysis, what we have here is a typical example of journalistic news communication, of A's reporting and interpreting recent events to such readers as C and D.

"I have been misunderstood by my readers," "My important work has not been appreciated by my readers": these are laments that issue all too often from the mouths not only of journalists but of all writers, even those who are fortunate enough to have an audience composed largely of highly reflective, knowledgeable, and imaginative readers. We can hardly attribute this vast mass of misunderstanding exclusively to careless reading and careless writing. We have to attribute at least a large part of it to human individuality. Of course, for some great writers, there is the consolation of believing that their works, too advanced for their own age, may someday receive a vindication that time alone can bring. But such consolation is not available to the typical journalist, who, unfailingly mindful of the fact that he is neither sage, philosopher, nor elegant belletrist, knows full well that future generations will not show the same willingness to revive ordinary periodical pieces on events now long past that they will show for works that take a view of matters under the aspect of eternity. Moreover, the typical journalist cannot afford to be misunderstood in his own age to the extent that the inspired author can; his publisher and his professional colleagues may be prepared to tolerate him if he occasionally offends his readers, but they will not allow him to carry on with his work if he consistently bores or baffles his readers.

Fortunately for the journalist, the immediate success of his newspaper or news magazine does not depend on him alone, and this is a major positive dimension of his being part of a cooperative endeavor. A publisher can often afford to keep on his payroll a journalist whose writing appeals to a relatively small but significant segment of the periodical's regular readership. If there are enough bald people and civil libertarians out there in the readership, Journalist A will manage to get by, notwithstanding the disappointing response that he gets from people such as Reader C. Major newspapers and news magazines are characterized by a large measure of diversity as well as of uniformity. It would be an exaggeration to say that the publishers and editors of major news journals want and expect their publications to be all things to all men. But it is certainly no exaggeration to say that almost all of them are constantly aware of the fact of the diversity of world views and value systems among their journalists and readers. One reader of the *Daily Mercury* will consistently pass over the political news and immerse himself in the newspaper's sports and business pages; another will do the opposite. A major newspaper may have full-time columnists specializing in the reporting of recent events in the worlds of chess, philately, gardening, or high society, even though these columnists write on matters of little interest to many or most readers of the publication. McLuhan has suggested that "British and American journalism . . . have always tended to exploit the mosaic form of the newspaper format in order to present the discontinuous variety and incongruity of ordinary life."[23] However sound this thesis may

be, there is a simpler and more important explanation of the newspaper's mosaic form: publishers and editors know that for every
regular reader who has a burning interest in gardening or the civil
rights of bald people, there are numerous other readers who do
not find such subjects particularly interesting or important.

Still, it would be a serious error to relate valuation to the news
process solely in such a way as to perceive only the effects of individuality upon the news process and journalism. If there is a single
worst error in the history of philosophy, it is the error of relativism,
the error of becoming obsessed with subjectivity to the point where
one loses sight of complementary dimensions of consensus, objectivity, and absoluteness. The person who sees the word *value*—or
judgment—and thinks immediately and exclusively of disagreement, subjectivity, and relativity may well be on his way to an irresponsible nihilism. With respect to the news process in particular, for
all the misunderstanding that inevitably infects it, those who participate in it are usually capable of understanding themselves and their
counterparts in the process, at least up to a point and on certain
levels. Reporter and receiver have a great deal in common as members of a community, or rather as members of several communities
(for example, a nation-state, a religious community, a community of
literate persons); and, of course, they have much in common as
members of what is perhaps the most important community of all,
the human community. The commonality of values (and empirical
and metaphysical judgments and emotional attitudes) that bridges
the gap between the journalist and his reader, and between all individuals, is most impressively illustrated in journalism by what Breed
calls the "traditional story." Among his examples of "traditional
stories," he includes "the weekend auto accident toll," "the lun-
cheon civic meeting," and "the child and his pet."[24] But we can
consider here all of the journalist's major news assignments: speech
reports and meetings, death stories and obituaries, stories about
people, accidents and disasters, crime and law enforcement, proceedings after arrests, trials and civil proceedings, and news of
government.[25] Of course, none of these matters are of universal interest; there are plenty of people who are not interested in the child
and his pet or in news of government. Nevertheless, while a journalist is mistaken if he believes that reports about gardening or discrimination against bald people are of nearly universal or even very
wide interest, he will rarely have to apologize to his editors and
readers for a lengthy series of articles on events that led up to a
recent industrial disaster in the region. If a journalist cannot afford
to assume that any event that greatly interests him will also interest

most of his readers, neither can he afford to assume that he is such a strange creature that he is wholly incapable of empathizing with his fellow citizens and fellow human beings. And before rushing to accuse a journalist of pandering to the public taste in his selection of subject matter, one should weigh the possibility that he shares the interest of his readers in the subjects on which he writes. For every sleazy gossip columnist who hates what he sees himself as having to do for a living, there may be a dozen who, perhaps despite outward professions of embarrassment and self-contempt, are absolutely enchanted with their assignment.

The journalist does not have to rely on empathetic intuition alone in determining what subjects that interest him will also interest a substantial portion of his readership. As a professional, he learns from experience and through the guidance of editors and senior colleagues. He actually learns, as Mott has observed, to apply certain tests of news importance: timeliness, prominence of the persons involved in the report, proximity, and probable consequence ("the expected or possible effect on his readers of a given event or condition").[26] Also, he comes to know relevant facts about the particular readership of his journal; for his readers are not just human beings as such, and not just individuals, but members of various identifiable groups. A contributor to the *Times* does not have to be very sophisticated sociologically to know that his readers, being literate and educated enough to be able to appreciate what the *Times* has traditionally offered, and being on the whole more traveled and more sophisticated than most readers of the competing *Sun*, will generally respond more enthusiastically than readers of the *Sun* to a feature on European wines or African politics. Indeed, he knows that people who are interested in European wines and African politics have traditionally turned to the *Times* for information on such subjects.

Some degree of specialization among newspapers and news magazines was an inevitable consequence of competition among such publications. Even if a newspaper publisher would like his publication to be almost all things to all men, he knows that it cannot be so; for all that readers of the *Sun* and *Times* have in common as human beings, and as Englishmen, they are sufficiently different in outlook to be able to appreciate one of the papers more than its competitor. The *Times* and *Sun* both report those traditional stories about the auto accident toll and the child and his pet, but they report them somewhat differently. When they go beyond the traditional stories and move into their particular areas of expertise, they invite some readers at the risk of alienating others. Of course, the regular reader

of the *Times* may be appreciative enough of one or two special features of the *Sun* to read the *Sun* on more than an occasional basis;
and some people studiously avoid becoming committed to any one
paper and opt for variety and adventure over consistency and familiarity. But there is a general tendency among readers to arrive at
the conclusion that, of all the newspapers and news magazines available, only a few are directed at an audience made up of people like
themselves.

Just as newspaper readers tend to gravitate toward a publication
with which, given their world view and their skills, they feel comfortable, the journalist appreciates the advantages of being on the
staff of a periodical whose readers will be interested in the subjects
on which he would like to write and will be respectful (though not
necessarily uncritical) of the particular approaches that he would
like to take to those subjects. Yet there are significant limits to the
degree of sympathy that participants in the journalistic news process
desire to share with their counterparts in the process. If reporter and
receiver do not at all challenge one another, they may end up boring
one another. The typical reader does not want to be enraged too
often by his daily newspaper, but neither does he want to feel that
he is being pandered to; he enjoys being reminded from time to time
that he is an individual with his own personal values and attitudes.
He may also recognize the need to widen his horizons and to be
open to exposure to new areas of knowledge and new ideas and
perspectives.

As for the journalist, his desire for self-respect—some would say
his vanity—disinclines him to think of himself as a mere panderer
who simply preaches to the converted and allows himself, for narrow materialistic reasons, to serve up to his readers whatever they
want to hear and nothing else. Hence, it is natural for him to write,
at least occasionally, certain things about certain subjects that he
thinks that he ought to write, regardless of how favorable they are
likely to be received by his readers. It is not necessarily sour grapes
that impels a journalist to reflect in retrospect that he does not regret having written a piece that was not properly or enthusiastically
received by his readers; he may sincerely believe, and rightly so,
that certain things needed to be said, not only for the good of society
as a whole but for the long-term good of the very readers who re-
sponded perplexedly or unsympathetically to his piece.

The journalist can never forget that he is professionally obliged to
provide a service, but how broadly or how narrowly he construes
that service depends partly on his personal value system and not
wholly on market forces or other factors beyond his control. He may

rightly feel that, like a competent physician, he must sometimes dispense bitter medicine in a way that his client will not immediately (or ever) appreciate, and that to do otherwise would not be professionally serving the client's needs. And he may rightly believe that society has provided him with the freedom and opportunity he has as a journalist in order that he may satisfy the needs, and promote the interests, not only of the paying customer but of society itself. Again, he must believe that through the proper practice of his craft, he is also serving his own needs—not just material needs (though these are certainly important) but also his needs as a moral agent with a clear vision of both the nature of the good life and the ideals of a civilized community.

Thus, even if the journalist were always in a position to give his readers pretty much what they want in the way of satisfaction of immediate, actual, and possibly unhealthy and socially worthless desires—and as we have seen, he is not always in such a position— his personal value system, with its concomitant implications for his conceptions of news value and his craft, would probably induce him, at least occasionally, to avoid doing so. Of course, the journalist, both as a professional and as a human being, is no more a totally free agent than anyone else is. Any number of determining factors contribute to the shaping of his ideas, values, attitudes, and behavior. As a journalist in particular, he must to some extent please publishers, editors, colleagues, readers, politicians, and policemen if he is to be allowed to carry on with his work. His approach to his craft is shaped, both consciously and unconsciously, partly by journalistic traditions and conventions and by the attitudes of fellow workers in his profession. As all of us are, he is in many ways the child of his age, of his society, and of parents who have brought him up in a particular way; and he is the product of one or more systems of education. But only a simple-minded determinist would choose to ignore the fact that he is also an intelligent human being capable of rational, reflective judgment, of existential commitment, and of learning from the wise as well as the worldly.

Journalism, even mediocre journalism, is, like almost all forms of professional writing, a vocation that calls for a considerable degree of intelligence. We all know how difficult writing can be even for people blessed with remarkable gifts; clear writing requires clear thinking, not just a spontaneous or mechanical ability. One has to have something to say, and one has to be able to say it in a disciplined and coherent manner. A person who is intelligent and talented enough to write for a newspaper or news magazine is not likely to be the sort of person who is ordinarily prepared to make himself readily available as an instrument for the promotion of values and ideas to which he is wholly antipathetic. Of course, many journalists have served trivial or ignoble causes, but so too have philosophers, clerics, scientists, dramatists, saints, and prophets.

One characteristic a journalist has in common with these people is a personal as well as a professional commitment to communicating; this commitment sometimes develops into a passion for communicating, and it merits some attention. There are obviously numerous practical considerations that motivate people to communicate with one another, and some people are so talkative that they make us wonder whether perhaps communicating can be an end pursued for its own sake alone. At the same time, we know that there are many relatively uncommunicative, taciturn, and secretive individuals, and that there are some who, though they would like to talk and write more often, usually find expressing themselves to be a difficult and painful task. Now, by the time he is ready to embark upon a journalistic career, a person knows that he is not only gifted at expressing himself in words but is the type of person who is likely to get satisfaction from such sustained expression. To be able to get so much satisfaction from this sustained expression, one must place a personal value on expression that stands apart from the conventional assessment. This point was much appreciated by William Hocking, one of the few philosophers to have taken a close look at journalism. While recognizing that the value of free expression has several dimensions, Hocking is careful not to neglect how free expression can satisfy what he calls a "will to power *through ideas*," and he suggests that, "This impulse is akin to the reproductive impulse; it is the instinct for mental self-propagation."[27] This may seem to be an extravagant claim, and those familiar with Hocking's characteristic pomposity and excessive fondness for the Germanic mode of expression might be inclined to dismiss it as pretentious rubbish. But perhaps there is a helpful insight here.

Hocking's use of the Nietzschean expression, "will to power," is particularly suggestive. The founder of Individual Psychology, Alfred Adler, also made use of this Nietzschean terminology, and Adlerian psychology at its most profound only confirms what acute psychologists long before Nietzsche and Adler already knew about human nature—that human beings are, if to varying degrees, striving at a fundamental level of motivation to overcome feelings of inferiority and to attain feelings of competence and self-worth.[28] Expression through verbal communication can perform many functions, but not the least important of these is its service as a field for the manifestation of one's presence as a talented, effective, and potentially useful or dangerous agent. Like political or military activity, it is a field for creative ambition and aggression that permits an agent to achieve not only respect and notoriety among his fellows but a personal confirmation of his existential significance. But Nietzsche meant to capture more with this expression. Nietzsche was impressed by the fact that the creative will to power is truncated in most people, and few people are honest, courageous, and stoical enough to allow it free rein. The creative will to power of journalists is truncated too, but every journalist is at least vaguely aware of the potential power and influence that his special gifts and position afford him. This awareness is capable of sustaining even the most frustrated journalist's sense of self-worth. For the superior journalist, it is an impetus to genuine creativity. The superior journalist recognizes that his greatest influence is to be exerted through the advancement of ideas and attitudes to which he is personally committed and not simply through service as the agent of those who already possess manifest power (publishers, editors, keepers of social institutions, or the Great Sophist itself).

Even the weakest of mediocre journalists is sufficiently aware of the potential power of journalism to be willing at least occasionally to exploit his writing as a vehicle for promoting those ideas and attitudes that he personally deems as having great worth. Of course, he often unconsciously manifests his biases in his reporting and interpreting, but that is another matter altogether. So again, the popular image of the typical journalist as someone who, being terribly venal or naive, merely gives the readership what it wants, or gives the readership what it has made him want to give back to it, is not entirely satisfactory. The Great Sophist influences the journalist in a variety of subtle but profound ways. But just like the philosopher, cleric, scientist, dramatist, saint, and prophet, the journalist himself is often readily given to proselytizing.

Like most philosophers, most journalists will recognize that Nietzsche's insight, helpful though it is, illuminates only one aspect of human motivation and morality. Exaggerating its importance, Nietzsche himself was led at times to nihilistic conclusions that no one should accept. A morally responsible individual does not look at social life as simply a field for the manifestation of his creative will to power. A healthy-minded journalist seeks much more than the thrill of knowing that he has contributed to the reshaping of his readers' world views. He wants his readers to be better people for having read what he has written for them. Unlike Nietzsche, he needs to be convinced of the objective soundness or at least the overall reasonableness of the particular ideas and attitudes that are being conveyed in his reports and analyses. On the other hand, he must be open-minded, responsive to intelligent criticism, unfanatical, and ever respectful of the difficulty with which profound truths, moral or otherwise, are grasped by people like himself. He must understand the difference between enlightening readers and merely propagandizing them, or between educating them and merely changing their view.

The news process itself imposes some salutary disincentives to overzealous journalistic proselytism. As we have seen, the journalist, both in his selection of subject matter and in his approach to that subject matter, must engage the reader's interest without alienating him. Like any writer of nonfiction, the journalist is engaged in something like an imaginary dialogue with his expected readers; he must to some extent anticipate the responses they are likely to make to what he has written. We are thus reminded of the other side of the coin: in his eagerness to avoid unwarranted proselytizing or propagandizing, or in his willingness to make concessions to his expected readers, the journalist may run the risk of moving too far in the direction of pandering.

Journalistic integrity involves a variety of virtues, but certainly one of the most important of these is the trained habit of bearing in mind, as one writes, the need to manifest a balanced and accurate appraisal of both one's own ideas and attitudes and those of the various elements in one's readership. This balanced and accurate appraisal is, in specific instances, rarely easy to make, and so it is difficult for even the most morally earnest yet open-minded of journalists to avoid consistently any propagandizing or pandering. When the journalist is acting as his own person, and not just as the agent or spokesman for his employer or some special interest group, then when he habitually overestimates his own wisdom or habitually underestimates that of his brighter readers, he is well on his way toward ending up as either an arrogant propagandist or an insincere panderer. When he habitually undervalues his own wisdom or habitually overvalues that of his duller readers, he is on his way toward ending up as a submissive panderer or an insincere propagandist. Journalistic integrity involves, among other things, a virtue that represents a mean between two extremes or vices, the disposition to propagandize and the disposition to pander. Cultivation of this virtue requires one to have some awareness of the full extent and the genuine limitations of both one's own insight and the insight of one's brighter and duller readers.

Of course, journalistic integrity involves much more. First, when thinking of the high-minded journalist, certain cases come to mind of exemplary behavior in which journalists have opted to inconvenience or even endanger themselves rather than violate what they and their colleagues take to be a special ethical rule of their profession. For example, many of us see journalistic integrity as having been manifested in the behavior of the journalist who has gone to prison rather than reveal a well-meaning but vulnerable source. Again, journalistic integrity is often simply a matter of habitually applying general principles of justice and morality to all of one's activities as a journalist. A journalist who is a good person is not necessarily a good journalist, but he is almost always a person who carries out his journalistic work with something that deserves to be characterized as journalistic integrity.

However, to reflect on these other aspects of journalistic integrity, is to no longer be considering the essential nature of journalism. Nor would it be considering the essential nature of journalism to reflect further on the specific values, aims, and interests that journalists and readers bring to the news process. The analyses of journalism and the news process that have been developed here have what I take to be fairly minimal content, and they are so abstract that they barely qualify as theories, if indeed they are theoretical at all. I regard them more as elaborations of lexical definitions than theories. Elaborations of lexical definitions serve well as starting points for theorizing; they establish a framework for further reflection. They are also valuable in their own right, not only in clearing up possible conceptual confusions but in drawing our attention to how theory-laden an informal conception can be.

Consider this statement by McCormick: "The newspaper is an institution developed by modern civilization to present the news of the day, to foster commerce and industry through widely circulated advertisements, and to furnish that check upon government which no constitution has ever been able to provide."[29] This comment might strike a casual reader as innocuous common sense, but even allowing for the fact that McCormick is talking here about newspapers and not directly about journalism or the news process, we see that he is in deep theoretical waters. McCormick's claim that a newspaper exists to present the news of the day is virtually tautological, but his other claims betray his personal biases and perceptions. First, is it necessarily one of the three major aims of a newspaper "to foster commerce and industry through widely circulated advertisements?" Is it not possible, after all, for a newspaper to have a small circulation, to have few if any advertisements, and to be produced by publishers, editors, and journalists who have no interest whatsoever in fostering commerce and industry? Second, is it necessarily one of the three major aims of a newspaper "to furnish that check upon government which no constitution has ever been able to provide?" Is it not, in fact, possible for a newspaper to be produced by people who are sympathetic to, or even slavishly supportive of, government policy? Is it not possible for a newspaper to be produced by people who are mainly concerned with furnishing a check instead upon big business interests, organized crime syndicates, terrorist and anarchist groups, overreaching ecclesiastical institutions, or foreign enemies? Third, why are these two possible functions of a newspaper more important than all of the others on that long list of Breed's that were considered earlier? Those familiar with McCormick's own publications will immediately suspect that his description of the newspaper is a dubious piece of self-justification. One does not have to know anything about McCormick, however, to recognize that his description of the essential nature of a newspaper is somewhat arbitrary and slanted, though it may well fit the particular newspapers that he himself was instrumental in producing.

Generalizing now, it may be said that awareness of the relative emptiness of these analyses serves as a reminder to us of the great diversity of uses to which journalism as such can be put. It indicates to journalists, editors, publishers, readers, and even those outside the journalistic news process that the function of journalism is not a single, inflexible, immutable given but rather something determined under concrete circumstances by particular agents who have their own specific aims, interests, and values. For the journalist, it can be an incentive to reflection on his own activity. The journalist who has such an awareness will not simply imitate his colleagues and predecessors but will regularly ask himself, as he undertakes his various projects, what exactly he is doing and why he is doing it. He will ask himself such questions as: Will my readers be interested in this report? Ought they to be? Should I be aiming here mainly to entertain, mainly to instruct, or to do both in roughly equal parts? Am I promoting my own values and attitudes in this article? Ought I to be doing so? Am I furnishing a check on certain overreaching politicians? Ought I to be doing so? Am I furnishing a check on certain overreaching interest groups? If so, precisely which ones? Why do these groups need to be checked? Am I the one who should be doing the checking? In my selection of subject matter, have I shown an excessive regard for the concerns of my publishers, editors, and colleagues, or those of my likely readers? Is my regard for the concerns of these various people perhaps insufficient? Am I promoting the importance or respectability of the particular individuals and groups about which I am writing? Am I diminishing it?

Ought I to be doing so? Am I defending the status quo or encouraging reforms? Is it my proper role as a journalist, or as a civilized human being, or as both, to do so? Am I paying too much (or too little) attention to my professional advancement? Have I made it clear enough to my readers what it is that I am trying to do for them by providing them with this information and insight? Will readers whose values and attitudes are very different from my own be able to understand what I am doing here and why I am doing it? Do I risk evoking the resentment of my readers, and if so, is such a risk worth taking? Would such resentment be salutary for them and their fellows?

Readers too can be stimulated to reflect on their own activity, and indeed they are as active in their own way as journalists are. Once they appreciate the diversity of uses to which journalism can be put, they will not be so inclined to rely on a single, narrow criterion as a guide to whether the writing that they are reading is good or bad journalism. As they move from one section of a periodical to the next, they will ask themselves such questions as: Why am I reading this material? Should I be reading it more carefully or passing over it entirely? Am I merely killing time now or am I actually accomplishing something personally advantageous and socially constructive? To what extent do I want to be challenged, and to what extent do I merely want to have my convictions confirmed? Does what I am reading call for direct action on my part or merely passive recognition of certain facts or possibilities? Are these journalists proselytizing and propagandizing, or are they making a sound case for the importance of their subject matter and the reasonableness of their approach to it? Are they attempting to pander to people like me or to some other segment of their readership? Do they understand the world view of people like me? Should I be reading this periodical, or could I get more helpful information and analysis from some other periodical or some other news medium? Do I have a right to expect something more to my liking from a periodical that has been produced by people who have aims and interests that I can now see are somewhat different from my own?

Publishers and editors can be stimulated to ask themselves some of the questions that journalists will be asking themselves, but they will also have to give special attention to the question of the extent to which they are promoting journalism proper and the extent to which they are promoting extrajournalistic interests, such as the money-making that could be just as well accomplished through the selling of furniture or motorcars. They may be stimulated to consider the related questions of whether they have been promoting a sound balance of journalistic and extrajournalistic interests, and if not, what could be done to achieve such a balance. As for those outside the journalistic news process, their appreciation of the diversity of uses to which journalism as such can be put will enable them to make more informed judgments about the principal roles that journalism ought to play in the social life of a civilized community. Regardless of to what extent they participate in the journalistic news process, citizens have a civic as well as a general moral responsibility to participate in checking the actual and potential abuses of journalism and to encourage improvements in the institution of journalism. Few of us are saints, and even if we were, we would still have to apply our moral vitality in many different spheres. But if journalism falls too short of what it ought to be here and now, that is partly because too many of us are too often silent about its failings. I grant, however, that if the journalist, reader, publisher, or outside observer becomes obsessed with constantly posing for himself the kinds of questions outlined above, he will become paralyzed to the point where he is no longer able to fulfill his proper role with respect to the journalistic news process. There comes a time for one to stop asking questions and get on with one's endeavors.

If one brings to the journalistic news process a narrow, overly specific conception of the function of journalism, and if one fails to appreciate the wide range of uses to which journalism is and can be put, one will often fail to understand the situation of one's counterpart in the news process and will be unable to exploit effectively what the process offers to both him and his counterpart. There is a danger that awareness of the emptiness of these analyses will lead us to become comfortable with an ambiguous conception of the function of journalism, or even with the view that ultimately we are better off without any clearly formulated ideas about journalism. Even limited, narrow, and unimaginative ideas about the uses of journalism may be better than none at all; and yet recognition of the emptiness of these analyses of journalism and news can be a disincentive to making the effort to determine what is going on in the mind of one's counterpart in the journalistic news process. That is, one could be led to the conclusion that because journalism can have so many very different kinds of value, both to the writer and to the reader, one is foolish to believe that one can successfully attain an insight into what his counterpart in the news process hopes to accomplish, or even into what he himself hopes to accomplish. And even if the journalist and reader were to spell out for each other in precise detail what they believe the primary value of the journalistic news process to be, then despite their sincerity, they might well be lacking in the self-knowledge necessary for making a full and accurate revelation.

It is not enough then to be able to distinguish journalism as such from the uses to which it is and can be put. Nor is it enough to realize that there is a wide diversity of uses to which it is and can be put. One must also have some reasonable idea of what specifically are the most important and valuable actual and possible uses of journalism to the various parties who stand to be affected by it. Here a list like Breed's is helpful, as are the relevant analyses by social-scientific and philosophical observers. But these are no substitute for the imaginative insight that, when disciplined, ultimately provides us with the deepest possible understanding of our own world view and the most profound empathetic understanding of the situation of counterparts in the journalistic news process whose world view may be quite different from our own. A good way for participants in the news process to begin improving it would be to describe, as carefully as possible, for both themselves and their counterparts in the process, what they themselves take to be the primary uses of journalism, and what they take to be their counterparts' views of those primary uses. Nothing at this time could have a more salutary influence on journalism than the regular exchange of such descriptions and the critical evaluation that would spontaneously follow. Whatever the limitations and inadequacies of such descriptions and evaluations, publishers and editors should see to it that a fair and representative sampling of them is regularly published in the pages of their periodical.

Insight that is disciplined as well as imaginative is not easy to come by. Given the many problems and anxieties that already confront us in everyday life, we are generally disposed, despite our dissatisfaction, to accept journalism for what it is, whatever that may be. For most people, journalists and readers alike, complaints about the periodical press, while common, are made in roughly the same spirit as complaints about the weather. With respect to the essential nature of journalism, that is ordinarily the appropriate spirit, for in a sense there is even less that we can do to change the essential nature of journalism than to change the weather. As to the uses to which journalism can be put, that is another matter entirely.

3

The Journalist and the World of Plato's Cave

Most attempts to understand what journalism is sooner or later bring one into the domain of theory. If someone seeks to know what the word *journalism* means simply because English is not his native language, he will be satisfied if we translate the word for him into its equivalent, if there is one, in a language that he speaks; we tell a person whose native language is Spanish what journalism is by informing him that the English word *journalism* has pretty much the same meaning as *el periodismo* in Spanish. When a child is in the process of learning English as his first language, we explain for him what journalism is in terms of words and concepts that he already understands, and if we are not too confident that we can do so adequately, then we read to him from a dictionary. As luck would have it, the definition of journalism that we find in a standard dictionary is given in relatively plain language, though as we have seen, a more serious investigation of the meaning of journalism calls for some elaboration upon the lexical definition. However, when people want to know what journalism is in the sense of knowing what it is all about or what it is really about, that is, when they want to have some deeper insight into the nature of journalism than a standard dictionary affords, then even an elaboration of the lexical definition is not likely to satisfy them; they are interested in some kind of theory.

What kind of theorizing is appropriate here? Obviously it is not the kind of theory with which physical scientists are associated, for journalism is not the kind of object or process about which a physicist, chemist, or geologist theorizes, even though journalism involves various physical objects and physical processes. Journalism is a human phenomenon. A biologist, particularly a modern sociobiologist, might have a few interesting things to say about it. But it is mainly behavioral and social scientists—especially social

70

psychologists, sociologists, and political scientists—who are interested in theorizing about phenomena like journalism. Indeed they have amassed a considerable amount of empirical data on journalism and have organized and interpreted the data into theories that are themselves extensions or applications of more general behavioral or social-scientific theories to which these investigators have been committed. Sometimes these investigators acknowledge, either with deep satisfaction or deep regret or a casual and matter-of-fact attitude, that their theories of journalism and the wider theories under which they may be subsumed have a certain philosophical dimension. The social-scientific literature on journalism is quantitatively and sometimes qualitatively impressive, but philosophers themselves, as previously noted, have not had very much to say about journalism.

The behavioral or social scientist might pointedly pose the question of what the philosopher could add to what behavioral and social scientists have had to say about journalism. Some of them hold the view that behavioral and social scientists are the successors to old-fashioned moral and social philosophers and now perform the role that was once performed, rather unscientifically, by such philosophers. But some behavioral and social scientists still believe that the kind of theorizing that moral and social philosophers do is helpful in its own peculiar way, and they might be puzzled as to why philosophers have been so reluctant to indulge in bold speculations and prescriptions about something as potentially important and influential as journalism.

At the beginning of my inquiry, I suggested some ways in which a properly philosophical investigation of journalism might be useful to journalists, scientific students of journalism, and philosophers themselves, but a further word is in order here about what philosophy has to offer. What I have to say may make certain philosophers, as well as critics of philosophy, wince in annoyance, yet it needs to be said. First, philosophers are humanists who have been trained to draw, in an especially informed way, on the history of very important ideas. Other inquirers draw on the history of those ideas too, but for the philosopher, familiarity with those ideas is a regular point of departure for most of his theoretical reflection. Philosophy is not simply the history of ideas, or even just the application of historical ideas to contemporary problems; philosophers regularly come up with their own ideas and apply methods of analysis and investigation that are largely independent of intellectual history. But the history of very important ideas provides a major part of the context in which the philosopher does his theorizing. Respectful yet appropriately critical of the philosophies of his predecessors, the careful philosopher is able to make use of their insights while avoiding the repetition of their mistakes. Secondly, on the basis of his historical studies, the philosopher has come to appreciate the importance of certain logical, linguistic, and phenomenological methods of analysis that, for any number of reasons, have not been cultivated with the same degree of enthusiasm and care by other scientific inquirers. Again, philosophers are virtually unique among scientific inquirers in their inclination to take a systematic and synoptic view of all things. When they discuss a particular subject, no matter how narrow, they try to bear in mind its relation to subjects that will normally strike the non-philosophical inquirer as only marginally relevant or perhaps not relevant at all. Finally, while many behavioral and social scientists feel a bit embarrassed when they get down to making concrete prescriptions and recommendations about how people should behave, philosophers usually feel that it is very much their business to provide such recommendations. It is clear then that whatever the value of what they will have to say, when philosophers get around to philosophizing about journalism, the theorizing that they do will look and be quite different from the kind of theorizing to which readers of behavioral and social-scientific literature are normally accustomed.

While there has been little philosophical literature on journalism, the great and lesser philosophers of the past have left us a repository of ideas that are in fact relevant to journalism. It is our great fortune that some of the most famous passages in the entire corpus of philosophical literature, those passages in the *Republic* in which Plato presents his parable or allegory of the cave, provide us with a particularly interesting framework in which to understand the deeper significance of a phenomenon like journalism. Journalism is but one of many phenomena that this rich parable illuminates, but its applicability to journalism is transparently obvious, and it is not surprising that such a serious modern student of journalism as Lippmann chose to begin his *Public Opinion* by quoting from the cave parable and adopting some of its terminology and symbolism.[1]

The cave parable begins the seventh of ten books of one of Plato's longest and most comprehensive dialogues, and is a synoptic device that summarizes and systematizes the main themes that have been developed in the first six books of this most famous and most influential of all philosophical works. Plato characterizes it as an illustration of the degrees in which our nature can be enlightened or unenlightened, and he uses it to bring together various metaphysical, epistemological, ethical, psychological, political, and educational

ideas. We are invited to consider the situation of people in an underground cave who, from childhood, have been chained down in such
a way that they can only see what is directly in front of them. Above
and behind them is a fire, and between the prisoners and the fire is a
wall that is a screen behind which some puppeteers are standing (or
walking) and over which they are showing their puppets. These puppeteers, some of whom are talking, are holding up various figurines
which, because of the firelight, cast shadows on the wall of the cave
that the prisoners are facing. The prisoners, who Plato cryptically
suggests are "like ourselves," recognize as reality only the shadows
that they see before them, and when they hear the voices of the
puppeteers, they assume that the voices must be coming from the
shadows on the wall. These prisoners are obviously wholly unenlightened with respect to the nature of reality.

Say now that one of these prisoners were liberated and forced to
look toward the light. This would be painful for him, for all his life
he had been accustomed to sitting in darkness and looking at
nothing but shadows on the wall in front of him. He would find it
difficult to perceive the figurines that had all along been casting the
shadows, and he would find it hard to believe that these puppets
were more real, so to speak, than their two-dimensional shadows,
which he had perceived so clearly. He would initially seek then to
return to his comfortable seat in the cave and resume his painless
perception of shadows on the wall. But with some effort, his liberator could make him realize that he was in fact better off, as well as
wiser, now that he could recognize the shadows for what they really
are, mere images of three-dimensional objects. The liberator could
then lead the former prisoner to look at the fire and appreciate the
circumstances in the cave that had led up to his previous and more
limited view of reality. And if the liberator took the former prisoner
out of the cave to see the objects of which the figurines themselves
are only images, the newly liberated individual, though dazzled at
first by the bright light and anxious to return to the cave, would in
time come to appreciate fully how unenlightened he had formerly
been and how unfortunate he had been to have so limited a conception of reality and so empty and deprived a life. Once he had become accustomed to seeing things in the sunlight, and the sun itself,
which illuminates and sustains all things of nature, he would feel
very sorry for those still imprisoned in the cave, even those prisoners who were honored in the cave for their keen perception of the
shadows on the wall and their understanding of the order in which
those shadows customarily appeared.

But say the liberated individual returned to the cave in order to

enlighten the poor prisoners therein. He would initially be blinded
by the darkness (as earlier he had been blinded by the light), and
when he began to explain to his former fellows that they were merely looking at images of images (and hence in need of enlightenment), they would laugh at him for not being able to discern the
shadows themselves clearly. They would ridicule his talk about becoming enlightened, and, as Plato suggests, in time they would
come to regard him as a dangerously arrogant meddler.[2]

There are some technical weaknesses in this parable, and some of
the Platonic themes that it is being used to promote—particularly
those related to Plato's metaphysical theory of transcendent Forms
or Ideas—are difficult for even some of Plato's greatest admirers to
swallow whole. Still, as an analysis of certain aspects of the formation of public opinion, the parable retains much of its value even
when divested of any metaphysical significance. This becomes clearer when one considers some of the points that Plato makes in interpreting and applying the parable in the passages that follow it.[3]

First, Plato is properly sensitive to several factors that contribute
to the enlightened person's difficulty in communicating his wisdom
to the unenlightened. He had already observed in the ship parable
that those who do not understand what navigation involves will be
naturally disposed to regard the true pilot as a mere stargazer. The
cave parable carries this theme further. For all his moral insight and
sense of moral obligation, the reflective, intellectual moralist will be
reluctant to return to the cave. The ivory tower offers satisfactions
to the truly enlightened person that the world of public affairs cannot. Thus the uselessness of the enlightened individual in a corrupt
society is partly a function of his own proclivity to escapism. It is not
only resentment or naiveté that deprives the thoughtful person of his
will to communicate with the ignorant but also the seductive charm
of the intellectual-spiritual-aesthetic life. The true pilot is not only
useless because the master and the sailors do not appreciate what he
has to offer them but because they can see for themselves what obvious delight he takes in his private, isolated, uninterrupted survey
of the heavens above.

Again, the enlightened person has learned, either from his own
experience or that of his predecessors, how exasperating or even
dangerous it can be to try to bring enlightenment to those imprisoned in the cave. He will initially be blinded when he returns to the
darkness of the cave, and hence unable to communicate with the
prisoners on their own terms. Having had his mind opened to a
higher truth and higher reality, he will not find it easy to grasp or
argue about the shadows of justice in a law court or elsewhere, and

so he will appear to the unenlightened to be an arrogant and deluded incompetent; for the prisoners know much about shadows but little about the higher realities of which such images are at best misleading adumbrations. Of course, when the wise person's eyes become accustomed to the darkness of the cave, he will then be able to communicate about the shadows. But he can never again see the shadows in just the way that the unenlightened see them. Thus, will it be worth his effort and pain to start thinking, talking, and behaving once again like a prisoner? Is his obligation to enlighten the ignorant so great that he should have to participate in a form of life that he knows to be so empty, so worthless, and such a diversion from the life that he could enjoy outside the cave? Plato believes that it is, but he also believes that some compulsion will have to be brought to bear on reflective, enlightened people if they are to be led back to the cave to free the prisoners as they themselves have been freed.

Plato also indicates in his explanation of the cave parable that too often a combination of arrogance, forgetfulness, and fatalism prevents relatively enlightened people from recognizing the extent to which their former fellows in the cave are capable of being enlightened. This is a Platonic theme that has received insufficient attention from even some of the most learned Plato scholars. Plato is so often thought of, and not without much justification, as an unrelenting proponent of an intellectual elitism based on recognition of degrees of innate intellectual aptitude that we sometimes underestimate the confidence that he had in the power of education to liberate the prisoners in the cave. Plato knew that some people in the cave could never be wholly liberated because they did not possess the requisite natural ability to grasp higher truths and realities. But for all his elitism, he was appropriately resentful of the failure of relatively enlightened people themselves to appreciate that many people in the cave could be liberated just as they had once been. They had not been liberated just so that they could selfishly enjoy a rich, rewarding life but so that they could also help others to enjoy such a life (or a life as close to it as their natural ability would allow) and to contribute to the advancement of their society and of humanity. Plato saw the self-perfection of individuals not only as something good in its own right but as the key to social and human progress. And he was perceptive in recognizing (as well as predicting) how quickly and conveniently enlightened people can sometimes forget that it was not their innate gifts alone that brought them to their present state of enlightenment, so that they are tempted to jump to the unwarranted conclusion that those still imprisoned are stuck in their situation because of their own innate limitations. When Plato criticizes the Sophists who claimed to be able to put knowledge into a mind that did not already possess it, he is alluding to some of his more curious metaphysical and epistemological ideas. He is also saying, however, that the capacity to learn exists to some extent in all minds, and that it is the job of the reformer, moralist, and educator to turn around the souls of the unenlightened so that they too can put that capacity to learn to proper use by directing it toward appropriate objects rather than mere shadows. As for the Sophists themselves, Plato here sets aside his customary resentment and expressed his deep regret at the fact that such people, who possessed superior innate gifts of keen apprehension and understanding, had not been liberated to the point where they could make proper use of those gifts.

Plato's interpretation and application of the cave parable may be seen as somewhat truncated or incomplete, and Plato had, to be sure, several reasons for not exploiting the parable in as much detail as he might have. Though in his exhortations and analyses he could be at times long-winded, Plato was often a sage enough literary stylist to allow a parable or illustration to speak for itself; he could see here that a single literary device, no matter how illuminating, palls when elaborated pedantically and excessively. Moreover, the cave parable is largely a summary and systematization of earlier material in the *Republic* and not meant to stand alone. Again, having witnessed the fate of Socrates, Plato was prudent enough to recognize the danger of identifying too explicitly those in his community who had kept the prisoners in the cave in chains and the puppeteers who performed in the cave. It remains for us then to do some of the interpreting that Plato himself declined to do.

The ship parable had been introduced primarily to illustrate why the enlightened person, despite his genuine suitability for leadership, is useless in corrupt societies, and so even in that simpler of the two parables it was necessary for Plato to provide some explanation both of degrees of enlightenment and of the formation of public opinion. The master, in his account, is somewhat deaf and short-sighted and hence easily narcotized by the drugs administered to him by the ambitious sailors who know well enough how to manipulate the master but are not educated enough to appreciate the full value of navigational skills. The drugs here obviously represent the devices of propaganda and mind-control that ambitious politicians, and their clever but unwise aides among the sophists (semi-intellectual professionals specializing in the shaping of public opinion, or as we would now say, in public relations) employ to promote their own selfish materialistic interests. Similarly, the prisoners in the cave are narcotized on two levels: first, they have been chained down so that they cannot make proper use of their capacity to learn (or to lead a full and rich life); and secondly, they have been kept occupied by a show of shadows on the wall that simultaneously entertains them and enables them to believe that they are engaged in a productive activity suitable for creatures with their perceptual and reflective gifts. As Plato indicates, the prisoners in the cave not only come to find their way of life sufficiently interesting and comfortable to be worth preserving (when initially confronted with the opportunity to look instead into the light) but allow their study of the shadows to develop into a field for the manifestation of personal competence. Developing the parallelism between the two parables, one could perhaps say that exploitative politicians and sophists have kept the prisoners in chains and occupied and pacified them with the show of shadows, thereby preserving their own artificial superiority and negating the possibility of a threat to their own free, unchecked pursuit of what they take to be the good life. In fact, Plato does not develop the parallelism in this (or any other) way, which is just as well, for one of the noteworthy features of the cave parable is that it does not give us any indication of what use puppeteers could possibly get out of people who do nothing but stare at shadows.

It may well be then that an alternative reading of the cave parable is in order. First, the prisoners, though individually capable of being enlightened, are, as a corporate body, as deaf and short-sighted as the master of the ship; their individuality is stifled as a result of their membership in a group that has imposed on them conventional standards of reality, morality, and competence. Their dependence on the group's world view reduces them to members of a herd that is not only susceptible to narcotization but perhaps even in need of narcotization. The individuals do not possess the will or natural insight necessary for divorcing themselves from the herd in the way that the puppeteer or liberator may once have done. In theory, the master of the ship could perhaps resist the attempts of the ambitious sailors to narcotize him, but he is only as independent as the individuals who constitute his essence are. Likewise, as members of a herd, most of the individuals are apparently unable to summon the imagination needed to provide them with the incentive to free themselves from their own chains and to resist the charms of the drugs administered to them by their manipulators. If potential liberators will not make a sustained effort to free them, then they will have to get by with what the puppeteers have to offer them. Liberated, they could perhaps reach the heights; but lacking the creative will to intellectual power, practical imagination, and self-assertiveness, they remain in chains, and remain as deaf and short-sighted as the master of the ship of state, himself kept deaf and short-sighted not only by his composite nature but by the failure of creativity and imagination that marks the individuals who constitute his essence.

But what of the puppeteers? Who are they, and what motivates them to create their play of shadows? Though Plato has told us remarkably little about these puppeteers—the focus of the cave parable being on the freed prisoner's ascent to the heights and his subsequent encounter in the cave with his former fellow prisoners—there is a clear contrast between the behavior of the puppeteers and that of the liberators. The liberators are the heroes of the parable. Having been to the heights, they understand the true nature of reality and of the best life for a human being. They suffer inconvenience and even risk danger in order to free prisoners so that these pathetic human beings can attain the wisdom, freedom, and fulfillment that the liberators have already attained. In doing so, they not only help the individuals that they free but elevate the intellectual, moral, and spiritual condition of the entire community, which is gradually being transplanted, piece by piece, into the world outside the cave, the world illuminated by the sun. In contrast, the puppeteers, who are freer than the prisoners and also wiser—they are unchained and have familiarity with, at very least, the puppets that cast the shadows—decline to emulate the behavior of the liberators. Instead, they keep the prisoners in their unenlightened state; when they could be liberating the prisoners, they instead offer them a show of untruths and unrealities. They entertain the prisoners and occupy their attention to the point where the prisoners have become comfortable with their situation, so much so that the prisoners will initially resist the attempts of liberators to enlighten and free them. It is not clear whether the puppeteers are working on their own or as agents for someome else, but what is clear is that, working together, the puppeteers are involved in a conspiracy against both the prisoners and those who would liberate them. Thus their behavior would seem to be anything but heroic; indeed, it would seem to be quite reprehensible.

The puppeteer, however, is actually a morally ambiguous figure. Consider the somewhat analogous situation of the ambitious sailors in the ship parable. Here are people who are drugging the master and standing in the way of the true pilot's taking command of the ship. While looking down at their venality, selfishness, and materialism, one should not forget that, though relatively clever fellows, the sailors lack the moral and political understanding that only the true pilot possesses. While involved in arrogant and unwarranted self-promotion, they do not fully realize that their behavior is wrong. Unlike the true pilot, they do not properly understand the difference between right and wrong, although they have almost certainly given some thought to the matter. They see that the ship is at sea and in need of direction, and since they hardly appreciate the true pilot's skills more than less ambitious people do, they have convinced themselves that if they are bright enough to be able to narcotize the master, they are also bright enough to do the best job of steering the ship, or at least determining who should do the steering. And in the end, they will suffer as much as their less aggressive fellows, as much as the master, when the ship wanders into perilous waters.

Consider again Plato's characterization of the corrupt politician and the corrupt sophist who serves his ends. Plato's words for these people are often very harsh; he cannot afford, after all, to take lightly their selfish manipulativeness and the dangers and abuses to which they have subjected their fellow citizens and the ship of state itself. But when Plato rises above the spirit of resentment and recognizes the futility of being highly judgmental, his view of these people is purer and more philosophical. In the first book of the *Republic*, he presents a vivid and disturbing picture of the sophist at his worst in the character of Thrasymachus, a slick operator who has managed to convince himself that there are no moral absolutes and that justice is whatever is in the interest of the powerful and aggressive, or whatever such people take to be in their interest. Disposing quickly of this incoherent position, Plato goes on in the *Republic* to sympathize to some extent with the plight of sophists, bright and talented individuals who are themselves hardly freer than those they manipulate. For all their shrewdness, sophists do not know enough, and in the last analysis, their world view is at best only a slightly refined version of the Great Sophist's, and their life is at best only a trifle more fulfilling than that of their less clever fellows. Lacking insight into the higher truth that makes people genuinely free, they delude themselves when they believe that their power over the less ambitious is significant.

I return then to the puppeteer, a figure almost as shadowy as the images he has cast on the wall. Who is he, and why is he doing what he does? What does he intend to accomplish by his puppetry, and to what extent is he succeeding? He does apprehend more than the prisoners. But is his life so much richer and more rewarding than that of the prisoners, whom in his own fruitless and inept way he is actually serving? Is the power that he possesses over the minds of the prisoners a significant one, and worth cultivating and taking pride in? We could say perhaps that the puppeteers are simply the corrupt politicians and sophists of the world and leave the matter at that; but then we would not be paying sufficient attention to the moral ambiguity of the puppeteers. Plato was especially fond of thinking in terms of hierarchies. He saw reality itself as admitting of degrees, and he saw the degrees of human enlightenment as corresponding to this metaphysical hierarchy. The puppeteers stand intellectually and morally as well as effectively between prisoners and liberators. True, they lack the innocence of the prisoners as well as the heroism of the liberators. Yet they are more enlightened than the prisoners in more than a technical sense, despite their being influenced by the Great Sophist's ideas, values, and attitudes. For all of their apparent egoism (and egotism), the superior political operators of classical Greece, such as Pericles, and the superior Sophists, such as Protagoras, were men of considerable moral stature, as Plato himself was sometimes willing to concede. The inferior political and rhetorical operators could be dismissed by Plato with a few clever comments, but men like Pericles and Protagoras could not. There are shallow puppeteers and then there are more imposing puppeteers, all caught up in an undefined role somewhere between the prisoner's and the liberator's. Plato was able to see that not all of the politicians and sophists of preceding generations (and his own) were wholly unconcerned with ameliorating the situation of their fellows and with enhancing the civilization of their society. While the superior puppeteers wre not liberators, it would be inappropriate to dismiss them as wholly ignorant and exploitative incompetents.

The puppeteer does not dwell in sunlit heights where he may occupy himself by contemplating timeless, transcendent essences. He is down in the darkness of the cave, entertaining the prisoners, keeping them occupied, feeding their misplaced sense of accomplishment. It is not hard to imagine how such a person could come to conceive of himself as sustaining those people, as helping them to live out a life that is, under the best of circumstances that he can conceive, a hard and unfulfilling one. If he undervalues the intellectual and moral potential of the prisoners, he is not so different in this regard from the fully liberated individuals who need to be compelled to return to the world of the cave. He may indeed take satisfaction in his relative superiority to those prisoners and in the strange power that he has over their minds; but perhaps there are moments when he has a vague awareness of the extent to which, on several levels, they have contributed to making him what he is. There are puppeteers who will look with smug contempt upon the prisoners, there are others who will be moved more by pity, and perhaps there are some who will be filled with an existential despair or with some combination of awe, wonder, and hopelessness. Some puppeteers will envy the innocence and passivity of their charges, and some will even end up as liberators. Prisoner and liberator alike have been freed of existential doubt; their path has been clearly laid down. But the puppeteer, an individual who knows both too much and too little, may well be plagued by doubts and anxieties.

Why then does the typical puppeteer not himself follow the liberator out into the sunlight so that he too can know the true, the real, and the good, and learn how to conduct himself properly in the cave? How are we to account for his lack of courage, adventurousness, creative imagination, natural insight, and ability to appreciate what the liberator has to offer? Why can he not divorce himself as thoroughly from the values of the herd as the liberator can? To all such questions, Plato might have been inclined to give an answer that is more practical than psychological: lacking wisdom as does, the puppeteer is really not all that different from the prisoner, and despite his superiority to the prisoner, he is nearly as much in need as the prisoner is of a patient but forceful liberator. Like the prisoner, the puppeteer has become accustomed to the life that he has been leading; in a sense, he is comfortable with it, despite any doubts and anxieties that may plague him, and hence he is not prepared to follow some mysterious adventurer who offers him something nobler and more satisfying if he will turn his back on the life he now has. The puppeteer is thus constrained by invisible chains.

But how did Plato's teacher and hero, Socrates, manage to become a liberator? Considering the case of Socrates, Plato must have been prepared to allow that every so often an independent-minded genius can arise from out of nowhere, thanks to the beneficence of the gods. However, here Plato's *ressentiment* had caused his perception to be vitiated: Socrates did not come from out of the blue but learned to be a philosopher and moralist by watching the Sophists closely, making astute judgments about what was noble and what was ignoble in their activity, and imitating what was noblest and elevating it to a new and higher order. Unable to appreciate fully the debt owed to the Sophists by Socrates (and by himself), Plato was left irritated and perplexed when he heard the detractors of Socrates characterize his beloved teacher as merely the shrewdest of sophists.

However disposed he might have been to emphasize the similarity of the puppeteers to the prisoners, Plato could never completely forget that the brightest of the Sophists were worthy rivals to the Socratic philosopher. Such men, after all, were not merely effective manipulators and unwary creatures of the unenlightened souls on whom they preyed and by whom they were preyed upon in turn. They were at least semi-intellectual figures who, though they could never be satisfied with a life of contemplating transcendent Forms, were perceptive enough to appreciate the pragmatic value of some concentrated reflection on moral and political subjects. I observed earlier that Plato's cave parable is illuminating even when divested of its deeper metaphysical and epistemological significance; it is all the more illuminating when we consider it in the context of the fundamental philosophical disagreement between Plato and the Sophists. However puzzled or unmoved one may be by Plato's pet theory, the Theory of Forms, one can still appreciate Plato's more fundamental commitment to the view that human beings are in need of metaphysical and moral absolutes to guide them in their thought and action. If there is no objective metaphysical or moral truth, and if truth as such is not objective, then anything goes, and a figure like Thrasymachus can see his way clear to being an apologist for virtually anything in the way of belief and behavior. Surely Plato was right in holding that the systematic relativism adopted by the Sophists could breed an excessive tolerance of political despotism and personal injustice, a disrespect for the power of reason to provide a sound resolution of moral and political disagreements, a cynical overvaluation of the need for manipulativeness, and a belief that education is ultimately nothing more than clever indoctrination and conditioning. But to a thoughtful sophist like Protagoras, radical subjectivism and the relativism that follows from it were not simply convenient justifications for self-promotion and exploitation but profound metaphilosophical and humanistic truths about the role played by thinkers and agents in the determination of reality, truth, goodness, and justice.

The most reflective of the puppeteers in the cave may look with wry indulgence at the self-professed liberator who claims to have attained intellectual access to a realm of timeless, transcendent absolutes; they may see the would-be liberator as a well-meaning but naive and somewhat dangerous fellow whose desperate need to believe in absolutes has led him into a self-deceptive hallucination. If Protagoras's teaching had helped to bring about monsters like Thrasymachus and Callicles, the teaching of Socrates also had much to answer for, being associated by much of the Athenian public with the political mischief of schemers like Alcibiades and Critias. Protagoras, in fact, was no apologist for despotism; he was inclined to promote the democratic ideal. Plato, an unwavering advocate of aristocracy, regarded democracy as a system of government second only to despotism in its maleficence. When Protagoras stressed the importance of consensus and reasonable conventions as the foundations of the healthy polis, Plato could only throw up his hands in disgust at what he took to be a bland acceptance of the world view of the herd and a calculated refusal to acknowledge the possibility of genuine enlightenment. But the more reflective followers of Protagoras simply could not be convinced that someone like Plato could really have intellectual access to a realm of timeless, objective truths, and neither perhaps could Socrates himself ever have been so convinced, for unlike his most famous student, he remained to his death a man of many questions but very few answers.

So perhaps the puppeteer can have intellectual and properly moral motives for looking to the world of human beings rather than to a world of transcendent essences for guidance on how to shape the minds of his charges. He is not necessarily a panderer if he takes human values as they are as the starting-point for a refinement of the conventional world view, and he is actually less likely than the self-proclaimed liberator to be a self-deluded propagandist.

The puppeteer is of particular interest because the ambiguity of his role in the cave corresponds in no small measure to the ambiguity of the journalist's in our own society. Of course, here I am putting Plato's symbolism to a use that he might not have sanctioned; he might not have been too happy with some of the interpretation that I have already provided. The noted classicist, F. M. Cornford, suggested in an earlier generation that, "A modern Plato would compare his Cave to an underground cinema, where the audience watch the play of shadows thrown by the film passing before a light at their backs."[4] But we cannot really know how a modern Plato would translate the cave parable into a more modern symbolism, nor can we even be sure that he would find some version of the parable appropriate for modern readers; indeed, I confess that, unlike Cornford, I find it hard to form an image in my mind of a modern Plato. The best I can do here then is to exploit Plato's rich symbolism for my own purposes, while trying to avoid violating the general spirit of the original parable. Of course, Plato was not familiar with anything quite like journalism as we now understand it, and it would be inaccurate to characterize the typical journalist as a modern sophist (as well as unfair to both the typical journalist and the brightest of ancient sophists).

In considering the similarities between the typical journalist and the puppeteer in Plato's cave, one may begin by observing that even the least influential and least capable journalist, regardless of how little regarded he and his work are, is no mere prisoner in the cave. Regardless of how trivial his subject matter, he has a noteworthy ability to alter the world views of his readers—their conceptions of reality, emotional attitudes, and value systems—and through the influence that he exerts on the judgment of his clientele, he has a wider influence on his community and on humanity. Lippmann overstates this point, I believe, when he writes in *Public Opinion* that, "Universally it is admitted that the press is the chief means of contact with the unseen environment."[5] The power of the press in this regard is not universally admitted, and with good reason: the press, even broadly understood as made up of past and present nonjournalistic writers as well as contemporary journalists, has worthy rivals in this sphere, such as the clergy, the professoriate, and the broadcasting profession. The journalist does tell us about what is going on in the world beyond our personal perceptual field, but so do others, and in any case, the "unseen environment" about which even journalists write involves more than just recent events and occurrences. When Plato talks about Forms, the preacher talks about heaven, the physicist talks about nuclear particles, and the journalist talks about the mentality of the Soviet leadership or the cultural traditions of the Japanese, they may well be providing us with valuable insights into the unseen environment. Still, journalists are clearly opinion makers, or at least judgment shapers, to be reckoned with, even if, as some observers such as Hennessey have suggested, their influence is all too easily overestimated.[6] And journalists are ordinarily well aware of their potential influence as judgment shapers, even though for various reasons they sometimes pretend not to be.

The journalist's power as a judgment shaper is sometimes underestimated too. I suggest that there are three main reasons for this. The first is that this power is often realized in subtle, imperceptible ways. Unlike the prisoner in the cave, the reader of a news periodical knows that other human beings are producing the images that he is accepting as realities, and he is prepared to acknowledge that not everything that journalists report is objectively true. But his faith in the general reliability and accuracy of the news periodicals he reads, as evidenced not merely by his habitual reading of the periodicals but also by the confident tones in which he passes on to others the information that he has read in them, suggests that he is only very rarely prepared to consider the possibility that he has been significantly misled. The naiveté in this regard of even sophisticated readers—who, of course, only allow themselves to be misled by sophisticated journalism—would appear on close examination to be almost universal, even though it is masked by the professions of skepticism about the periodical press that have come to represent a cultural institution of most advanced societies. Even the professional critic of journalism who appreciates, as a theorist, the great amount of valuation that goes into the journalist's selection of subject matter and approach to that subject matter, manages somehow to convince himself, as he reads his favorite newspaper in an ordinary, unprofessional way, that most of the reporting therein is fairly objective. Journalistic bias is usually so subtle in its manifestations that normally it is even unrecognized by the journalist himself, who is usually earnest when he contends that ultimately he is simply a slave to the facts. Occasionally we come across an article in the paper on crime, fashion, or even chess and are suddenly struck with an awareness of the fact that the writer of the piece is, consciously or not, an apologist for some far-reaching political ideology or philosophy of life; but as a general rule, we do not draw out any lesson from what we take to be a curious journalistic anomaly.

A second reason that the journalist's power as a judgment shaper is underestimated is that we are not accustomed to thinking of journalists as particularly extraordinary. In a society in which we regularly mistake for our sages the physicians, lawyers, and professors who have survived supposedly grueling educational demands and have been rewarded with impressive titles and credentials and an aura of personal authority, only the most visible of journalists are seen as possessing gifts that place them above the herd. As Lippmann observed, "Reporting, which theoretically constitutes the foundation of the whole institution, is the most poorly paid branch of newspaper work, and is the least regarded. . . . The rewards in journalism go to specialty work, to signed correspondence which has editorial quality, to executives, and to men with a knack and flavor of their own."[7] We often find it difficult to think of the ordinary journalistic laborer as having the courage, intelligence, and imagination necessary for being a judgment shaper; he is simply not an imposing figure. Yet as I observed earlier, the skills that go into regular written communication about events of the day that are quite often complex and multidimensional should not be undervalued; and even a journalistic journeyman can influence the moral and political ideas of his clientele in a way and to an extent that no ordinary physician or lawyer can. In addition, the journalist, by virtue of his professional status, has access to many kinds of information that other people do not.

The third and most important reason the journalist's power is underestimated is that, unlike the prisoners in the cave, we are cognizant of the influence that we as readers, news consumers, and fellow citizens have upon the puppeteers. Sometimes, in overvaluing this influence, we are led to a corresponding undervaluation of the puppeteer's autonomy. We also know that there are employers, colleagues, and political and other interest groups that the journalist is required, persuaded, or conditioned to serve as an agent, and in overvaluing their influence, we again are led to a corresponding undervaluation of the journalist's autonomy. Plato was inclined to undervalue the potential autonomy of sophists and other puppeteers, both in their relation to the Great Sophist and in their relation to the powerful politicians whose interests they are presumed to serve; often we simply repeat Plato's error. Bernard Hennessey, who believes that political leaders are mistaken in their traditional belief that the mass media of communication are highly political and politically very important,[8] sees what he takes to be the relative insignificance of journalistic influence in America as partly a function of the mediocrity of both American journalists and their clients: "The fact is that most producers and consumers of newspapers prefer mediocrity to intellectual challenge. There is a dearth of talent in American newspapers—a dearth of talented writers and a dearth of talented readers."[9] Hennessey thus attaches much importance to a particular factor limiting the journalist's potential influence:

> Why do newspapers . . . exist? For one thing, they make money for their owners and producers. . . . From the perspective of the consumer, however, the mass media provide three main functions: (a) entertainment; (b) a guide and orientation for daily living; and (c) a source of information and opinion about public events. It is undeniable that the third is least important for the majority of media consumers. Much of the intellectuals' criticism of the mass media misses this point: *Most mass-media consumers neither want nor appreciate the subtleties of political discourse.*[10]

Yet Hennessey also believes that,

> The major daily newspapers and TV network (and large urban independent) news departments are the main channels for the democratic dialogue in all political communities of size. Activist groups and their speakers can suggest, demand, implore, deplore, and confront, but their efforts will fail unless the newspapers and television pay attention to them.[11]

Thus, while it is often more derivative than it can and ought to be, and while it is often used more sparingly than it can and ought to be, the journalist's power as a judgment shaper is a force in its own right, a force with which to be reckoned.

To recognize that the journalist is no mere prisoner in the cave, however, is to see only half of the relevant picture, for it is just as important for us to appreciate the typical journalist's disinclination or inability to be a liberator, an educator. The typical journalist, who sees it as his vocation to provide valuable information and insight, will resist most attempts to characterize him as a professional educator. He will grant that what he does professionally has certain affinities with what an educator does professionally, and if he is not afraid to appear slightly pompous and self-important, he may even grant that in his own special way he contributes in some measure to the advancement of civilization by promoting in his readers a fuller, more accurate understanding of reality and an enhanced capacity to make informed, intelligent value judgments. But he will normally cap such an admission with the insistence that he is not an educator as such but a journalist. How are we to account for his reticence in this regard?

First, we may sometimes see in it a reasonable modesty. The title of educator often confers on those to whom it is applied, even in its less significant senses, a certain honor and authority to which the typical journalist may feel that he is not entirely entitled. If he is not skeptical in the way that the classical sophist was about the possibility of the superior intellect's coming to know absolute moral and metaphysical truths, he still may feel that he has no access to such truths and hence is not in a position to impart them. Whatever his estimation of genuine scholarship, he would say that he is no scholar and that he has never had the patience necessary for joining reflective sages in their difficult, and perhaps futile, quest for insight into moral and metaphysical absolutes. Nor is he attracted by the life of the educators who toil in classrooms, dispensing established truths to minds that are not fully formed.

In addition to modesty, fear of responsibility may be a factor that discourages the journalist from thinking of and portraying himself as a full-fledged educator. Regardless of whatever confidence he may have in the overall soundness of his personal world view, he may not want to be held responsible for the moral and intellectual malformation of his less estimable clients. Here he would appear to differ from the classical Sophist, who prided himself in his ability to transform his disciple in such a way that the disciple would be successful in the social world. Yet even the classical Sophists made clear, if not always clear enough, that they were no liberators in the Platonic sense, and that it was not their business to provide either support for or an alternative to the properly moral instruction offered by the traditional Athenian religious and cultural authorities. In any case, unlike the Sophist's, the journalist's influence is indirect and impersonal and thus difficult to control, so his desire to avoid responsibility is not only prudent but also more justifiable than the ancient Sophist's.

At the same time, the journalist may well share the Sophist's view that it is the puppeteer rather than the self-proclaimed liberator who, for all practical purposes, has the real, concrete power to shape the judgment of the prisoners in the cave. Journalists have been known at times to ridicule and show contempt for intellectuals, academics, and visionaries, and to feed the prisoners' conviction that would-be liberators are deluded characters who have little to offer them. More often, I believe, the journalist prefers to serve up platitudinous cant about the importance of the denizens of the ivory tower and the lonely reformers out in the field, while simultaneously reflecting somewhat smugly on the fact that he reaches audiences that few scholars and prophets can hope to attract. He reflects as well on the fact that he is the channel through which such people must work if they are to make a significant mark in the cave. Whatever his own estimation of the value of what the self-proclaimed liberator has to offer those who will never be willing or able to leave the cave, and despite the fact that most people in an advanced society are prepared to acknowledge that the educator is in a sense an honorable person who has something to offer, the journalist-puppeteer is enough like the prisoners to be resentful about (and feel threatened by) the liberator's claim to be morally and politically enlightened in a way and to a degree that the ordinary cave dwellers are not. Moreover, if too conservative to alter the established rhythm of his professional and personal lives by trying out the role of scholar-liberator, the journalist-puppeteer may justify to himself his refusal to grow by dismissing the true sage's practical wisdom as "sour grapes." In coming to perceive the sage as a rival who poses a threat to whatever power and influence he himself enjoys in the cave, he has all the more reason to promote an unflattering, or at least ambivalent, view of the sage in his own mind and in the minds of the prisoners.

If the journalist were actually willing and able to make a sustained effort to become a liberator, he would have to do more than merely refine his puppetry. No matter how sharp the images on the cave wall are, they are still only images, not realities. To have intellectual access to higher truths, the puppeteer would have to get out of the cave. This would require him to abandon, at least temporarily, his comfortable situation in the cave. Once he reached the sunlit world, the prospect of returning to his puppetry in the cave would hold no attraction for him, for an enlightened person can only be induced to return to the cave if he is convinced that he can perform there the noble role of liberator. The enlightened person will have no interest in puppetry, for he is cognizant not only of the relative worthlessness of the images on the wall but of the extent to which his puppetry would be shaped by both the values of the herd to which his work would have to appeal and the values of the political and business leaders who control the instruments of puppetry.

So the journalist, bright and talented enough to be a judgment shaper rather than a prisoner but disinclined or unable to attempt the journey to the heights so that he can perhaps return to the cave as a liberator, is left in his ambiguous situation in the cave. Neither prisoner nor liberator, he finds himself possessing a strange sort of power, undefined and largely derivative, with which he is not entirely clear what to do. How then does he end up handling it, and what motives impel him to use it in the ways that he eventually does? If he is not too reflective or imaginative, he will use it to satisfy the narrow, materialistic desires that he has partly absorbed from the herd. If, however, he attains even a small part of the vision of the liberator, he will have at least some interest in the socially constructive purposes for which that power can be harnessed.

For the journalist, his professional work is, among other things, and certainly not least importantly, his way of getting on in the world. His writing keeps him occupied, provides him with feelings of competence and self-respect, and, of course, puts bread on his kitchen table, clothes on his body, and a roof over his head. It is his sustenance, his livelihood. One does not have to adopt a capitalistic or Marxist ideology to see journalism as very much an economic phenomenon, a business which has far-reaching effects on other businesses and on the general condition of the economy in a given society. The journalist himself is not as such a businessman, but a wage earner whose economic situation depends on businessmen, both those who employ him and those who sustain an economy that leaves room for people like him to practice their craft and be remunerated for doing so. Among the latter, advertisers, of course, are of particular importance. Desirous of getting on, and also of getting ahead, the journalist-puppeteer all too readily accepts the necessity of selling out by allowing news consumers, publishers, and advertisers to make the primary determination of the tunes to be piped; if sensationalism, flattery, and escapist triviality are the tunes in demand, then the piper can oblige, leaving it to the liberator to dispense the unpleasant medicine.

Though an overgeneralization, McCormick's remark that, "A newspaper is a daily publication conducted for profit,"[12] speaks volumes about the professional mentality of many of those involved in the production of journalism, including journalists themselves. The journalist is the agent not only of the Great Sophist but of various commercial, industrial, and political leaders who expect to profit from the puppeteer's show. In return for sustaining the journalist and enabling him to satisfy his hunger for self-expression and self-advancement, publishers, advertisers, and politicians expect the journalist to help them to attain greater power, wealth, and prestige. Because Plato does not tell us much about the puppeteers in his parable, we may overlook the fact that Plato was much impressed by the leading Sophists' personal familiarity with (and dependence upon) the big-time political operators of their society. If the politicians of ancient Athens were sometimes given to attacking the Sophists—in the same spirit as modern politicians so handily make whipping boys of the journalists who promote their glory and importance—that was something that the Sophists had to accept as part of the power game. Politician and journalist generally need each other to promote their respective careers. They have always been capable of putting the same power that they normally use to promote one another's status to the use of ridding oneself of a particularly pesky counterpart. Still, even in a so-called free society, in which journalists routinely make a show of criticizing certain policies and practices of the government of the day, journalists customarily pay their homage to those who have a power and authority of a higher order than their own. And their respect for politicians, publishers, and others whom they serve as agents is not based solely on their understanding of the economic order in which they operate but also on their fascination with authority figures.

Most of us are fascinated with celebrities, but many journalists are even more fascinated with celebrities than the rest of us are. It is not hard to see why. Journalists constantly find themselves writing about celebrities, studying them, thinking about them, interviewing them, creating them, and socializing with them. Thus they have a special relationship with those celebrities on several levels, and the relative depth of this relationship is ordinarily a principal determinant of their own social status and self-esteem. The closer and more intimate a journalist's access to celebrities, the greater will be his social status and his self-esteem, the closer he will be to being a celebrity himself, the more vivid will be his images on the cave wall, and hence, the greater will be his remuneration for his services. And of all celebrities, those who are the principal objects of fascination are the ones with some kind of authority. Commenting on the built-in bias of the Canadian press, Fulford has suggested that it has rel-atively little to do with party political loyalty; rather, "The struc-ture of the press and the character of the men who staff the news-papers both force the press to lean in one direction, and only the most persistent and vigorous opposition can offset this. The bias I refer to is in the direction of Authority, and in this case Authority means anything which is organized, which has a name, and which gives speeches."[13] "Politics, in the newspapers, means party poli-tics. Culture means what the National Ballet Guild is doing. . . . This policy of concentrating on official action affects newspapers' judgement of what is news."[14] Of course, the journalist's respect for authority involves more than a fascination with a certain kind of celebrity, just as his fascination with celebrities is not confined to authority figures; but celebrity and authority have a way of enhan-cing one another, particularly in the eyes of a journalist.

The authoritarian theory of journalism is, of all theories, the "most pervasive historically and geographically."[15] This is the theory, according to Fred Siebert, that, "The units of communication should support and advance the policies of the government in power so that this government can achieve its objectives."[16] Even in the most liberal democracies, journalists find themselves taking their cue from politicians in various ways. For example, as Lippmann noted, "Democratic politicians rarely feel they can afford the luxury of telling the whole truth to the people. . . . The men under them who report and collect the news come to realize in their turn that it is safer to be wrong before it has become fashionable to be right."[17]

Still, where the journalist's sustenance, livelihood, and self-advancement are concerned, his authority of authorities is in a sense his publisher. Though he overstates his point, Kingsley Martin emphasizes an important dimension of journalism when he writes that, "The ordinary journalist is dependent on the mercy of the proprietor's whim."[18] As supportive and tolerant as his publisher may be, the journalist is still the publisher's vassal, even if the pub-lisher is a corporate institution rather than a single personality. While being a vassal means being limited in one's autonomy, it brings with it the advantage of being limited in one's responsibility. As was indicated (with some overstatement) in the report of the Hutchins Commission, "No public service is more important than the service of communications. But the element of personal respon-sibility, which is of the essence of the organization of such professions as law and medicine, is missing in communications. Here the writer works for an employer, and the employer, not the writer, takes the responsibility."[19]

While the journalist-puppeteer does much of what he does partly in order to satisfy the desires of the economic and political leaders for whom he is an agent, theirs are obviously not the only desires that concern him. Even if a submissive person habitually inclined to obey the voice of an authority figure, he still sees his work as promoting his own interests. At the same time, he may well have strong grounds for believing that he is in certain ways serving the interests of the prisoners, even if he is not fully aware of the extent to which his professional behavior is molded by the ideas and values of the Great Sophist. He has good reason to believe that the prisoners enjoy his show, and it is easy to see how he might be disposed to justify his activity in his own mind by concluding that it is not cruel, destructive manipulation but a matter of providing people of limited capability with something relatively innocuous with which to keep their minds occupied. Indeed, even his publisher wants him to keep the customers satisfied. We have already noted that a technical weakness of Plato's cave parable is that it does not indicate how passive prisoners, chained down and hypnotized by shadows on the wall, can be of much use to those who seek to control their minds and behavior. In the real world, however, the prisoners are much more active. They buy newspapers, purchase products advertised in those papers, and actively participate in various political and economic processes. Thus in the real world, those with political and economic power need the support of the prisoners, and so it is of great practical importance to them to create circumstances whereby those prisoners will be led to acquiesce to the world view that they want the prisoners to adopt. One of the advantages of mind-control over brute force is that it can condition people relatively painlessly, even pleasantly. But precisely what kinds of satisfaction do people attain by occupying themselves with the journalist-puppeteer's images?

Analysts of the periodical press are often moved to speak of the entertainment value of journalism. We have already seen how Hennessey characterizes entertainment as one of the three main functions that the mass media provide for the consumer.[20] Peter Hood speaks of the aim of journalism "to amalgamate instruction and entertainment."[21] Kingsley Martin tells us that "we put into the hands of the people most clever at entertaining us the enormous weapon of propaganda,"[22] and that "we must face the fact that comparatively few people have a passion for truth as a principle or care about public events continuously when these do not obviously effect their own lives. People want to be pleased, and truth is not always pleasing. . . . Newspapers have always depended on their public, and the public hands out fortunes, not to those who present the truest possible picture of public events, but to the showman who can provide the most entertaining kaleidoscope."[23] McCormick points out that it is no coincidence that in most newspapers news is packaged together with various features: "News is the basis of the modern newspaper, but it cannot live by news alone. It must also amuse and serve. There are strips of comics. There are book and theatrical reviews. There are columns of advice on health, investment, radio, law, love, complexion, corsets, cooking, good manners; substantially all subjects that interest the general public."[24]

Such talk about the entertainment or amusement value of journalism does not in itself shed much light on why people find it satisfying to read a news periodical. Entertainment designates activities as diverse as playing Scrabble, dancing, listening to opera recordings, watching a hockey game, leering at exotic dancers, and engaging in vigorous intellectual debate. What the satisfaction of reading a newspaper has in common with the satisfactions afforded by these other activities may not be as important as some analysts seem to believe. In point of fact, such analysts often speak of the entertainment value of journalism when they need a summary and inoffensive way of characterizing those motives for reading a news periodical that they either cannot identify, cannot understand, or cannot take as seriously as what they consider to be the really important motives. Moreover, it seems inappropriate to characterize as entertainment the bad news that makes up so many traditional stories about violent crimes, disasters, accidents, wars, economic decline, political corruption, and quarrels among celebrities. Yet ironically, it is the sensationalistic reporting of such grim events that appeals most to those readers who supposedly want above all else to be entertained by their newspaper. There are some very serious forms of entertainment; in its own way, viewing a performance of *King Lear* is as much a matter of being entertained as viewing a hockey game or a burlesque show is, even if it does not evoke peals of laughter or squeals of delight. Yet it still seems inappropriate to characterize the reading of a detailed account of a grisly airplane disaster or sex crime as even serious entertainment.

Mott would seem to be more cautious than some analysts when he characterizes soft news as being interesting and exciting rather than as entertaining. "The chief fault and failure of American journalism today—and this applies to all media of information—is the disproportionate space given to the obviously interesting news of immediate reward ('soft news') at the expense of the significantly important news of situations and events which have not yet reached the stage of being exciting for the casual reader ('hard news')."[25] Yet again it seems inappropriate for Mott to locate the secondary value of journalism for the casual reader in its power to excite him; it is more likely that such a casual reader reads his favorite paper more for relaxation than for excitement. Cinema and television have fixed firmly in our minds such pleasant images as that of the tired breadwinner sitting down in his armchair after a hard day and clutching a daily paper that he expects to offer him respite, and that of family members chatting at the breakfast table about reports in the morning paper as they prepare to go out once more into the world to face their vocational and academic obligations. However, when Mott refers to the capacity of news to be interesting, he would seem to have hit upon the safest term for characterizing that function of journalism which other analysts associate with journalism's entertainment value.

Unfortunately, the term *interesting* is even less informative here than the term *entertaining*. I was once asked to give a young artist a candid appraisal of her paintings, and when I tactlessly described them as interesting, I was met with the indignant but fair reply that it was somewhat insincere of me to offer so empty and neutral an evaluation. Still, the term is not wholly lacking in significance, even if we sometimes treat it as if it were. The fact is that people do not take lightly the capacity of journalistic writing to do something so fundamental as draw and maintain our attention. The competent journalist's pieces, like the shadows on the cave wall, have the capacity to occupy our attention, often for reasons of which we are quite aware, sometimes for reasons which even the most erudite psychologists have not yet been able to explain. Of course, all sorts of things, many of them rather unpleasant, can occupy our attention, and we cannot afford here to set aside the question of why people find it as satisfying as they do to have their attention occupied by newspaper and news magazine articles in particular.

It is useful at this point to reconsider some of the items on Breed's list of functions that newspapers perform.[26] First, reading the newspaper can be a diversion; it can divert our attention away from professional and domestic matters that for the time being either bore us or fill us with anxiety. As Breed indicates, the newspaper can be a means of escape, even if we do not read it closely but merely become lost in it for a half-hour, staring semi-consciously at its pastiche of headlines and photographs of different sizes. Life offers us countless means of diversion and escape, but few are as safe, efficient, readily available, and reasonably priced as that offered by the light, portable object that regularly appears on our doorstep or on the shelves of the variety store around the corner. Reading about a famine in Africa or a bloody war in Asia can be sobering and upsetting, but there is a certain relief to be found in thinking about other people's problems rather than our own; reading about the misfortunes of others has, among other effects, that of reminding us how fortunate we are in our own way, regardless of the personal problems that have been weighing on our minds all day or all night. We rarely take cruel delight in the misfortunes of people who are essentially strangers to us, but we do regularly take pleasure in knowing that we are a good deal better off than lots of people in the world. And, of course, all news periodicals contain their share of upbeat, humorous, or uplifting stories, stories about animals that save the lives of their masters, juries that dispatch nasty characters off to prison, nonagenarians who have just earned their college diplomas, successful attempts by fellow citizens in another part of town to revitalize a neighborhood that had been written off as beyond the point of being saved, and the latest antics of eccentric but kindly English dowagers. Such heart-warming stories may be cloying after a while, and they may lead some people to adopt an unrealistically rosy view of the state of the world, a view that blinds them to their obligation to help remedy the evils and injustices of that world; still, they sometimes represent a much-needed diversion and even a constructive check to paralyzing cynicism.

A related satisfaction offered to the readers is that derived from the semi-authoritative confirmation of their judgments that news periodicals generously (and often intentionally) provide. We have already noted Lippmann's observation that journalists come to see that it is safer to be wrong before it has become fashionable to be right, but this is only one aspect of the matter. Another is that most journalists want to be widely read, admired, and quoted, for not only is positive recognition by a significant portion of the public an important key to their professional advancement—and to the financial success of the businessmen they serve—but all other things being equal, it is better to be admired than despised or ignored. To enjoy the rewards of autonomy and independence, the journalist must have a thick skin and be able to deflect the complaints and threats of offended readers and the pleas and threats of worried publishers and colleagues. Most journalists, however, tend to be rather thin-skinned in this regard. Furthermore, as we have noted several times, the puppeteer, lacking the insight of the fully liberated individual, derives much of his world view from the herd, considerably more of it than he realizes. McCormick writes that, "Newspaper editors come from the ranks of the normally educated. The first newspapermen's minds were moulded by the prevailing education. Newspapers have not altered this standard."[27] Of course, the published opinions of journalists can never mirror or confirm those of all their readers; they mirror and confirm the opinions of what I have described as a significant portion of the public, or more precisely, of their readership. Fulford's comments about Canadian journalists also apply to journalists in many other societies: "In a country dominated by its middle class, where all our important institutions reflect a middle-class point of view, the newspaperman is now pre-eminently a middle-class citizen. His attitude is not far from that of the dead-centre suburbanite: an attitude which looks to organizations to sustain it."[28] These comments apply, of course, to journalists who write for publications with a general readership. Journalists who write for publications with a narrower, specialized readership—say, Roman Catholics, businessmen, or veterans—may be less concerned with typical middle-class attitudes, but their published judgments also mirror and confirm the opinions of a significant part of their readership. At the same time, one should not overestimate the influence of the herd's beliefs and values on the kind of journalist who, lacking the courage to offend his readership, writes things with which he does not whole-heartedly concur, or even with which he may substantially disagree.

Thus it is hardly surprising that, as Breed has pointed out, newspapers so easily perform the functions of maintaining the status quo and providing a pleasant picture of the community. Regardless of what positive and negative social effects follow upon their doing so, it is clear that newspapers bring a certain satisfaction to their readers in the process. Even when they point to corruption, injustices, and other weaknesses in the communal way of life, they usually tend to do so in such a way as to enhance the moral status of the community as a whole. They may suggest that nasty, crooked characters are anomalous figures who abuse the privilege of being citizens of a basically sound polis populated mainly by generous, hard-working, upright individuals like the readers themselves. Angered and troubled though they may be by reports of corruption in their community, readers are pleased to be reminded that they are among the honorable and worthy class of citizens, and they are also pleased to be reminded that they live in a community in which there exists a free press to expose the bad apples for what they are.

Journalists often confirm the opinions and advance the causes of special interest groups. Sometimes they are motivated to do so by purely prudential considerations, as when they strive for an interesting subject matter, to attract new readers from an interest group, to please their publisher, or to promote their own moral stature. Sometimes their motives are more noble, as when they are led by a proper or misplaced compassion to come to the aid of the lowliest prisoners in the cave. Even the most cynical puppeteer is capable of compassion as well as happy to have occasional opportunities to manifest his power and nobility by promoting the situation of those prisoners in the cave for whom he has developed a special personal concern.

The journalist also provides his readers with a convenient outlet for their intellectuality and a painless method of enabling them to think of themselves as knowledgeable. When I first read the cave parable, I thought that Plato seriously underestimated the average individual's desire to be educated, and I reflected that most people do not resist attempts at educating them but usually jump at opportunities for educational advancement. Do not ordinary people appreciate the prudential value of education, I asked myself. More importantly, do not all people take delight in attaining a higher degree of understanding of all sorts of things? Did not Aristotle himself, as much an apologist for intellectual elitism as his teacher, Plato, allow that all men by nature desire to know? Yet I think now that my argument against Plato rested on premises almost as extravagant as Plato's own; for Plato's position, though overstated, is illuminating. All people do have purely intellectual needs apart from and beyond their needs for practical knowledge. They are inquisitive, they prize knowledge for its own sake, and they look favorably upon someone who can increase their knowledge. But the intellectuality of most people is truncated; it is not strong enough to nerve them to follow the liberator out of the cave. Thus they are both intellectual and anti-intellectual up to a point: they want to be knowledgeable about the shadows on the cave wall, and they admire those who are experts on the shadows, but they are afraid to undertake the painful and dangerous trek that the liberator has commended to them, and they justify their cowardice and laziness in their own minds by dismissing as useless the supposed insights that the learned person promises await them. So how then can they satisfy their intellectual drive, and how can they convince themselves of their own relative knowledgeableness? Only by becoming experts on the shadows.

Newspapers and news magazines, as Hennessey notes, provide the desired illusion of keeping up with public events.[29] They provide their readers with a set of facts (or putative facts) that can be memorized and served up with show at the appropriate moment in casual conversation. The education that the news periodical provides is often less painful than that which the school or university provides. Reading the newspaper requires an important set of skills, the skills involved in literacy, but often little more. It is education without teachers, tests, homework assignments, external supervision, and the application of standards. I remember how impressed I was as a child at the ability of some of my classmates to rattle off the batting averages of every player on the local professional baseball team; here, I thought, are fellows who cannot pass a mathematics or history test and yet seem so much more sophisticated and clever than I am. When I got older, it was only those who could quote theater and book reviews and discuss European and Asian politics who seemed sophisticated and clever to me. What the scientific student learns, for example, is usually too specialized to be of interest to many and too technical to be discussed with laymen. But everyone has, and thinks that he ought to have, some interest in what is going on out there in the world. In the cave world of cocktail lounges, social clubs, coffee shops, and dinner parties, it is the regular newspaper reader, with his wealth of information, who shines. Even if the expert on shadows does not have concrete opportunities to display his learning, he still has the twin satisfactions of believing that his intellectuality has been adequately channeled and that he is in the know to a degree that other members of the herd are not.

Journalism is a branch of literature, so it stands to reason that journalism offers the reader certain satisfactions comparable to those that are offered by other forms of literature. Journalism can offer the reader the occasion for abstract reflection that philosophical literature does. Its affinities with historical and biographical literature also are obvious, for it focuses the reader's attention on people and events. Newspeople sometimes are portrayed as writers who describe and interpret history in the making, and if this portrayal is not wholly accurate, the fact remains that the superior journalist is writing something akin to the history of recent events. A perusal of the standard literature on the philosophy of history will indicate how different critical history is from the "scissors-and-paste" variety of history that newspaper reporters ordinarily serve up.[30] Even so, it is fair to assume that the reading of news journalism offers certain satisfactions comparable to those offered by the reading of thoughtful, well-crafted historical literature. It also must be remembered that the news journalist does not have the time (or distance from events) needed for the writing of critical history. It should also be noted, however, that the typical reporter has not carefully cultivated the intellectual habits of the professional historian and that the motives that impel him to write are substantially different from the historian's. Finally, as Arthur Schopenhauer has said, journalism is characterized by many of the weaknesses and limitations that mark even the most disciplined historical writing.

Less obvious but perhaps more interesting are the affinities between news journalism and fictional literature. This is not the place for literary aesthetics or even a quick survey of what satisfaction people derive from reading novels, short stories, dramas, and poems; it need only be noted that the journalist is very much a story-teller, and that the stories he tells can have much in common with those told by creative writers.[31] The news journalist finds himself in the position of having to make the affairs of his fellow human beings as interesting as possible, so often he is inclined to render his accounts in somewhat dramatic fashion. He mirrors the fictional writer in his preference for writing about interesting people (the powerful, the wealthy, the beautiful, the stylish, the well-connected, the well-born, the eccentric, the colorful, the profound, the heroic); even when he writes about ordinary people, he is often inclined to do so in such a way as to either ennoble them or hold them up as representative of some curious or otherwise noteworthy human tendency, particularly some virtue or vice. He deals in much the same archetypes as the creative writer does, and he confirms traditional myths and invents new ones. (This is perhaps most obvious in sports journalism, I believe, where writers regularly make relatively uninteresting people doing relatively unimportant things seem like epic heroes engaged in earthshaking struggles.)

McCormick sees the news journalist as "subject to the temptation of all story-tellers," which he associates with credulity: "Perhaps newspaper men are naturally credulous. It may seem to their interest to be credulous. Believing and wanting to believe have an affinity."[32] I doubt whether news journalists are as naturally credulous as McCormick suspects, but certainly they are subject to various temptations of storytellers, the most important being the temptation to distort the truth in order to present a more interesting or more satisfying story. Plato certainly counted the dramatic and epic poets among the puppeteers in the cave; in various places in the *Republic*, and especially in the dialogue's last book, Plato goes to great pains to portray creative writers as rivals of the philosopher who seduce people with distorted pictures of reality, truth, and morality that further disincline people to make the effort to attain genuine understanding through the cultivation of reason. Whatever their other motives, such deceivers crave the glory that comes from recognition as authors of appealing stories. In the case of the journalist, however, distortion and deception are all the more dangerous and maleficent, because the journalist claims that he is dealing exclusively in fact rather than fiction and is thus neither entitled nor presumed to make use of the kind of license allowed to the poet. The reader of journalism expects the journalist to establish that fact is, if not literally stranger than fiction, at least roughly as interesting in its own way, but this is often a rather severe and unrealistic demand to make of the journalist, who thus sometimes feels compelled to embroider the truth. The rare journalist who is caught inventing complete, outright fabrications is duly censured by his colleagues and editors, but journalists routinely take liberties with their subject matter that are accepted in their trade as matters of journalistic business that are necessitated by, among other things, the need to construct interesting and appealing stories.

Thus the distortions of truth that characterize so much journalistic writing cannot all be explained away as the result of inadvertent bias, cold manipulativeness, or deficient craftsmanship on the part of the journalist, and I have in mind here such traditional sins of journalism as incorrect attribution, loaded words, libel, omission of relevant details, reliance on unsubstantiated rumor, and, last but not least, sensationalism.[33] McCormick queries that "if sensationalism in itself is an objection, how much of literature can escape?"[34] But there is the problem in a nutshell: when Gloucester's eyes are plucked out in *King Lear*, that is pretty sensational stuff of which old Plato would have much disapproved, but still it is the creation of someone who professes to be neither more nor less than a dramatic poet. Journalism, however, is not dramatic poetry, and journalism is not simply one more genre of creative literature. The journalist's puppetry is more akin to the sophist's than the creative writer's is, so when he acts as if he were entitled to something like poetic license, he risks compounding the deceptiveness of manipulative sophistry with the deceptiveness of poetry in a dose that is doubly lethal to his client's chances of attaining sound understanding of the highest truths.

As if this were not bad enough, the journalist is normally at a disadvantage in relation to the creative writer when it comes to embodying moral and philosophical themes in his work. For all of his mistrust and jealousy of the poets, even Plato himself was willing to grant that at their best, poets could provide a certain amount of salutary moral instruction. There is obviously a good deal more to *King Lear* than Gloucester wandering about with blood streaming from his eye sockets; *King Lear* is pretty weighty material, even if lightweight in comparison with the *Republic*. But the journalist rarely has the time or occasion to work the deepest moral themes into his writing, and he knows all too well that those who read his work will not make the effort to dig out whatever philosophical significance is imbedded in it in the way that they will routinely do so for *belles-lettres*. Hence, the stories that the journalist tells can only rarely have the depth that the finer creative writer's stories have; dramatic though they may be, his stories can only rarely be interesting on the higher plane that good fictional literature can be.

Still, the news journalist's stories must not be undervalued. In addition to providing diversion and limited moral insight, they offer the opportunity for vicarious experience and certain forms of practical guidance. It is likely that almost every puppeteer has, at least occasionally, an existential vision of the importance of the vicarious experience that he offers to his audience. Whatever his other attitudes toward those whose attention he keeps occupied, the puppeteer in the cave cannot always avoid feeling sorry for those lowly, powerless creatures whose chains, self-imposed or otherwise, have robbed them of the opportunity to live as full and rich a life as that of those who are unchained. By offering the prisoners shadows on the wall at which to stare, he gives them a life that is at least richer than one of looking at a blank, unchanging wall; he gives them something to talk about, to become knowledgeable about, and around which to organize an aspect of their lives and to build complex social criteria of competence and honorableness. The latter feature of cave life is what Plato had in mind when he spoke of the prisoners' practice of honoring those of their fellows with the keenest understanding of the shadows. The journalist, ever mindful of the fact that most of his readers do not have the opportunities for adventure, excitement, and glory that are routinely enjoyed by many of the figures about whom he writes, allows them to participate to some extent in the stories that he tells. He realizes that his readers will, by various methods of imagination, put themselves into the stories that they are reading, much as the reader of a novel does. They will relate to certain figures in certain of the situations described, they will speculate about how they would behave in such situations, and they will even occasionally indulge in the fantasy of actually being in those situations. Without such vicarious experience, even the life of the relatively free and sophisticated person would be much harder to bear. One danger of vicarious experience is that it can be made a substitute for real, lived experience that is potentially far more fulfilling, but there are times when vicarious experience is the most fulfilling as well as the most satisfying available to us, and these times are all the more numerous for those in chains. All of us, no matter how reflective or unreflective, are sometimes burdened by an existential ennui, by an uncomfortable feeling that life is tedious and pointless. While reading a news periodical may exacerbate this situation, it can often offer an antidote to it by means of the vicarious experience that it provides.

Turning to the matter of the practical guidance that a news periodical can provide, one is no longer even remotely concerned with what analysts sometimes inaccurately and misleadingly characterize as the entertainment value of journalism. A consideration of the potential contribution of journalism to intelligent personal and social praxis on the part of readers seems to be a turn to the really important side of journalism, to its primary value. The appearance may be deceptive; once one reflects on the practical value of journalism, one may be led by one's value system to conclude that in the last analysis it is really not personally or socially more important than the so-called entertainment value of journalism. Still, it may be properly distinguished from the latter, even when the two overlap and intertwine. The most obvious practical value of journalism resides in the information that it provides in order to help us to do (or do better) the various things that we are disposed to do in everday life. This information is sometimes characterized as "service news" and includes everything from weather information that suggests how we should dress for the picnic to medical information that suggests how we may be able to prolong our lives.[35] In real life, we need to make many more decisions and practical judgments than the prisoners in Plato's cave parable do, and here the journalist might seem to be able to serve us in a way that the puppeteer cannot serve the prisoners in the cave. However, because the shadows that really interested Plato were the shadows of justice, it can be said that Plato was very concerned with the praxis of the prisoners, even if his literary device was not wholly adequate to the purpose of indicating so.

Of course, what would have interested Plato in this regard is not such service news but rather the most general ways in which journalism shapes the behavior of readers. Breed has referred to journalism's power in this regard as "standardizing thought and action."[36] Journalism does not only give us a glimpse at the lives and world views of political gods, cultural giants, and criminal monsters, it gives us, if often in very indirect ways, ideas about how ordinary folks think and behave. We read advertisements and draw certain conclusions about products that people such as us really ought to own, we read the travel pages and learn where people such as us ought to visit. However special we may want to feel, and however critical we may be of those who slavishly follow the manners and fashions of the herd, most of us do not want to be (or seem) too different from out fellow tribesmen, and so we need to know whether to buy a long dress or a short one, a wide tie or a narrow one, and airline tickets to California or to Kansas. Determining how to live a life, whether simply as an individual or also as a member of a community, ordinarily requires more than spontaneous intuition, casual observation, and independent reflection. One of the services that the journalist performs for his readers is to help them to orient themselves in life. Making big decisions is often very difficult, and even the most independent-minded of thinkers cannot get very far if they do not take certain conventional ideas about reality and value as starting points for critical inquiry. So here the journalist enters, ready to supplement, build upon, and correct the practical instruction of parents and teachers; and he offers direct and indirect suggestions to his readers about how normal people in the tribe live, about what people such as themselves want, about what is really important, and about what success and social competence involve. Those suggestions may well be bad suggestions—bad, that is, when assessed from some relatively lofty moral and axiological perspective—but they are useful nonetheless. They save the intellectually weak from total confusion, they give the sophisticated thinker something about which to be skeptical and critical, and they provide society with some degree of requisite intellectual uniformity through the establishment of that somewhat mysterious phenomenon, public opinion.

The political aspects of the orientation that journalists help to provide are obviously particularly important. When they read the stories told by journalists, readers are led to draw certain conclusions about the nature of the polis and their proper place and role in it. Indeed, journalists convey to readers the distinctly Platonic message that political matters are the most important of all practical matters, though unlike Plato, journalists do not give much in the way of direct advice on how readers can involve themselves in the political process. In democratic societies, news periodicals do routinely suggest, in the editorial pages and elsewhere, how readers should vote in a given election, but unlike Plato, journalists typically fail to appreciate the extent to which the just society is established through the cultivation of personal justice by individual citizens. Hence, for all of their emphasis on political news, newspapers and news magazines offer surprisingly little in the way of genuine political education.

The political orientation that newspapers help readers to attain has less to do with political news than is commonly believed. It may be granted that, as Breed has observed, newspapers are sometimes successful in "crusading for causes," "watchdogging," and "arbitrating."[37] For the most part, however, political news concerns matters over which readers have little, if any, control. Consider first news of foreign affairs. The reader of a North American or Western European newspaper is daily bombarded with news about Asian, African, and South American conflicts that, even if he is sincerely and profoundly troubled about—which ordinarily he is not—he is not in a position to do much about. Of course, he may choose to vote or work for a political party whose foreign policy he finds attractive, but even if he is willing to make foreign policy rather than domestic policy the basis of his decision here, foreign policy is terribly complex, and the voter might find himself in the position of having to endorse indirectly an Asian policy of which he disapproves in order to support an African policy of which he does approve. In other words, no party will offer him exactly the combination of foreign policy options that he wants. And in any case, despite the dramatic rhetoric of politicians in the Western democracies, the actual foreign policies of powerful democratic governments ultimately tend to be more subtle and more pragmatic than those on which they campaign in order to be elected.

And what about news of domestic political affairs? Such news does, of course, often influence how citizens of a democratic state vote, but here again it may not be as influential as it initially appears to be. The typical reader who is incensed by newspaper reports of his government's mistreatment of, say, ethnic minorities, small businessmen, or the handicapped, will wail for a while, but in the end he will usually still vote for the party that promises to promote a handful of economic and social policies that are of immediate, direct, personal interest to him. The pious Roman Catholic obsessed with the immorality of abortion on demand may well vote for the anti-abortion party even if doing so means tolerating that party's callousness toward certain ethnic minorities and small businessmen; the farmer ordinarily will accept, if somewhat regretfully, a party's callousness toward the handicapped if that party promises tax relief for farmers. Most political news is, with respect to its actual content, less of practical value than of entertainment value (in the wider sense outlined earlier); only rarely does such news ignite sufficient passion in a reader to alter substantially his political values and voting pattern. Journalistic watchdogging and crusading have contributed to the elimination of various social abuses and injustices, but even at their noblest and most hortatory, they have fairly consistently failed to nerve the overwhelming majority of readers to take forceful political action against morally weak governments that have trafficked with, encouraged, behaved as, and condoned the barbarism of military mass murderers, slaveholders, imperialists, robber barons, international criminals, and gestapo thugs.

Thus it is at another level entirely that journalism ordinarily helps readers to attain some socially useful political orientation. Political journalism in democratic societies promotes limited participation in the political process. On one hand, it promotes some participation: it encourages people to vote, or even to become somewhat more active in the political process, and it outlines a variety of issues that can serve as a basis for political involvement. In doing so, it promotes the stability of whatever democratic institutions prevail in the readers' society, and it thus serves as a check against extremist factions in the community that would radically alter the structure of the polis and the way of life of the typical citizen. On the other hand, by clearly indicating the complexity of political matters, both foreign and domestic, it discourages the typical reader from engaging in fruitlessly quixotic political adventures, while it warns the more ambitious reader of the pragmatic realism he will have to adopt if he is to succeed in the political arena.

If these indeed are the principal ways in which the periodical press has helped readers to attain a political orientation, then the periodical press has clearly failed to live up to the high expectations of it shared by lofty democratic theorists and the more idealistic political journalists. Lippmann argues in *Public Opinion* that such high expectations are simply unreasonable; he writes there that the periodical press "is very much more frail than the democratic theory has as yet admitted. It is too frail to carry the whole burden of popular sovereignty. . . ."[38] Continuing, he says "Acting upon everybody for thirty minutes in twenty-four hours, the press is asked to create a mystical force called Public Opinion that will take up the slack in public institutions. The press has often mistakenly pretended that it could do just that."[39] Nevertheless, the periodical press can and does participate in the formation of public opinion, even if not in the grand manner that certain political idealists would like it to. An older and wiser Lippmann was more hopeful about the potential of the periodical press to embody and promote a sound political philosophy and more disposed to emphasize the distinction between what political journalism has been and what political journalism can be. It is perhaps no coincidence that in later years he became more of a Platonist and more inclined to worry aloud about the weaknesses inherent in the democratic system itself.

Plato held democracy in very low regard. He saw it as mob rule, anarchy, and the worst possible form of constitution with the exception of despotism, into which, being unstable, democracy must inevitably degenerate. Plato did not adequately appreciate the strengths (and potential strengths) of democracy, and he was not farsighted enough to be able to envision the sophisticated forms that democracy would eventually come to take. (Plato might have regarded the democracies of our own day as more like oligarchies than pure democracies.) But for all his misunderstanding of the nature and possibilities of democracy, Plato had a keen insight into certain features of democracy, and among them, the complex relationship in a democracy between the Great Sophist and the puppeteers. How can the puppeteer, having declined to become a true liberator, provide anything in the way of genuine political education when his political ideology is so extensively shaped by the political, moral, and empirical views of the Great Sophist? If the journalist-puppeteer does not possess genuine political knowledge, then the stories that he tells will result only in shadows on the cave wall, regardless of how serious and important their political content is. Political news may in the end be virtually meaningless data, a set of transient, ephemeral empirical appearances, unless it is organized according to some pattern, and if that pattern is not a properly philosophical one, determined on the basis of knowledge and understanding, then it may be determined largely by the Great Sophist. The shape of the political news that the journalist-puppeteer serves up to his readers is affected by the world view of the Great Sophist in three ways. First, the journalist-puppeteer's most basic personal political beliefs and values are largely derived from those of the herd; secondly, he must sell his political news to the herd in order to sustain and advance his career; and thirdly, even the more idealistic, independent-minded puppeteer may well come to the curious moral conclusion that it is his social responsibility to give the prisoners political news in the shape they prefer, or at least the shape that he thinks they prefer.

Still, if democracy is not as bad as Plato thought, and usually it is not, then there are strict limits as to how much we should lament the journalist-puppeteer's dependence on the values and attitudes of the herd. Those of us who have been trained to appreciate the positive dimensions of democracy can see that Plato's descriptions of the ignorance of the masses and the wisdom of philosophers are exaggerations. Plato's elitism is not a little repugnant to anyone whose study of history has taught him about the cruelties and evils that have been perpetrated by proponents of this or that form of ideological elitism. Even if Plato's own elitism is more reasonable and less maleficent than others, it shows an unwarranted and dangerous disrespect for the judgment of the common man. Where Plato could only see prisoners in chains, other learned and reflective social theorists have been able to see naturally decent souls guided by generous affections, moral intuitions, and a common sense unencumbered by dogmatic ideology. Their portrait of the common man is also a caricature, but no more exaggerated than Plato's.

The confidence of democratic theorists in the moral and political judgment of ordinary, politically unlearned people is in part a reaction against authoritarian political ideologies that have contributed to the promotion and acceptance of the most reprehensible forms of exploitation, injustice, and cruelty. History has taught these theorists a lesson that Plato could never learn—that sincere, idealistic authoritarianism can degenerate even more quickly into vicious despotism than democracy does. There are never enough real liberators around, and usually it is a good thing that the journalist-puppeteer depends more on the judgment of the common man than on that of some self-professed liberator.

To a great extent, the periodical press "takes on the form and coloration of the social and political structures within which it operates."[40] Plato would not have abolished the periodical press; he would have reorganized it and put it to different purposes. The uses to which despots, tyrants, and dictators have put the periodical press are well known. Political journalism in a democratic society tends to reflect and then reinforce the democratic institutions and attitudes that constitute its context. If the domain of democracy is the world of the cave, then the typical journalist therein will be nothing more than a mere puppeteer. If the domain of democracy is nobler than the world of the cave, then the typical journalist therein will be much more than a puppeteer. If the domain of democracy is sometimes like the world of the cave in certain ways and at other times nobler, then the typical journalist therein will sometimes be a puppeteer, sometimes something nobler.

Plato's political theory, though overstated at key points, is still instructive, and particularly so for those of us who have been mesmerized, indoctrinated, or at least charmed by the rhetoric of classical democratic theory. As obnoxious as the political theory underlying the cave parable may be, it effectively counterpoises sentimental but dangerous myths about the natural wisdom and kindness of the masses, the political acumen of simple folk, the reliability of the judgment of the people, and the overall integrity and trustworthiness of a democratic society's free press. We continue to be inspired by the words of Locke, Rousseau, and Jefferson because we have a clear image in our minds of the selfish, exploitative aristocrats of pre-Enlightenment Europe. That image tends to be sharper in our minds than the image of wild mobs sadistically persecuting members of innocent, civilized minorities. When both images stand out clearly in our consciousness, we may think, like Spinoza, that while democracy is perhaps the best of all political systems realistically available to us, "The fickle disposition of the multitude almost reduces those who have experience of it to despair, for it is governed solely by emotions, not by reason . . . ."[41]

In all fairness to Plato, it should be said that his view of human potential, even the potential of the common man, was not as cynical as that of Hobbes, and that he could never have endorsed Nietzsche's (or Thrasymachus's) view that the common man is simply an object to be used by the superior man for whatever purposes the latter sees fit. In addition, if relativism is a false and maleficent doctrine, then it may well be that among those who profess to be able to liberate us, there are some who actually possess the knowledge that will enable them to perform the task through any of various means, perhaps even through the vehicle of journalism.

4

The Journalist as Educator

It is not surprising that Arthur Schopenhauer, that most pessimistic, most misanthropic, and (after Nietzsche) most abusive of eminent philosophers, had little respect for journalism and hardly any confidence in its chances for improvement. In characteristic lines, he writes:

> Newspapers are the second hand [of the clock] of history. This hand, however, is usually not only of inferior metal to the other two hands, it also seldom works properly. The so-called "leading articles" in them are the chorus to the drama of current events. Exaggeration in every sense is as essential to newspaper writing as it is to the writing of plays: for the point is to make as much as possible of every occurrence. So that all newspaper writers are, for the sake of their trade, alarmists: this is their way of making themselves interesting. What they really do, however, is resemble little dogs who, as soon as anything whatever moves, start up a loud barking. It is necessary, therefore, not to pay too much attention to their alarms, and to realize in general that the newspaper is a magnifying glass, and this only at best: for very often it is no more than a shadow-play on the wall.[1]

The last line in particular points to the influence of Plato upon Schopenhauer. Unlike Plato, of course, Schopenhauer was familiar with the institution of journalism.

If we return now to certain observations of more recent (and more serious) students of journalism, we may see in them something akin to Schopenhauer's pessimism. Recall, for example, Hennessey's remark that, "The fact is that most producers and consumers of newspapers prefer mediocrity to intellectual challenge. There is a dearth of talent in American newspapers—a dearth of talented writers and a dearth of talented readers."[2] Or consider again Kingsley Martin's lament that, "No, we must face the fact that comparatively few people have a passion for truth as a principle or care about public events continuously when these do not obviously affect their

109

own lives. People want to be pleased, and truth is not always pleasing. . . . Newspapers have always depended on their public, and the public hands out fortunes, not to those who present the truest possible picture of public events, but to the showman who can provide the most entertaining kaleidoscope."[3] However discouraging their assessments may be, such writers as Hennessey and Martin do not appear to be committed to an ideological pessimism like Schopenhauer's, and they seem to allow for the possibility that journalism could perhaps one day be a much greater force for the advancement of civilization than it now is.

Schopenhauer's contempt for journalism is not merely a function of his ideological pessimism, however, nor even of a pessimism combined with a recognition of journalism's status as an inferior department of historical writing; it also involves Schopenhauer's sensitivity to certain limitations of historical writing. Notwithstanding his view that, "Clio, the Muse of History, is as thoroughly infected with lies as a streetwalker is with syphilis,"[4] Schopenhauer was able to see some positive value in historical writing, yet he also saw history as something of an inferior rival to philosophy in much the same manner as Plato saw sophistry and poetry as such rivals. There is more than a little wisdom in Schopenhauer's view that,

> History has always been a favourite study of those who want to learn something without being put to the effort demanded by the true sciences, which require the exercise of reason; but in our own time it is more popular than ever before, as is demonstrated by the countless history books which appear every year. Since I cannot avoid seeing in all history nothing but a repetition of the same things, as when a kaleidoscope is turned you see only the same things in differing configurations, I cannot share this passionate interest, though I do not go on to censure it: my only objection is that many want to make history a department of philosophy, indeed to identify it with philosophy, in that they believe it can be substituted for it, and this is ludicrous and absurd.[5]

Schopenhauer's attitude here is quite Platonic: he sees all historical writing, journalism included, as concentrating on "individual things for their own sake,"[6] on fleeting particulars in the world of appearance that have not been properly considered in their relation to timeless truths and realities. For Schopenhauer, as for Plato, philosophy is the only form of intellectual inquiry that offers the prisoners and puppeteers in the cave a realistic opportunity to be liberated through education, for only philosophy can turn people's minds away from interesting but insignificant particulars and focus their attention instead on the worthiest objects of apprehension.

Still, Schopenhauer would have almost surely been prepared to follow Plato in his belief that education must necessarily proceed in stages; thus, it is likely that both philosophers would have been prepared to grant, if pressed, that thoughtful, high-minded journalism could play a role in preparing the mind for loftier forms of reflection, and even could indicate certain features of the relation between fleeting particulars and higher principles.

Before considering the possibilities of journalism as an instrument of education, however, a few words are in order about the Platonic association of liberation with education, because questions could fairly be raised about a possible arbitrariness in this association. A minimal defense of this Platonic association would be one that confined itself to asserting that education, the turning around of the soul, is the particular kind of liberation that is Plato's primary concern in the *Republic* (or in his philosophy as a whole); such a defense, however, would not only be weak but would fail to do justice to Plato's unqualified view that education is, in fact, the primary and most important kind of liberation. To the extent that a Plato or Schopenhauer emphasizes intellectual liberation, or any liberation of the mind, at the expense of other kinds of liberation that perhaps ordinarily come to mind sooner—such as, say, the economic liberation that is trumpeted by so many revolutionary movements—he is open to the charge that his idea of liberation is too much tied to an idealistic metaphysic and an intellectualistic conception of self-realization. Why should we endorse such idealistic and intellectualistic views, especially if doing so will lead us to undervalue concrete forms of political and economic liberation that would seem to be rather more urgent than intellectual liberation to most of the oppressed and exploited poeple of the real world?

This is a question many journalists would certainly be tempted to ask, and they might well want to argue that even if they are disinclined to be (or incapable of being) educators in the lofty and somewhat abstract Platonic sense, they routinely do a great deal more in the concrete ways of liberating than an intellectualistic critic might recognize. Many such journalists could fairly insist that they have done more in their own way to promote concrete social reforms than most abstract theorists or speculative ideologists have. Here again come to mind the various functions of journalism on Breed's list, such as crusading for causes, watchdogging, and arbitrating, as well as the traditional importance of journalism as an instrument for the dissemination of revolutionary (or reactionary) propaganda. Moreover, however much one may admire the high speculations of a Plato or Schopenhauer, one must recognize that such an intellectualistic idealist all too often shows a gratuitously arrogant disregard for the concrete problems of ordinary human beings and makes a naive and unrealistic appraisal of our material and emotional needs. Finally, the idealistic metaphysic of a Plato or Schopenhauer is itself riddled with questionable philosophical assumptions.

Even so, two major points can be made here in Plato's behalf. First, Plato rightly sees intellectual liberation as very closely related to more concrete forms of political and economic liberation. Education not only can contribute to some extent to the prisoner's personal political and economic liberation but can provide him with insights that enable him to play a more intelligent, effective, and constructive role in promoting social justice. Plato makes it clear that prisoners are to be liberated not only for their own good but for the good of the commonwealth and of their fellow citizens; the liberated individual is obliged to return to the cave to help others enjoy the best way of life available to people with their particular capacities. Also, while due acknowledgment must be paid to the concrete social reforms that have been instituted by passionate and compassionate activists who have been guided more by gut feeling than by reason, it should not be forgotten that as a general rule, lasting social reforms have largely been the work of those who are intellectually liberated, and that well-meaning but ignorant and irrational revolutionaries and would-be reformers have, overall, done more harm than good. Thus, if the political and economic liberator must not necessarily be someone who has already been intellectually liberated himself, the fact remains that the most significant and lasting advances in civilization have largely been the result of moral education. Secondly, even if we cannot endorse all of Plato's views about the essential nature of self-realization and the good life, we can appreciate his general view that where the mind is enslaved by superstitious and arbitrary beliefs, uncontrollable passions, and shallow desires, other forms of freedom are hollow. There are perhaps some materialistic hedonists who see unobstructed access to materialistic satisfactions as the zenith of human freedom, but most of us are apt to agree with Plato that freedom of the mind, or the spirit, has an ultimacy about it, if not an urgency about it, that other freedoms do not, and that education is, with the possible exception of religious experience, the most important means of attaining it. One could agree with Plato on this point even if obliged to reject his metaphysic as too idealistic, his ethic as too intellectualistic, and his educational theory (with its emphasis on the need to apprehend timeless, transcendent essences) as too narrow and too speculative.

So while the journalist can do much concrete liberating without taking upon himself the role of educator, he cannot thereby fulfill his potential as an agent of civilization. Moreover, while there may be a genuine nobility, and a concrete value, in his efforts to ameliorate the situation of certain oppressed individuals or groups, he will have failed to establish conditions for the maintenance of his reforms (and others) if he has not argued for such reforms in some properly educational context. Now, few people or institutions realize anything even close to their highest potential, and a journalist who has done his fair share of crusading, watchdogging, and arbitrating may well be offended if he is chastised for not having taken upon himself the additional responsibility of educating his readers. Still, given the nature of his work, it may well be that others have a right or even an obligation to expect more from a journalist than he expects from himself, or than others expect from other craftsmen in our society. When a teacher, physician, or statesman falls far short of fulfilling his potential, more is normally at stake than when an athlete, businessman, or entertainer does, and though all individuals ought to strive to carry out their chosen vocation as conscientiously and honorably as possible, a journalist may well have greater responsibility than most.

The 1947 report of the Commission on Freedom of the Press urges us to recognize that "the agencies of mass communication are an educational instrument, perhaps the most powerful there is; and they must assume a responsibility like that of educators in stating and clarifying the ideals toward which the community should strive."[7] One may feel that one can detect in these lines the ideological biases of the figure most often identified with the work of the Commission, Robert M. Hutchins, who was an outspoken advocate of certain classical (his detractors would say medieval) political, ethical, and educational ideals, and, as Margaret Blanchard says, whose "main theme then and throughout his career as a press critic was the power and importance of the press as an educational tool and how the press was not meeting society's needs."[8] As noted in chapter 1, many journalists at the time were resentful of the Hutchins Commission's high-minded, abstractional criticisms of their work; but some of the most gifted thinkers and journalists of his day also supported Hutchins's thesis.

When people buy and read a news periodical, they do so on the understanding that they will personally benefit from doing so. In addition to being entertained by that periodical (in both the narrower and broader senses of entertainment considered earlier), they also expect, in some sense of the word, to be educated by it. As noted earlier, the journalist provides his readers with a convenient outlet for their intellectuality and a painless method of enabling them to regard themselves as knowledgeable. While I have granted, in Plato's defense, that the intellectuality of his prisoners is significantly truncated, I have also observed that he underestimated the intellectuality of his prisoners. In any case, while some regular newspaper readers may be hesitant to characterize their newspaper-reading as an educational experience, most will at least allow that they do not simply read the paper for fun but also because they believe that it is something that a civilized person ought to do, and they think this way because they see the paper as providing them with information and insight that not only make them better citizens but better human beings, too. Even a relatively shallow, materialistic reader expects the newspaper to make him just a little wiser, not only for the good of his society but for his own sake as well. The reader does not buy and read the newspaper only so that a crusading journalist may be able to ameliorate the situation of this or that oppressed individual or group, he sees the journalist as doing something directly for him. Faced then with what is an implicit demand that he offer something at least akin to education, the journalist must decide whether he will do the job thoughtfully and whole-heartedly or carelessly and half-heartedly. This is not always an easy decision for the typical journalist to make, for as discussed earlier, various interests may lead him to choose to pander to readers who do not want him to do too much in the way of enlightening them, and he may well believe, perhaps rightly, that he is not in the position to offer much in the way of enlightenment.

That journalist-puppeteers can and should become liberators, or at least trustworthy partners of liberators, is a notion that is apt to be met in many circles with the same scepticism as Plato's Socratic paradox that philosophers should be our political leaders. I have already presented some of the reasons why our new "paradox" would be met with resistance by the larger part of the reading public, by most journalists themselves, and by philosophical critics of journalism like Schopenhauer. That the notion may well seem to be of almost paradoxical proportions is evidenced by a mischievous but potent rhetorical question raised by McLuhan: "Is not the essence of education civil defence against media fall-out?"[9] We can hardly be blamed if, as we ponder McLuhan's query, all the sins of all the journalists we have ever read pass before our minds. Yet, it was this very same McLuhan who was later able to observe that "all media that mix ads with other programming are a form of 'paid learning.' In years to come, when the child will be paid to learn, educators will recognize the sensational press as the forerunner of paid learning."[10]

In *Public Opinion*, Lippmann offered this rather limp and unconvincing defense of the journalism of his day:

> Ethically a newspaper is judged as if it were a church or a school. But if you try to compare it with these you fail; the taxpayer pays for the public school, the private school is endowed or supported by tuition fees, there are subsidies and collections for the church. You cannot compare journalism with law, medicine or engineering, for in every one of these professions the public pays for the service. . . . It would be regarded as an outrage to have to pay openly the price of a good ice cream soda for all the news of the world, though the public will pay that and more when it buys the advertised commodities. The public pays for the press, but only when the payment is concealed.[11]

This curious mélange of sincerely articulated half-truths can be attacked on many scores, but here it need only be said that (1) it is ultimately a reading public interested in news that keeps the periodical press in business; (2) the typical reader has fewer illusions than Lippmann suggests about the moral failings of the periodical press (and of the church, the school, and the professions, for that matter); and (3) as much as they may carp, fairly or unfairly, about those moral failings, most readers believe in their heart of hearts that the periodical press, with all its faults, is, not much less than the school or church, one of the institutions that ought to and often does protect and promote the ideals of a civilized community. Despite the skepticism about the possibilities of journalism that constantly surfaces in various quarters, only the Schopenhauers among us would scoff at Kingsley Martin's passionate assertion that "the task of providing accurate news and intelligent comment is vital for the mental health of the public and. . . to entrust it to untrained and ignorant people is as dangerous as to rely on quacks and faith-healers."[12] Hence, for all the initial resistance that the notion of the journalist as educator is likely to meet, not everyone will regard it on reflection as preposterous, though even the most hopeful souls will be understandably troubled by the gap that exists between what journalism usually is and what it can and ought to be. Toward the end of his life, Lippmann himself became absolutely convinced that there is no excuse, economic or otherwise, that can justify the journalist's avoidance of his responsibility to promote a sound public philosophy.

What this responsibility involves may be more than initially meets the eye. Consider a possible response to the paradox of the journalist-educator that is quite different from the merely skeptical one. Say a journalist, reader, or theorist were to argue instead along these lines: "Of course, the journalist is something of an educator. He provides all sorts of information, some of it quite useful to the reader and the community. He advances interpretations and opinions that induce the reader to think about certain matters worth thinking about. He encourages the reader to make use of and develop certain intellectual skills. So even if neither journalists nor readers are accustomed to thinking of the journalist as an educator, they will probably grant on reflection that he is indeed something of the sort. Still, the education that he offers is a secondary, low-grade kind that falls short in comparison with the kinds of education provided by schoolteachers, professors, religious leaders, great authors, and other full-fledged educators, those who are educators in the highest, purest sense of the term. Moreover, it would be presumptuous and unrealistic for the journalist to attempt to offer more in the way of education than he already does: it is not his business to do so, he is not expected to do so, and he has not been trained to do so."

Before proceeding to swallow this argument whole, one should consider a few things. First, it cannot be known merely by intuition what the proper business of the journalist is, even if that intuition is based partly on an informed understanding of what journalism has traditionally been. Why, after all, should we rule out on principle the possibility of journalism's being (or becoming) a good deal better and more valuable than it has traditionally been? Again, why could not the journalist be better trained to provide a higher grade of education? And is it not gratuitous speculation to assume that any journalist who attempted to be an educator in the highest, purest sense would inevitably find that his well-meaning aspirations had been presumptuous and unrealistic? Also, while education does involve providing interesting, useful information, making people think, and helping people to develop certain intellectual skills, it goes beyond these particular tasks (or effects) and even beyond the combination of them. A journalist could provide interesting, useful information, make people think, and help people to develop intellectual skills and yet still be a puppeteer in the cave, just as a manipulative totalitarian propagandist could perform all these specific tasks and still end up as the polar opposite of a liberator.

If the journalist is to be an educator in anything like the highest, purest sense, perhaps he must do what the Hutchins Commission has enjoined him to do: he must continuously state and clarify the ideals toward which the community should strive. This is what the later Lippmann had in mind when he mused about the journalist's obligation to promote the public philosophy. This vision is in an important way a Platonic one.

If the tradition of associating education at its highest or purest with the promotion and clarification of certain ideals is followed, as I think should be the case, then one should at least be prepared to acknowledge that one is swimming in deep theoretical waters, for a straightforward analysis of how the word education is used in everyday language will not lead directly to a consideration of the importance of promoting the clearer apprehension of proper ideals. The term is in fact used to denote a much wider range of things than the term journalism is, and even a cursory survey of the history of educational philosophy will reveal that there is widespread and profound disagreement about the nature and aims of education. Some educational theorists have been satisfied to conceive of education as little more than the process of performing some of the specific tasks that we considered above, such as imparting information and promoting the development of intellectual skills. Some have seen it mainly as a matter of putting knowledge into a student's mind, while others have seen it more as a matter of drawing insights and skills out. Some have taken a largely utilitarian view of its significance, while others have associated it more with self-realization and self-development. Some have associated it with a relatively narrow form of socialization such as enculturation, while others have stressed its value in enabling the student to transcend the limited moral vision of his particular community. Not long ago, John Dewey achieved celebrity—and not a little notoriety—for his thesis that education should have no fixed aims at all, apart from the promotion of a vague sort of "growth."[13] All of these theories have been helpful in providing new perspectives of education and insights into aspects of education that might otherwise be undervalued or even ignored. The journalist is actually capable of educating in all of these various senses, so that a theoretical investigation of the nature and aims of journalism could be to some extent subsumed under the general philosophy of education. Still, while acknowledging that the journalist can be an educator in all of these forms, high or low, primary or secondary, I shall follow that tradition that attaches most importance to the relation of education to the promotion and clarification of ideals, and that accordingly would be inclined to stress the journalist's capacity to be an educator-liberator in this regard.

The guiding force behind the Commission on Freedom of the Press, Hutchins, was possibly the most prominent defender of his day of a classical theory of liberal education. President and later chancellor of the University of Chicago, and advocate of the famous great books program, he was a zealous promoter of various Aristotelian and Thomistic (and indirectly, Platonic) theories about the human condition, the good life, and the essential relation of education to self-realization. In *The Conflict in Education*, he says that the ultimate aim of education is always the same from age to age and culture to culture, despite technological and other advances in civilization, and that that aim is to improve man *as man*. Every man has a function as a man, and the primary object of education is to know (and help others to know) what is good for man; it is to know (and help others to know) the goods in their proper natural order, he proposes. Only those who act on the basis of an informed understanding of the proper hierarchy of values are capable of living well and contributing consistently and effectively to the maintenance of social justice and the advancement of civilization. It was this rather Platonic view that Hutchins brought to his work with the Commission on Freedom of the Press, and that is so much reflected in the tone of the commission's famous report.

When Lippmann's *Public Opinion* was published in 1922, he could hardly have had much sympathy with such an outlook. Still much under the influence of a certain pragmatic kind of liberalism, he would have regarded such an outlook, and the related belief by thinkers like Hutchins in natural law, as too rigid and abstract, elitist, speculative, dogmatic, and generally illiberal. But over the years, Lippmann's views on politics, education, and the proper mission of journalism underwent an interesting transformation. Summarizing some of the main themes of *Public Opinion*, the liberal historian, Arthur Schlesinger Jr., writes:

> For most people, Lippmann argued, the world they were supposed to deal with politically was "out of reach, out of sight, out of mind." The real environment was replaced by a "pseudo-environment," compounded of ignorance, distortion, tradition, emotion, stereotype, and manipulated consent. . . . Public opinion, in consequence, became primarily "a moralized and codified version of the facts." Nor would liberation of the facts by itself affect a cure, since few people were prepared to absorb them or to assess them at their proper significance. What was necessary was some means of making the facts intelligible, and this less for the people at large than for the few who had to make large decisions. Most people Lippmann felt obliged to dismiss as "outsiders," without the time, or attention, or interest, or equipment for judgment.[14]

The first half of *Public Opinion* is a penetrating analysis of subjectivity, bias, prejudice, stereotype, and code; at the same time, it is a Platonic uncovering of the dark side of pure, unrestrained democracy.[15] The second half of the book begins with a close examination of the periodical press, and here Lippmann's observations are no more encouraging. If the author was once able to see his fellow journalists as potential liberators in some sense,[16] experience has taught him that most newsmen are no more than puppeteers in Plato's cave. But Lippmann does not blame the periodical press for public ignorance; indeed, he is critical of those who expect too much from it, and in memorable lines he concludes:

> For the troubles of the press, like the troubles of representative government, be it territorial or functional, like the troubles of industry, be it capitalist, cooperative, or communist, go back to a common source: to the failure of self-governing people to transcend their casual experience and their prejudice, by inventing, creating, and organizing a machinery of knowledge. It is because they are compelled to act without a reliable picture of the world, that governments, schools, newspapers, and churches make such small headway against the more obvious failings of democracy, against violent prejudice, apathy, preference for the curious trivial as against the dull important, and the hunger for sideshows and three-legged calves.[17]

Public bias, group bias, and journalistic bias are all symptoms of the same disease, a disease that cannot be cured by replacing journalistic bias with a bazaar of biases. If the diagnosis here is right, then the appropriate remedy is clear: self-governing people can and must transcend their casual experience and their prejudice by developing a machinery of knowledge. The facts must be liberated and made intelligible; in the last chapters of *Public Opinion*, Lippmann makes a Platonic appeal to us to promote the method of reason.

Lippmann never lost confidence in the ability of reason to lead enlightened decision makers to a reliable picture of the world, and he never ceased to believe that liberal democracy is salvageable, but having become as skeptical about social-scientific experts as he had earlier been about majorities and about newspeople, he eventually realized that he would have to move on from the position that he had developed in *Public Opinion*. Interestingly enough, his approach to his traditional constellation of problems actually became more Platonic rather than less so, though he came to draw more on Plato's metaphysic than on Plato's social criticism. As Schlesinger observes:

> In *The Phantom Public.* . . , Lippmann's note of hope against the irreducible pluralism of the world was "the maintenance of a regime of rule, contract and custom." In 1925, this was for Lippmann a procedural conception. But in the years thereafter, what began as a functional necessity was somehow hypostatized into a transcendental faith—and then employed to abolish the very pluralism which had originally produced it.

The invocation of due process grew into "a universal order on which all reasonable men were agreed," "a common conception of law and order which possesses a universal validity," natural law, the public philosophy. By this he meant the realm of essences ("I am using the ambiguous but irreplaceable word 'essence' as meaning the true and undistorted nature of things"), a world of "immaterial entities. . . not to be perceived by our senses," but nonetheless more real than anything else . . . . In the name of the public philosophy, Lippmann spurned his pluralism of the twenties. A "large plural society," he argued, could not be governed "without recognizing that, transcending its plural interests, there is a rational order with a superior common law."[18]

Lippmann came to believe that "it was the responsibility of intellectuals to propagate the public philosophy,"[19] and he could not have desired journalists to propagate any other.

Schlesinger and others have expressed reservations about Lippmann's Platonic notion of the public philosophy, and not without reason.[20] It is noteworthy, however, that this reflective philosopher-journalist who knew all about stereotypes and codes and biases ended up by adopting so metaphysically Platonic a position. Even when he wrote *Public Opinion*, there was a pronounced strain of Platonism in Lippmann's thinking; during this phase of his reflection, he was concerned with the mistaking of images for reality, the reduction of journalism and opinion shaping to a kind of sophistical puppetry conforming largely to public demands, the need for reason and an organized machinery of knowledge, and the necessity of infusing a large dose of Platonic elitism into the politics of the democratic state. Yet, during this phase, Lippmann associated knowledge with the interpretation of facts gathered by social-scientific experts; and he was inclined to attach a great deal of importance, in Protagorean fashion, to a pluralism softened by convention, consensus, and social contract. In the end, however, while still committed on some level of political consciousness to democratic liberalism, he found himself unable to carry on his theoretical program without appealing more and more to the hypostatized moral essences that Plato characterized as Forms; he came to believe that the paramount social obligation of all agents of civilization, whether they be teachers, statesmen, churchmen, or journalists, is to know the Forms, to promote that knowledge to whatever extent possible among the prisoners who constitute the majority in a self-governing public (and who ultimately do possess the greatest real power in a democratic society), and to apply that knowledge in reasonable public analyses of the great moral and political issues of the day. Thus, while Lippmann was ultimately prepared to grant that even the ordinary man and woman are capable of a significant measure of moral insight and reasonable moral judgment, he also came to appreciate more and more the journalist's capacity and obligation to function as one of the community's educator-liberators.

By adopting such a position, Lippmann might seem to have left himself open to the charge of having encouraged his fellow journalists to become propagandists, and indeed some journalists who adopt Lippmann's final outlook will end up as propagandists. But before indicting Lippmann on this count, one must bear several things in mind. Lippmann rightly recognized from the start that there is no such thing as neutral or objective reporting or news journalism. Both in the earlier and later phases of his reflection, Lippmann stressed that a journalist never simply reports the facts but presents facts in the context of a framework of certain moral, political, metaphysical, and scientific attitudes that to some extent reflect personal and cultural biases, as well as the biases of professional colleagues and interest groups. So what is commonly and often unilluminatingly classified together under the label of propaganda manifests itself in news reporting and analysis on many levels. But as he matured, Lippmann became increasingly convinced that the typical news journalist, along with many other members of the polis, is capable of understanding the differences between good and evil, right and wrong, just and unjust, real and unreal, true and false, beautiful and ugly, civilized and barbarous. Hence, Lippmann came to see that if the journalist is to exploit his influence properly, he must develop and refine this understanding and apply it in his work. One is not a propagandist for the good, the true, and the civilized in the way that one is a propagandist for the pet schemes of a certain political, religious, or economic group, and to argue that all attempts to promote the good, true, and civilized inevitably degenerate into the propaganda for such pet schemes is to endorse uncritically a sophistic relativism. To reinforce a public convention, consensus, or social contract, without paying appropriate attention to its degree of soundness and reasonableness, is to leave oneself more open to the fair charge of propagandizing than to play intelligently the role of educator-liberator is. Not all systems of morals, politics, metaphysics, or theology warrant the same degree of journalistic promotion or reinforcement, and the popularity of any such system in a particular community is not in itself prima facie evidence of its soundness or reasonableness. Of course, a would-be liberator can bungle the job, and a journalist who bungles the job may end up as being a more dangerous propagandist than the colleague who allows himself to be nothing more than an apologist for the ideas, values, and attitudes adopted through communal convention, consensus, and contract. Nevertheless, fear of bungling the job is hardly an adequate defense of having performed another job that, though less risky, is morally unsatisfactory in its own right, even if it is perhaps often an adequate defense of one's having avoided the profession of journalism completely.

I have already noted the journalist's susceptibility to adopting a sophistically conventionalistic position toward morality itself and toward his own professional role in society. In addition to the more obvious pressures that compel him to pander to the whims of the public and his publishers, I have said the journalist-puppeteer is very much the creature of the Great Sophist for more profound psychological reasons. Now, whatever the weaknesses of conventionalistic moral and epistemological theories, such theories do at least have the merit of representing a defense against the kind of unrestrained ideological pluralism that threatens to plunge a society into anarchical chaos. Those who stress the importance of convention, consensus, and contract have at least this much in common with Plato, Hutchins, and the later Lippmann: they fear the social consequences of the kind of radical, thorough-going ideological pluralism that goes together with pure relativism. Yet there are some who would argue, often in the name of tolerance, that radical pluralism is ultimately a good thing for a society.[21] The application of this view to journalism has been given the name of *multiperspectivism*. Consider a fairly clear and potent defense of this view offered by the sociologist, Herbert J. Gans.

In his book, *Deciding What's News*, Gans endorses multiperspectivism, which he characterizes as a news philosophy that seems to offer a partial solution to the problem of news distortion without detracting from the integrity of the journalistic enterprise.[22] He recommends that "the news, and the news media, be multiperspectival, presenting and representing as many perspectives as possible—and at the very least, more than today."[23] The fundamental justification for multiperspectival news, he says, is its "potential for furthering democracy."[24] And, although it is not designed to gain supporters for a particular political cause, neither is it apolitical, "since making the symbolic arena more democratic is a political goal."[25]

The solution to the problem of news distortion might seem to involve making journalists more knowledgeable and more articulate, but if Gans is right, it is naive to believe that the journalist can ever transcend bias:

News can be judged as distorted *in relation* to a specified standard (or ideal) of nondistortion. However, the standards themselves cannot be absolute or objective because they are inevitably based on a number of reality and value judgments: about the nature of external reality, knowledge, and truth; about the proper purposes of the news; and more often than not, about the good nation and society.[26]

Moreover,

In the prototypical homogeneous society, which has never existed, everyone shares the same perspectives; but in a modern society, no one sits or stands in exactly the same place. Consequently, perspectives on reality will vary. Poor people experience America differently than do middle-income people or the rich; as a result, their attitudes toward government will also vary. Different perspectives lead to different questions and different answers, thereby requiring different facts and different news.[27]

Since people who come from different backgrounds and live under different circumstances have different perspectives, different world views, they view different things as important. Nothing is objectively important. What matters a great deal to certain journalists or news editors may matter very little to most readers. Were the problem of news bias primarily a matter of false reports, working for objectivity would be the appropriate solution. But if "the issue is what facts should become news," as Gans suggests, striving for an unattainable objectivity is pointless.[28] Thus Gans suggests that national news and news media present and represent as many perspectives as possible. News must be made multiperspectival: the journalists' perspectives cannot be falsified, but they can be to some extent neutralized by being juxtaposed with different perspectives.

Gans recognizes that omniperspectival news is impossible. so which perspectives should be included, and which should be excluded? And who should be making such judgments? If the leadership is largely racist, should multiperspectival news include information of special interest to racists? Should editors and journalists go to great pains to present and represent the perspectives of Presbyterians, adulterers, Masons, the color-blind, astrology buffs, and people who resent having to think for themselves? Should they decrease their coverage of the oppression of certain minority groups on the grounds that those groups represent a very small part of the population? And should news executives recruit as editors and journalists more Presbyterians, adulterers, and so forth? Whoever had the power to make such decisions would be able to do considerable damage with his own biases.

Gans assumes that even if many perspectives cannot be presented in the news, it is better to have more than the national media now present. But a Roman Catholic or Jew who resents the secularism of a certain newspaper may be even angrier if that paper balances its secularist perspective with, say, a fundamentalist Protestant perspective.

Multiperspectivism is not merely a putatively practical solution to the problem of how to reduce bias in the news media; it is a news philosophy that concentrates on what it takes to be the essential and necessary subjectivity of the journalist's perspective. The kind of journalistic bias that multiperspectivism is concerned with is nothing over and above the subjective elements constituting perspective. Multiperspectival news can be seen, then, as multibiased news. In such multibiased news, the various biases presented and represented do not necessarily neutralize one another. The combining of various biases into a package is done by necessarily biased people for necessarily biased people. The news editor's conception of what constitutes an appropriate combination of biases is likely to displease many members of the readership who do not share his values, perceptions, or overall perspective. Indeed, many readers will be more critical of a newspaper that pretends to do justice to their perspective than one that is more obviously opposed to their perspective. It is, after all, easier to detect genuine bias in a uniperspectival periodical than a multiperspectival one.

The typical news journal is perhaps rather more multiperspectival than might appear on the surface, for it involves various journalists with unique perspectives writing for various readers with unique perspectives. What troubles a multiperspectivist like Gans is that though every journalist has in some sense a unique perspective, most influential journalists share certain key values and perceptions. Gans is especially concerned with the various professional, social, and personal political values and perceptions that such journalists share. He tells us, for example, that "the high value placed on civil liberties is almost an instrumental necessity, since journalistic autonomy depends on freedom of the press,"[29] and that the political values of journalists have some relation to the upper-middle-class status of most journalists.[30] (Gans makes the same observation as Fulford about the journalist's typical association with the middle class.)

The judgment of journalists does reflect, of course, their educational background and professional status. But before dismissing

their judgment as the result of just one more of many possible
biases, one should reflect on what is involved in being a highly educated professional. It is not clear that newspapers would be better if
publishers and managing editors entrusted the job of informing the
public to uneducated amateurs. There is a very important sense in
which the educated person's bias is superior to the uneducated person's; many would even say that the educated person, even if he has
not been fully liberated, tends to be less biased than the relatively ignorant person. Even the puppeteer is no mere prisoner. It is
also widely believed that professionals are generally superior to
amateurs in the practice of a craft, though the radical multiperspectivist might want to dismiss even this belief as just so much Platonic
dogma.[31]

Indeed, it is here that the contrast between the outlook of the
multiperspectivist and that of people like Plato, Hutchins, and the
later Lippmann comes into bold relief. According to the classical
model, a major purpose of education is to make people better human beings and better citizens. The study of philosophy, literature,
and history ought to give a person deeper insight into the human
condition, into the nature and potential of human beings, and it
ought to help him to empathize and sympathize and to see things
from other people's perspectives. If journalists do share many key
values and perceptions, that is at least partly because they have
generally been educated to some extent to be reflective, logical, fair,
and somewhat compassionate, and they have arrived at similar conclusions partly as a result of carefully analyzing data. The philosopher who sees the journalist as having the capacity and obligation
to participate in the educational liberation of his fellows will see the
multiperspectivist as unjustifiably assuming that the common perspective of journalists—to the extent that one can exist—must necessarily be primarily a result of the same hidden determinants that
shape the perspective of a relatively unreflective, irrational person.

The term *bias* itself is subject to various interpretations, but when
used in such expressions as *journalistic bias* and *news bias*, it normally has pejorative force. In ordinary discourse, the statement, "They
are biased in their reporting," carries with it the implication that
those responsible for the reporting have done their job badly. Journalistic bias is usually associated with injustice and incompetence. It
is often associated with dishonesty and self-serving motives. Gans
offers what is, in effect, a stipulative definition of the expression,
journalistic bias, when he associates such bias with perspective. But
it is not doing justice to either ordinary language or common sense
to suggest that the very act of reporting or interpreting, necessarily

based on a somewhat subjective perspective, is probably badly done and quite possibly unjust, dishonest, and self-serving. To treat a high-minded social worker's interpretation of the situation of the poor as being as essentially biased as the callous corporation president's interpretation is to do violence not only to ordinary language but to ideals of civilization that even the most cynical among us do respect in our finer moments. Similarly, to reduce pro-Nazi and anti-Nazi perspectives to the epistemologico-ethical status of pro-Nazi and anti-Nazi biases is to confuse ordinary speakers of English and perhaps to be indiscriminately tolerant of barbarism.

Bias belongs to a family of concepts that includes intolerance, bigotry, discrimination, ethnocentrism, racism, prejudice, dogmatism, and close-mindedness. In analyzing the related concept of prejudice, I have observed elsewhere that when people talk about prejudice, usually they do not have all prejudgment in mind but only false and maleficent prejudgment.[32] A similar point can be made with respect to bias: in most cases, a perspective is not seen as qualifying as a bias unless it satisfies the conditions of being epistemically and/or ethically unacceptable, based on false presuppositions and/or productive of harm or evil. Hence, in dealing with the problem of journalistic bias, we should worry much less about the question of how many perspectives the news media present and represent than the question of what constitutes an epistemically and morally reasonable perspective by which to report and interpret events. To reject the latter question outright as being unanswerable in principle is to embrace relativism of a very radical and dangerous kind. If such relativism is right, then the moral judgments of Socrates and Albert Schweitzer are not superior to those of Caligula and Hitler.

Gans says that the fundamental justification for multiperspectival news is its potential for furthering democracy. His motive for advocating multiperspectivism would thus seem to be an admirable one, for in our society, *democracy* tends to be a positive word in much the same way as *bias* tends to have pejorative force. It is important that we clearly distinguish between the pro-democracy and anti-bias motives for favoring multiperspectival news. Gans does not argue that there is a direct and necessary connection between being in favor of democracy and being opposed to news bias. There is indeed no such connection. Someone who has little or no interest in the potential of multiperspectival news for furthering democracy— or even someone who is anti-democracy—can still enthusiastically promote multiperspectival news on the grounds that it offers a partial solution to the problem of news bias. Similarly, one who is deeply concerned about the need for furthering democracy may be quite willing to tolerate the most common forms of journalistic bias.

To insist that the two motives simply be distinguished may be to understate a key point. A critic of news bias could build an impressive case for the position that a large part of such bias exists precisely because the major news media are already too democratic. Far from being a manipulative elitist, it could be argued, the typical newsman or news executive is someone who must consider, reconsider, and in one sense at least, respect the values, perceptions, needs, and wants of those who comprise his readership. The journalist-puppeteer is frequently given to pandering, both consciously and unconsciously; even the journalist-liberator has to learn to speak to the prisoners on their own terms if he is to induce them to follow him out of the cave. On one level, democracy seems to be a matter of everyone's having a say in political decision making, but on another level, it seems to be a matter of popular perspectives taking precedence over unpopular ones. In reflecting the worst as well as the best values and perceptions of the Great Sophist, the general public, newspapers and news magazines leave themselves open to many criticisms, but normally not that of being undemocratic.

When Gans says that multiperspectival news can help to further democracy, he is thinking of its value as a means of bringing more people into the ranks of the decision makers; multiperspectival news will provide relevant information to those who have not been able to make much use of the type of information that the news media now provide. While I share Gans's view that a healthy democracy is one that involves the active participation of members of diverse groups (and respect for the rights of members of diverse groups), I worry about the importance that much democratic theory attaches to what is popular. To the extent that furthering democracy is a matter of promoting popular perspectives, multiperspectival news is effectively undemocratic, for while it gives power of expression to some who have hitherto been denied such power, it takes power away from majorities in the process. This form of redistributing power is quite different from the form usually associated with democratization; that is, shifting power from a minority to a majority. It is somewhat misleading, then, to say that multiperspectival news furthers democracy. Rooted in a more extreme theoretical relativism than conventionalism is, multiperspectivism aims to some extent at undermining convention, consensus, and social contract. On the other hand, the value of furthering democracy is itself something that must constantly be considered and reconsidered in the light of concrete circumstances. Oppressed minorities have often received more benign treatment from political elites than from the mob. One can appreciate this point even if one is not prepared to endorse the radical Platonic arguments against the democratic system of government.

Gans also suggests that "the interests of diverse groups have priority over the needs of nation and society."[33] This extraordinarily ambiguous statement epitomizes the confusion inherent in multi-perspectivism. The nation is not just a collection of groups but is itself a group, and so too is the human race. To be a citizen of a nation or a member of the human race is to have certain rights and responsibilities. When gross injustice is committed by or against our fellow nationals or our fellow human beings anywhere in the world, the fact is newsworthy, regardless of our individual and cultural biases and perspectives. When newspapers and news magazines hide these truths behind a screen of conflicting perspectives, they cease to function as instruments of civilization. News journals, in any case, do not constitute the entirety of the public forum, so that even when they do not offer accurate reporting and sound and reasonable interpretation of current events, there may well be liberators in other domains to promote wisdom, justice, and the other ideals of civilization. Such domains are the schools and universities, book publishers and electronic media, churches and legislatures. Nevertheless, there is no good reason to write the news journals off and take the fatalistic view that journalists can never perform the task of promoting civilization in a way comparable with the performance of it by the best teachers, professors, authors, broadcasters, ecclesiastics, and statesmen. Indeed, once cynicism leads us to write the newspapers off, it may not be long before it leads us to write off the other institutions as well.

Despite the journalist-puppeteer's complex dependence on the prisoners on several levels, he normally has a certain degree of autonomy in relation to those for whom he performs his show. Whatever its failings, and they can be very great, his show at least has the virtue of having the order and coherence that derives from its being directed. Multiperspectivism gives the prisoners only a random barrage of images, and though it may give a certain type of participatory power to the prisoners, it threatens to leave them without an orderly pattern of images around which to organize their activity in the cave.

Even if one were prepared to grant all this, one would still have reasonable grounds for worrying about the fineness of the line that may separate promotion of the public philosophy of ideals of civilization from the dissemination of propaganda. A manipulative, self-serving propagandist could hide his true motives behind the pretense of participating in the classical program of educational liberation. A misguided fanatical ideologue could convince himself and others that he is participating in that program. (Plato himself has often been attacked as such an ideologue, and thinkers like Hutchins and Lippmann have not been immune to a subdued version of this criticism.) We all know how often lofty motives are proclaimed by those who, deliberately or not, are agents of barbarism rather than civilization, and we all have our pet examples of how journalists have abused their power as opinion shapers. Still, the fact that such power can be (and has been) regularly and significantly abused does not in itself justify the refusal to attempt to exercise that power creatively and beneficently; and it should not escape our attention here that the charge of propagandizing has been directed, sometimes fairly and sometimes unfairly, at all those involved in the classical program of educational liberation, not just journalists.

The term *propaganda* has a special historical association with religious teaching: its initial reference was to the Catholic church's efforts to propagate the Catholic faith. History teaches us how religious proselytizing often degenerates from noble witnessing into a deceptive, dishonest, and generally vicious exercise It is not hard to see how propaganda came over the centuries to be viewed in a negative light by many high-minded liberals. What is sometimes forgotten, as I have previously written, is that proselytizing can be ethical or even noble under certain circumstances.[34] What applies to religious proselytizing also applies to its most conspicuous secular counterpart, ideological proselytizing.

However, merely to compare the situation of the journalist-liberator with that of another kind of educator does not indicate the key problem here, which is that any kind of educational program may be regarded, fairly or unfairly, as the dissemination of propaganda. In fact, any educator—whether author, elementary school teacher, professor, or philosopher—can be seen as a puppeteer in the cave. Consider the case of Plato himself: here is someone widely regarded as one of the world's greatest philosophers, writers, and educators, yet often taken (and even by some of his admirers) to be a propagandist for certain regrettably authoritarian ideas and institutions.

In books 2 and 3 of the *Republic*, Plato outlines a program of primary education for future leaders, and in the process, he advocates censoring Homer's epics for school use and preventing students from listening to certain kinds of music. Some critics have accused Plato of encouraging arbitrary censorship and techniques of mind control. Whether or not Plato's particular recommendations are sound, it should not be forgotten that all formal education involves a systematic process of selection and rejection: certain ideas, values, experiences, texts, and skills are offered to the students, while others they are encouraged to avoid and still others are deemed by their teachers to be of no special relevance to the program. Such selection and rejection can be heavy-handed, propagandistic, and destructive, but it is not at all clear that the selection and rejection is necessarily so. When a teacher tells his students that the Holocaust is a myth invented by Zionist bankers, the words *propaganda* and *indoctrination* appropriately come to mind, but our value system and use of language have gone awry when we characterize as a propagandist the elementary school teacher who encourages her students to manifest a sympathetic concern for those less fortunate than themselves.

Fears about high-minded journalism inevitably deteriorating into propaganda may be somewhat assuaged if it is remembered that any reasonably thoughtful person can, with some effort, sensibly distinguish certain characteristics of education from the defining characteristics of such processes as propagandizing, conditioning, indoctrinating, manipulating, and brainwashing. Some of the distinctions that could be drawn here would involve reference only to the lexical definitions of these terms, definitions that indicate how in fact the terms are used in ordinary discourse. As we observed earlier, an interpretation of the journalist's potential as liberator could be given in the context of a general philosophical theory of the nature and aims of education. We could argue, for example, that as one fundamental aim of education is to help those being educated to think critically and analytically for themselves instead of relying exclusively on the unchallenged testimony of self-professed political experts, the journalist who performs this task responsibly, and with proper regard to other aims of education and to sound moral ideals in general, is no mere puppeteer, propagandist, or entertainer, but a participant in the classical program of educational liberation. In contrast, the journalist who promotes his friends in political power by appealing to the emotions of his more manipulable readers with flashy rhetorical images, appeals to force and pity, and clever half-truths is a puppeteer and propagandist, no matter how much positive utilitarian value his influence may have. Again, the journalist who encourages his readers to reject outright whatever political leaders say is not participating in a program of educational liberation.

In determining how his reporting and analysis could be put to educational use, the journalist would be wise to take various cues from the extensive classical and recent literature on educational theory. However, he would normally find it more convenient to take cues from educators themselves. The journalist should, as a matter of course, carefully scrutinize the writings of the great journalists of past ages and his own; I have in mind here not the writings of journalists who have merely been popular or well placed in the profession, but rather the writings of those journalists who have left a powerful positive influence on the character of individual readers. (When someone tells a journalist that reading the work of a certain columnist cured him of certain entrenched racist delusions or opened up his eyes to grave environmental problems that he hitherto could not take seriously, the journalist should give serious consideration to making it his business to see how such a columnist has gone about his work.) But the journalist should also take as models humanistic writers in fields as diverse as fiction, literary criticism, social criticism, historical writing, and philosophy.

To be capable of liberating others, one must have been liberated oneself, and to be liberated oneself, one must take advantage of the traditional institutions by which liberation can be accomplished. Plato learned much from his revered teacher, Socrates, and by founding his Academy and leaving his philosophical dialogues to posterity, Plato passed on intellectual methods and insights first to students like Aristotle and ultimately to all future generations. The educational resources available to a modern journalist are vast. It has become common for young journalists to study in institutions of higher learning. With the passing of time, more and more young journalists may see the relevance of their humanistic studies in university to their work in reporting and analyzing current events that may on the surface seem rather more trivial and uninstructive than they are. We took note earlier of the kinship between journalism and both belles-lettres and historical literature. Even the best modern journalist does not moralize on the level of a Thucydides, Erasmus, Lessing, or Milton, but if he studies the works of such writers carefully, he may well find that both the style and the content of his pieces on local politics, fashion, or sports can be elevated somewhat.

If we are to think of the journalist as an educator, we have to banish from our minds the image of an educator as an elderly gentleman with a long black gown and a square-topped academic cap standing in front of a blackboard with a pointer. The journalist has different ways of passing on valuable information, helping his readers to develop moral and intellectual virtues and skills, and increasing the power of those readers to participate intelligently and constructively in the social life of the polis. Still, in attempting to help his readers to become wiser and generally better human beings than they are, the journalist-liberator is no more patronizing his reader than any other educator is patronizing his charges. He remains the reader's servant, even if he refuses to give that reader exactly what the latter wants (if the latter even knows what he wants) in the short term. The journalist who remains suspended at the level of puppetry can be seen as rather more patronizing, since he has a lower estimation of his reader's potential for personally satisfying and socially constructive self-development.

Consider a specific example, that of sports reporting. While I believe there are all too many pretentious, long-winded, self-important sports reporters who blow out of all reasonable proportion the events that take place on the baseball diamond or in the hockey arena, I agree that good sports reporting involves much more than simply describing the key plays of last night's games. High-quality sports journalism concentrates on the human element in athletic competition rather than on mechanical occurrences. It not only relates sporting activity to other aspects of life, but it draws our attention to the many ways in which such activity is related to values, as, say, in being a field for personal achievement, the overcoming of adversity, the application of closely reasoned strategy, the appreciation of cooperativeness and sportsmanship, and the constructive application of disciplined training. The archetypal figures that we encounter in the sports columns, though often broadly drawn, are not altogether unlike those that we encounter in the political columns, or for that matter, in great novels, history books, or even sacred works: the aging competitor who must capitalize on his savvy because his physical vigor is naturally declining, the rebellious young prospect who squanders his talents through lack of self-discipline and of appreciation of the importance of cooperating with his teammates, the authoritarian manager and the one who prefers to be one of the boys, the star who cannot cope with his heavy responsibilities or his own success. Many people who dismiss the newspaper's sports pages as unimportant fail to recognize the continuity between those pages and the important pages in constituting a synoptic vehicle by which moral ideals can be illustrated, promoted, and sharpened. And the reading of high-quality sports journalism calls for critical moral reflection and judgment on the part of the reader, as well as a variety of intellectual skills. High-quality sports journalism is not the random compilation of statistics and tidbits of trivial gossip, and we do not do it justice if we characterize it as mere entertainment even in the widest senses of the term.

I am not suggesting that sports journalism or any other kind can provide the reader with moral and political insights as profound as those that can be derived from reading the *Upanishads*, *War and*

Peace, or the historical works of Mommsen and Parkman, or from witnessing a well-crafted production of *Prometheus Bound* or *Othello*. Yet the insights it can provide are at least comparable in certain important ways, and a journalist who is familiar with great literature will have more to say and will be able to say it better than he otherwise could.

The fact is—and alas, Plato himself was all too often blind to it—that the study of all great works of literature, and not just philosophical works, leads the reflective person closer to an apprehension and understanding of the moral ideals that, as they are more closely seen and more consistently applied, lead one to be wise rather than merely clever, happy rather than merely satisfied, just rather than merely prudent, honorable rather than merely prominent, and civilized rather than merely active. Because of the positive influence that he is in a privileged (though not unique) position to exert on his fellows, the journalist has a special obligation to make himself conversant with the humanistic tradition, and if he never produces great literature himself, he can nevertheless play a larger part than most of his fellows in carrying out the program established by great authors and teachers. But if he thinks of himself as essentially an entertainer, or an agent of the powerful, or as someone who has simply found a relatively painless and convenient way to get on in the world, or as someone who can invent at will his own standards of truth and goodness, or as someone who ultimately must tell people what they want to hear, then he will only be the slave of the Great Sophist and his other masters, a puppeteer whose central mission in life has been to project shadows on the cave wall.

The view we have just taken of the journalist's potential as an educator-liberator is a truncated one, however, for it exaggerates one dimension of the journalistic endeavor at the expense of others. Exaggeration can be a useful pedagogical device, firmly establishing in our minds a point that, were it made more cautiously, might completely elude us. That is why so much study in the history of philosophy concentrates on philosophical systems that both initially and ultimately quite properly strike the thoughtful reader as implausible; the exaggerations involved in such systems help us to grasp in a quick, painless, and effective way the kernel of insight in each of them. So it is with Platonism, which, for all its profundity, obscures important dimensions of reality and the human condition, and ultimately, even of something like journalism. Although its emphases on timeless essences and human self-realization are salutary when combined with other reflections, the Platonic model, even when polished up and renovated by a Hutchins or Lippmann, will only take us so far. Whatever truth there is in Alfred North Whitehead's famous suggestion that all of Western philosophy is essentially a series of footnotes to Plato's work, the footnotes contain some rather potent and effective criticism of the master's pet themes, and they are especially valuable in reminding us about all sorts of practical matters of which the master, looking toward the heavens, has lost sight.

Both philosophers and enemies of all philosophy have objected to such aspects of Platonic idealism as its extreme hypostatization of moral ideals, its excessive devaluation of our material needs, its disregard of individuality and historicity, its authoritarianism, and its failure to appreciate the existential predicament in which real human beings find themselves. Reading an author like Pascal, Hume, Nietzsche, Marx, or Freud can help to cure one of the spiritual indigestion that comes from consuming too much Platonism for one's own good.

As for the journalist himself, he needs to emphasize the ways in which his own style of educating differs from that of other educators (poets, novelists, historians, statesmen, philosophers, religious teachers, for example). The news journalist is not a second-rate philosopher; he has a special role to play in advancing civilization and retarding barbarism that no lofty idealist gazing into the heavens can ever hope to play. For unlike his fellow educators given more to abstract modes of thinking, the news journalist is both obliged and equipped to deal with the here and now, the events of the day, and the concrete interests of flesh-and-blood human beings as they suffer both the slings and arrows of outrageous fortune and the cruelties inflicted upon them by their fellows. Troubled by the abstractness of much philosophical discussion, William Gass has lamented that often, "in the rush to establish principles, to elicit distinctions from a recalcitrant language, and to discover 'laws,' those lovely things and honored people, those vile seducers and ruddy villains our principles and laws are supposed to be based upon and our ethical theories to be about are overlooked and forgotten."[35] When the philosophers get lost in the stars, the journalists can and must step in to indicate the links between ideals and current events, principles and the world we now live in, laws and the people and institutions that we encounter in everyday life. In defense of his own mission, the journalist may be moved to echo the words of Milton: "I cannot praise a fugitive and cloistered virtue, unexercised and unbreathed, that never sallies out and sees her adversary. . . . ; the knowledge and survey of vice is in this world so necessary to the constituting of human virtue, and the scanning of error to the confirmation of truth. . . ."[36] A human being is not simply an ideal type but our neighbor in the field, the marketplace, and the prison. Ideals must be made to animate our perception of, and our response to, current events involving real people in the real world that we live in; and here is a task that a competent journalist can perform a good deal better than a mere theoretician. His type of educating, of informing, can be of immediate, direct utilitarian value in establishing the field for moral action in which ideals need to be realized at this very moment; he cannot afford to forget, as the thinker of deep thoughts is so often inclined to forget, that the ship is at sea.

5

The Ideal of a Free Press

In the *Republic*, Plato sends us two different messages about freedom, or liberty, that may or may not be consistent. The first of these messages is transmitted most directly in the course of Plato's critique of democracy in book 8, where he complains that in a democratic society, people are free and can say and do whatever they want. Plato does not approve of this kind of freedom; he associates it with license, anarchy, permissiveness, intemperance, inconsistency, and kindred phenomena. Plato believes that when people are free in this sense, they tend to do what they want to do instead of what they ought to do; and in a society in which people are generally thus free, people who lack wisdom and other virtuous dispositions have the same voice in the decision making of the community as do the wise. In the *Republic*, Plato specifically singles out freedom of speech or expression (whereby every citizen, regardless of how much knowledge or ability he possesses, has an equal right to express himself and be listened to) as one of the worst features of democratic society.[1]

Yet only a few pages later, in describing the rewards of leading a just life, Plato argues that the just person is free and not a slave to his passions and appetites. He takes for granted throughout this discussion that freedom is itself one of our highest moral ideals and that it is something that people generally value, and indeed ought to value, very highly.[2] Any apparent contradiction between Plato's two messages could perhaps be explained away by saying that Plato is talking about two different kinds of freedom. Still, these two supposedly different things have enough in common to be classified together as freedom or liberty. And Plato's mixed feelings about freedom are mirrored in our own, for nowadays we still extol freedom as a great good while lamenting that there are not enough limits to the abuse of freedom in our own troubled society.

In our own society, freedom of the press is generally considered to be one of the most important modes of freedom of expression, which is itself generally taken to be a great good, both intrinsically and pragmatically. It is considered one of the fundamental freedoms or rights of a healthy polis, and one which contributes greatly to protecting the others. Many would argue that a free press is an important symbol and defining condition of a civilized community. Yet most of the people who would defend the abstract ideal of a free press can frequently be heard complaining that the press—and more specifically, the periodical press—is allowed to get away with too much, needs to be checked and regulated in various ways, and is not responsible enough to be trusted with unlimited power.

Freedom of the press has regrettably come to be so widely identified with journalistic freedom alone that, when discussing this freedom, we are sometimes inclined to forget that public journals represent only a part of what is published. The free press also publishes, for example, novels, poems, philosophical and historical works, sacred books, science and mathematics textbooks, almanacs, travel guides, and dictionaries. But my interest here is in news journalism, and I shall consider freedom of the press solely with reference to the material written for and published in public journals.

There is no dearth of journalists and students of journalism who are prepared to testify eloquently to the importance of a free press. As Kingsley Martin has observed, it was a basic argument of Milton and Mill "that truth can only be established by the clash of argument and the exposure of error, that the goal of man is virtue through freedom, and that of all liberties the right to free opinion and free publication is most essential to good government."[3] Freedom of the press is a mode of freedom of expression, which, according to the Hutchins Commission, is "unique among liberties: it promotes and protects all the rest."[4] Hocking, who saw freedom of expression as valuable in various ways, placed special emphasis on the social value of free expression, for "without expression, there is no society."[5]

Yet, in the view of many keen observers, the freedom of the periodical press that journalists and some citizens proclaim themselves to be vigilantly protecting is, for the most part, a mythical phenomenon. According to Innis, "freedom of the press" is generally a "catchword" and "illusion."[6] There is no true competition in the marketplace of ideas, he says; what is generally proclaimed to be freedom of the press has, if anything, contributed to the monopoly and mechanization of knowledge.[7] "Freedom of the press," Servan-Schreiber suggests, "perhaps because of the obstacles it meets in practice, remains one of our great myths [in Western democracies]"; "the myth gives to the capitalists who own the media the cachet of those who serve the public interest," and it turns ordinary journalists into "knights in shining armor, defenders of the man in the street, if not sacred cows."[8] Publishers and journalists often exploit the myth in order to protect and extend their own power and influence. As Servan-Schreiber puts it: "Anyone who attacks journalists is likely to be pilloried as a murderer of freedom."[9] The idea that the press in modern Western democracies is basically free, then, may be not only something of a myth but a dangerous one too.

If we scrutinize these and similar claims closely, we find that several different assumptions are being brought into question: (1) the assumption that freedom of the press, despite a continuous stream of threats to it, is an institution that more or less prevails in some form in the modern Western democracies in which its importance is widely as well as officially proclaimed; (2) the assumption that, even if it does not exist in any contemporary society, a rather pure freedom of the press could exist in a future democratic society not much unlike contemporary democracies; (3) the assumption that freedom of the press is an institution that is necessarily, or at least ordinarily, beneficial to a society; and (4) the assumption that *freedom of the press* is an expression capable of being grasped and analyzed in a reasonably straightforward way, an expression that characterizes a fairly clear and stable social idea. Both those who extol freedom of the press and those who have grave doubts about the clarity and viability of the ideal tend to blend these assumptions together and to treat them almost as if they constituted a seamless unity.

It does not take much courage for a North American or Western European to argue that the periodical press in his country is freer than that in authoritarian or totalitarian countries. But it takes more courage and self-confidence for him to argue that the periodical press in his country is basically free. For one thing, it is illegal for newspapers and news magazines to publish certain kinds of material, such as "top secret" government documents putatively containing sensitive material related to national security, libelous statements, copyrighted material from which permission to quote has not been obtained, personal journals and correspondence that have been improperly obtained, certain articles that are deemed by people in power to be highly seditious or promotive of racial hatred, and obscene material. And, of course, there is a great deal of material that is legally publishable that a publisher will nevertheless not feel free to publish because of strong social sanctions. A publisher who, for example, allows the publication of an article advocating the liquidation of mentally retarded children, will not only lose a large chunk of his readership but friends and colleagues as well. Or, a publisher may not feel free to allow the publication of material that will offend powerful political, business, labor, ecclesiastical, orga-nized crime, or other interest groups. A journalist may not feel free to write material that will offend his publishers and editors. Clearly, such obstacles to journalistic freedom as these cannot fairly be dis-missed as being of marginal importance, even if they are not as dramatic or extensive as the obstacles to journalistic freedom in au-thoritarian or totalitarian states.

However, observers of freedom of the press such as Innis and Servan-Schreiber are primarily troubled by an obstacle to journalis-tic freedom of a different order: they draw our attention to how, even in the most liberal democracy, accessibility to the really influential and effective organs of journalistic judgment shaping is confined to relatively few people, and how this matter of accessibility is involved on several levels with both economic power and prestige. Innis writes, "Publishers demand great names and great books particular-ly if no copyright is involved. The large-scale mechanization of knowledge is characterized by imperfect competition and the active creation of monopolies in language which prevent understanding and hasten appeals to force."[10] In a more general vein, Servan-Schreiber (who we have already noted sees the influential media in the West as being in the hands of capitalists) observes that, "People now realize that freedom of expression is useless without the means to exercise it."[11] Kingsley Martin tells us that, "Historically the free-dom of the press also covers the right to start a newspaper without government licence. In practice this freedom can now only be exer-cised by a millionaire. As a right for the citizen to-day, therefore, it has as little meaning as the right of a worker in a Sheffield factory to start a steelworks in competition with a steel combine."[12]

What forum in the public journals is available to the person who has something important to say to his fellow citizens but does not have powerful connections in the business world or the journalistic profession? He can write a letter or article in the hopes that it will appear in the editorial section of a leading newspaper, but that piece may be rejected as unsuitable by an editorial assistant, or it may be published in a truncated, poorly edited form that trivializes or obscures its message. Even if it is published in its original form, it is not likely to have the same impact as certain other pieces in the newspaper, for it will probably be thrown in with a parcel of infor-mal contributions that will be assumed by most readers to be highly subjective observations. The person can probably place his piece in a small, local paper, but he will then only reach a small, local read-ership. Of course, he is free, more or less, to have his work dissemi-nated in a periodical published at his own expense, but even if he has money to burn (or has a wealthy patron), how much of an audience can he ordinarily be expected to reach in this way? Small newspapers do sometimes, by a quirk of fate, attract wide, respectful attention; still, only a naive sentimentalist would assume that if something is truly worth being published, it will inevitably reach the readership that it deserves. There is, of course, yet another option available to the person: he can become a professional journalist. Doing so would require major sacrifices on his part, and even as a professional journalist he would not have the kind or degree of accessibility that he craves and merits. Even so, this option is worth taking seriously.

In typically high-minded fashion, the Hutchins Commission concluded that "it is the whole point of a free press that ideas deserving a public hearing shall get a public hearing and that the decision of what ideas deserve that hearing shall rest in part with the public, not solely with the particular biases of editors and owners. In any populous community a vigorous trimming-out process among ideas presenting themselves for wide public hearing is obviously essential; but freedom of the press becomes a mockery unless this selective process is free also."[13] The commission continued: "The free press must be free to all who have something worth saying to the public, since the essential object for which a free press is valued is that ideas deserving a public hearing shall have a public hearing."[14] All this is very well, but how is such a state of affairs to be brought about, especially in light of how entrenched the phenomenon of imperfect competition has become in the journalistic sector of contemporary Western democracies? Responding to the dangers of concentration in the media,[15] the Hutchins Commission first addressed a plea to journalists and publishers themselves: "We recommend that the members of the press engage in vigorous mutual criticism."[16] But recognizing that this is hardly enough, the Hutchins Commission turned, interestingly enough, to *government*: "We recommend that government facilitate new ventures in the communications industry, that it foster the introduction of new techniques, that it maintain competition among large units through the antitrust laws, but that those laws be sparingly used. . . ."[17] What makes this recommendation particularly interesting is that, as the Hutchins Commission was well aware, and as all journalists and publishers are well aware, government intervention has traditionally been perceived—and rightly so—as the greatest *threat* to journalistic freedom.

So far I have considered only one side of the problem. Let me now flip the coin, as the Hutchins Commission itself did, and as Plato would have expected me to do, and consider the dark side of freedom: license, the abuse of unlimited freedom, the accessibility to journalistic influence of corrupt and confused puppeteers. The Hutchins Commission longed for a free and responsible press. In its concern with journalistic responsibility, it became associated with the famous "social responsibility theory" of the press, a theory perceived by its proponents as an Aristotelian mean between the extremes of pure authoritarianism and pure libertarianism. While recognizing that, "The press must be free from the menace of external compulsions from whatever source," whether it be "financial, popular, clerical, institutional,"[18] the commission warned that "the moral right of free public expression is not unconditional."[19] The commission did not regard responsibility so much as something that checks freedom as something that is a condition of a genuine freedom. Thus, in its report, it indicated its belief that only an accountable press will be able to fulfill the ultimate aims of a free press.[20] Here the commission was surely much influenced by the views of Hocking, who held that, "Freedom without limitation is a chimera. Concrete freedom is proportional not to the absence of rule but to the amount of rule it can absorb and turn into a ladder to achievement."[21] In a similar vein, Lippmann observes in *Essays in the Public Philosophy* that, "If there is a dividing line between liberty and license, it is where freedom of speech is no longer respected as a procedure of the truth and becomes the unrestricted right to exploit the ignorance, and to incite the passions, of the people. Then freedom is such a hullabaloo of sophistry, propaganda, special pleading, lobbying, and salesmanship that it is difficult to remember why freedom of speech is worth the pain and trouble of defending it."[22]

What then are the responsibilities that the periodical press must fulfill in order for it to be capable of being free in a profound sense rather than in the sense of being simply unlimited or unrestricted? According to the Hutchins Commission, the periodical press is both free and responsible when it is able to satisfy the fundamental social needs that it was developed as an institution to serve. The view here is clearly Platonic: the periodical press is free and responsible when it is efficiently performing its proper function and, at the same time, not endeavoring to usurp the role of any other institution in the polis. And what are the social needs it was designed to serve? As the commission saw it: "Today our society needs, first, a truthful, comprehensive, and intelligent account of the day's events in a context which gives them meaning; second, a forum for the exchange of comment and criticism; third, a means of projecting the opinions and attitudes of the groups in the society to one another; fourth, a method of presenting and clarifying the goals and values of the society; and, fifth, a way of reaching every member of the society by the currents of information, thought, and feeling which the press supplies."[23] Here we have what is essentially a functional analysis of freedom and responsibility of the press.

But there is another dimension to a properly Platonic analysis of freedom and responsibility, one that Lippmann characterizes as "procedural." A free and responsible press is a rational press, a press that employs the method of reason. What Lippmann has in mind here, of course, is not merely clever, self-serving, rhetorical argumentation but full-blown dialectical reason of the kind that one finds in sincere, disciplined, high-minded philosophical discussion. "Because the dialectical debate is a procedure for attaining moral and political truth, the right to speak is protected by a willingness to debate."[24] The dialectical debate that guarantees expression that is truly free, as Lippman sees it, requires logic and the rules of evidence to prevent it from degenerating into sophistry and propaganda.[25]

These two Platonic approaches to the matter of freedom and responsibility of the press provide us with the philosophical core of the "social responsibility theory," a theory which stresses that, "Freedom carries concomitant obligations; and the press, which enjoys a privileged position under our government, is obliged to be responsible to society for carrying out certain essential functions of mass communication in contemporary society."[26] What troubles many libertarian theorists, however, is the kind of practical strategy that certain social responsibility theorists propose as a remedy to journalistic irresponsibility. In fact, the most visible social responsibility theorists do not believe that it is enough for journalists and publishers to be reminded of what their special responsibilities are. They argue, in addition, that if the periodical press fails to fulfill its social responsibilities, "some other agency must see that the essential functions of mass communication are carried out."[27] It is not hard to see why a libertarian is apt to be troubled by such an argument; for once the activity of the periodical press is subject to intervention from some agency external to the press itself, it ceases to be free, in one sense of the word, even if it is putatively freer in some idealistic sense. And, of course, the agency toward which social responsibility theorists find it most convenient to turn, as we have seen in the case of the Hutchins Commission, is the government, the traditional archenemy of the free press in authoritarian states. Now, the government of a relatively democratic state is generally not as heavy-handed in its intervention as that of a relatively authoritarian state. But the potential for abuse is still there, and even if it is the public that ultimately calls the shots, the libertarian still has reason to worry. Indeed, he may have even more reason to worry, for as I have observed on several occasions, a political elite may well be more enlightened than a mob.

The traditional solution to the problem of abuse of power in a liberal democracy is a system of checks and balances. If the press, Thomas Babington Macauley's "fourth estate,"[28] carries on irresponsibly, it may need to be checked by an agency external to itself. But if in the process of being checked, it actually becomes subordinate to that external agency, whether the agency be political or ecclesiastical or whatever, then its own power to check the abuses of that particular agency will be seriously diminished, and thus it will not be able to carry out one of its most important responsibilities. The social responsibility theorist realizes that the checking of journalistic abuses must not be allowed to emasculate the periodical press by depriving that press of its own checking function. But the libertarian will argue that the social responsibility theorist's ideal is not realizable, so that society must allow the periodical press to proceed as it wishes even if it acquires the nasty habit of behaving somewhat irresponsibly.

In a lively attack on the social responsibility theory, J. C. Merrill writes that, "American journalism is becoming so institutionalized and professionalized and so immured with the nascent concept of 'social responsibility,' that it is voluntarily giving up the sacred tenet of libertarianism—'editorial self-determination'—and is in grave danger of becoming one vast, gray, bland, monotonous, conformist spokesman for some collectivity of society."[29] Indeed, Merrill continues, "Journalistic philosophy, where it is seriously considered at all, is leaning toward a press which has its concept of responsibility socially determined rather than *self* determined."[30] Merrill sees Lippmann, Hutchins, and their ilk as "Platonic élitists."[31] He points out that for all of his wisdom, Plato was a no-holds-barred proponent of authoritarianism, and was indeed the primary source of all subsequent authoritarian theory.[32] Against the social responsibility school, Merrill argues that "a libertarian press system . . . is (for me) socially responsible *for the very reason that it has little control from outside and much autonomy.*"[33] Moreover, he adds "Since, in a nation such as the United States, there is no ready definition for 'social responsibility,' there is really no standard to which our media seek to conform—even though, without a doubt, they would all conceive of themselves as socially responsible."[34] For the libertarian theorist, the only satisfactory cures for the disease of journalistic irresponsibility are healthy competition in the marketplace of ideas and rigorous self-criticism.

Merrill's passionate defense of libertarianism brings up several things that ought not to be forgotten: that libertarianism developed as a response to an authoritarian theory of the press that was used as a justification for emasculating and misusing the press and thereby retarding the growth of civilization; that the strategies advocated by social responsibility theorists can quickly degenerate, in the hands of careless or manipulative agents, into arbitrary and destructive interventions in journalistic affairs; that social responsibility theorists often are inclined to underestimate the capacity of journalists and publishers to regulate their own affairs in a sensible and responsible manner; that fear of being or appearing socially irresponsible can intimidate journalists and publishers to the point where they are no longer capable of carrying out socially productive tasks; and that thoughtful, reasonable observers do not necessarily agree with social responsibility theorists about precisely what genuine social responsibility consists of. Nevertheless, there are at least three important reasons for concluding that Merrill has overstated the case against the social responsibility theory.

The first is that the logic of his argument inevitably requires Merrill to undervalue the abuses perpetrated by irresponsible journalists. Merrill is not sympathetic to purely utilitarian ethics, and has adopted what he considers to be a modified Kantian position with strains of existentialism and rational humanism.[35] Yet, he is not consistently oblivious of the fact that the assessment of journalistic philosophies requires in part the consideration of the consequences of society's adopting each of those philosophies. He is not so rigid in his "modified deontologism" as to believe that libertarianism should be adopted even if it results in the greatest evils; in torture, genocide, and barbarism. Underlying his attack on the social responsibility theory is the assumption that, in the long run, a periodical press that does not have to be accountable to external agencies will do more to realize the ideals of civilization than a press that has to be thus accountable. Yet, Merrill not only is as passionate in his attack on journalistic irresponsibility as in his attack on the social responsibility theory, but he underscores the point that journalists and publishers have routinely failed to discipline themselves. He is particularly sensitive to how journalists hypocritically hide behind such slogans as "the public's right to know." Journalists routinely "pay lip service to professionalism," "insist that they have a right to protect the identity of their sources while they ridicule government secrecy," and "cling tenaciously to old journalistic clichés and practices," Merrill charges.[36]

Secondly, it is crucial that we distinguish the philosophical core of the social responsibility theory from the practical strategies that may or may not be appended to it. The core of the social responsibility theory is the principle that the press should be free and responsible, or alternatively, that the press can only be truly free if it is responsible. This principle in itself does not entail any particular conclusion about precisely how the periodical press should be accountable. In a democratic society, as in most others, every individual and group is required to be accountable in some ways. The accountability of citizens, at least in some abstract sense, is a sine qua non of a healthy and stable society; the very idea of society requires consideration of the contractarian elements binding a community together. Only in a despotic regime are some people largely able to avoid accountability. (Religious teaching often consoles us with the thought, however, that even arbitrary despots are accountable to a higher authority.) Now, we may disapprove of the policy of government intervention in press affairs, or of requiring public opinion to be the ultimate guide as to how journalists and publishers should conduct their business, or of any other particular strategy for promoting journalistic responsibility, but we are not thereby forced to conclude either that the philosophical core of the social responsibility theory is false or that journalists and philosophers should not be encouraged (or even compelled) to account for themselves in any way whatsoever. I will grant Merrill's point that groups like the Hutchins Commission are not always careful enough in formulating their recommendations about what kinds of practical strategy would most efficiently and least dangerously promote journalistic responsibility. But this does not force us to conclude cynically that outsiders cannot do anything useful to make the periodical press more responsible than it now is.

Thirdly, there is a disturbingly relativistic ring to some aspects of Merrill's critique of the social responsibility theory. His existentialist talk about self-determination should not be swallowed whole, even if there is an element of truth to it. Human beings do not simply determine, by an act of the will, what is right and wrong, or what they ought to do; at their best, they employ reason so that they can attain moral knowledge. This theme is in fact central to both the Kantian deontologism and the rational humanism in which Merrill professes to find so much wisdom. Again, while there are reasonable disagreements among reflective individuals about the precise scope of social responsibility, the term itself is not an empty cliché. When a barbarian such as Goebbels comes along and tells us that true social responsibility is such-and-such, one must remind one's fellows, forcefully and effectively, that this barbarian misunderstands the concept, is abusing language, and is advancing self-serving doctrines that should be refuted. There are, in fact, places in his discussion where Merrill, recognizing these truths, condemns relativism as vigorously as the "Platonic elitists" do. Rejecting what he takes to be the most sophisticated versions of ethical relativism, those of Dewey and Russell, he charges that such theories represent "non-ethics" or "anti-ethics," and he urges us to return to the "older classical philosophy."[37]

On one level, there is no satisfactory answer to the question of what kind of practical strategy would most effectively promote the establishment, maintenance, and development of a free and responsible periodical press; the question itself is so general that, in order to answer it adequately, one would almost be obliged to outline a utopian political theory. First, as the Hutchins Commission observed, "freedom of the press is certainly not an isolated value."[38] It should be noted that not only must certain freedoms be weighed against other freedoms, and certain people's freedoms be weighed against other people's freedoms, but freedom itself must be weighed against other values, such as justice, wisdom, security, prosperity, happiness, salvation, and so on. Second, though they overstated the point, Siebert, Peterson, and Schramm were not too far off the mark when they theorized that "the press always takes on the form and coloration of the social and political structures within which it operates. Especially, it reflects the system of social control whereby the relations of individuals are adjusted."[39] The would-be reformer of the periodical press of his society cannot afford to forget that whatever practical strategy he adopts will either have to complement prevailing social and political institutions, ideas, and values, or be treated as just one ingredient in a recipe for wholesale social and political reconstruction. Third, though institutions do in a sense have a life of their own, much still depends on the individuals involved with those institutions. So, for example, it is unlikely that reasonable, politically sensitive citizens will be as suspicious of the intervention in press affairs by an honest, dedicated, enlightened statesman as of the intervention in those press affairs by a politician who is transparently a self-serving schemer. Or again, public opinion should not be viewed the same way in a society with a highly educated majority as in a society dominated by an illiterate, vengeful, or bigoted mob. Still again, any assessment of the capacity of the periodical press to regulate its own affairs will partly be a function of our assessment of the intelligence and integrity of the most influential journalists and publishers in our own society.

If, however, compelled to specify some general political principle with regard to the matter of institutional press reform, I probably cannot do better than indicate the value of a system of checks and balances, which, as I have already suggested, is the traditional solution in a democratic society to the problem of abuse of power. For any number of reasons, such a system does not always work as well as we would like it to; all sorts of subjective factors enter into the act of balancing things as intangible as human interests, especially when those who find themselves having to do the requisite weighing have to consider both the short-term and long-term consequences of their adjustments. But after a review of history books, one is likely to conclude that no matter how noble or how corrupt the periodical press of our own society is, or the government of our society is, or public opinion in our society is, none of these elements in the polis should either be left unchecked and unaccountable or deprived of its power to check and demand accountability from the others. Plato held that in the ideal state, Guardians would not have to be checked, and attempts to interfere with their decision-making powers would be maleficent; but Plato also knew that such a state nowhere exists in this world.[40]

But, returning to the philosophical core of the social responsibility theory, I observe that people should not be encouraged— whether by journalists, politicians, political theorists, or anyone else—to behave as barbarians. In a civilized community, people are not free to torture or murder their fellows at will or to undercut the very foundations of a civilized community. Indeed, as I have suggested, there is a sense in which the barbarian cannot act freely at all, and the barbarian who insists that liberals should, to be consistent with their principles, allow him to do whatever he wants, does not understand either freedom or liberalism. There are misguided self-professed liberals who think that a free society is one in which even some barbarians should have wide latitude to carry out their projects. In the long run, they argue, interfering with the freedom of such barbarians will be more damaging to society than allowing those barbarians to carry out their pranks. Of course, while there is a wide consensus about the barbarism of torture and murder, there are profound disagreements among thoughtful people about whether such people as pornographers, abortionists, business executives, and military men are agents of barbarism, and we must all guard against ascribing barbarousness in careless generalizations. Yet, even a genuine liberal will see that there is something wrong when a free press makes heroes out of fanatics, terrorists, robber barons, neo-Nazi marchers, and charismatic despots who are supposedly freely exercising their will to power.

True liberalism requires a commitment to moral absolutes, to ideals of civilization. This is partly because true freedom is not the power to behave thoughtlessly, irrationally, and arbitrarily without regard for the interests of others; rather, it is the power to act on the basis of the intellectual and moral discipline that yields the moral insight that distinguishes purposive human action from random movement or from the movement that is determined exclusively by blind emotions, compulsive appetites, and unconscious drives. Because ordinary language is plastic and flexible, it could be argued that what I have just characterized as true freedom is just one kind of freedom. Perhaps this is so, but what I have characterized as true freedom seems to me to be the kind of freedom that people, on reflection, take to be a moral ideal, an ideal comparable in importance to justice and wisdom. Other kinds of freedom are essentially either instrumental or trivial viewed from a properly *moral* standpoint.

It is useful then to consider the whole matter of a free press on a level of analysis higher than that on which it is customarily approached. We should not dismiss as unimportant or irrelevant the instrumental varieties of journalistic freedom that have traditionally received the most attention. Obviously, a press that has been reduced, for example, to disseminating the self-serving propaganda of despots cannot be truly free. What is not always so obvious, however, and yet is at least as important, is that a press that is instrumentally free in the sense of having no obvious external obstacles to its self-determined activity may nevertheless be less than free in a more profound sense. The absence of external constraints does not in itself make a press free in the morally relevant sense of the term, though it may ordinarily be a condition of true freedom of the press. Ultimately, what makes a press truly free is that it is dominated by free men and women who draw on moral insight, intellectual skills, and their special gift of communicating clearly and impressively so as to educate their readers about important matters of the day and the relevance of those matters to the higher aims and ideals of a civilized society.

Servan-Schreiber suggests that, "Even though the press is not really free, what has nonetheless come to be called a free press plays a crucial role in the democratic process, because it does inform the public more freely and more objectively than other sources of information. It does so in an incomplete way, it is often biased and wrong—but, still, it informs."[41] His comment is a reminder that all ideals are only partly realized at any particular point in time, and only partly realizable by mere mortals. With its cynical tone, however, it may obscure the fact that the degree to which an ideal has presently been realized should serve as a reminder not only of the inevitable limitedness of human striving but of the agenda that represents a field for future achievement for courageous, creative individuals who have not allowed a fashionable cynicism to blind them to the real possibilities of personal and social progress. If journalists are not as free and responsible as they should and can be, then whether insiders or outsiders in relation to the press, the rest of us should do what we can—given our numerous other obligations—to help them to be better than they now are. If they have to be pushed out of the cave, so be it; if they can be induced to go freely, so much the better. But we are hardly being just with them (or with ourselves and our fellow citizens) if we allow them to believe that they should be free to indulge in whatever form of puppetry they choose.

Despite the misgivings that libertarian theorists have expressed, the role of outsiders here is crucial. When we consider both freedom and the press in a wider context than that in which, when examined in their relation to one another, they are customarily considered, it can be said that the press, and the individual journalist, are to a great extent what outsiders have made them. Writing in the late 1930s, Peter Hood, who thought then that, "'The freedom of the Press' is one of many clichés which are used more out of habit than by real conviction,"[42] also observed that, "It is a ready temptation to talk about responsibility, but in the present economic organization it is not at all easy to find a single individual anywhere, not being an actual owner, who could be held even vaguely responsible for the general voice of the Press at any time."[43] Journalists must operate under certain constraints imposed on them by both the institutionalized press in which they function as professionals and the broader social institutions in which they function as citizens. Some of these constraints are, as Hood has observed, economic; others are political in a more general sense, and sometimes ideological or even theological. At any given time, certain groups and individuals are freer and more responsible than others, and the typical puppeteer is potentially more autonomous than the typical prisoner in the cave, despite his complex dependence on the corporate body of prisoners. But to blame journalists and publishers entirely for their irresponsibility is to assume, mistakenly, that their professional activity is wholly self-determined. It is not entirely the puppeteer's fault that he has not been liberated. Given the entrenched social institutions of cave life, moreover, it is not entirely the liberator's fault that he cannot liberate others more effectively, more quickly, or more extensively than he does.

It is unreasonable to demand that a society's press be truly free and responsible when it must constantly defer to a government dominated by the unfree and irresponsible, and to the public opinion of readers and other critics who are unfree and irresponsible. I think back here to Lippmann's lament that the press is "too frail to carry the whole burden of popular sovereignty."[44] And as if this were not enough, it is also difficult for the individual journalist to be truly free and responsible when he must personally defer to colleagues, managers, and publishers who are unfree and irresponsible.

Freedom is a lofty and complex ideal, and the substantial realization of it even in a rather limited sphere such as journalism requires more than a little tinkering with a few laws, customs, and attitudes. Borrowing Plato's metaphor again, it may be said that personal freedom requires a "turning around" of the soul, that social freedom requires a "turning around" of the state, and that true freedom of the press requires a "turning around" of the press. The constraints that limit or prevent such actions can be internal or external; outsiders can facilitate or complicate the process.

It is also clear that those who wish to see the press freer and more responsible are obliged to work for the liberation of other elements of the polis—such as the government and the school system—for not only does the condition of those elements directly affect the condition of the press, but it influences the entire character of the polis of which the press is a part. However, though institutions have a life of their own, and impose constraints on (as well as provide sustenance and aids to self-realization to) the individuals who function in them, with them, through them, and sometimes in spite of them, the most important means by which institutions and whole societies are reformed is, according to Plato, through the moral and intellectual advancement of individuals, and most particularly, of ourselves.[45]

My remarks on liberalism, freedom, and a free press may strike many journalists and media critics as, if not platitudinous, at least unhelpfully abstract and thus largely irrelevant. Such a response might well be expected. But the journalist's impatience poses a great challenge to those who would play the part of the philosopher. As the ship of state is at sea, and social problems are more than theoretical puzzles, high-minded intellectuals must acknowledge that impatience is not necessarily a vice; it is perhaps unreasonable for intellectuals to expect their critics to be mollified by the Socratic defense that they follow that path that they earnestly believe will lead them to provide the greatest benefit to both themselves and their fellows.

There are academic philosophers who discourse freely, boldly,

and sometimes even knowledgeably about very specific moral, political, legal, and medical controversies in the news. If my conception
of philosophy is such that I cannot see my way to following their
lead, I leave myself vulnerable to the criticism even of my fellow
academic philosophers that what I have said about the ideal of a
free press is insufficiently concrete and relevant. Their complaints
could run along these lines: This scholar, though erudite and well-
meaning, handles the pressing problems of press freedom by speaking in generalities. He quotes from the writings of thinkers who are
dead, obscure, or out of the public eye. He undervalues the importance of the contemporary. He systematically avoids reference to
people and situations in the news. He underestimates the importance of the legal, judicial, and political dimensions of current media
controversies; he is hypnotized by ethical considerations and, even
worse, by metaphysical and epistemological ones. He does not
analyze particular cases, and he does not even bother to illuminate
the most important kinds of cases that have been increasingly per-
plexing journalists and jurists alike. He has obscured the urgent
matters in a haze of conceptions and principles; his very emphasis
on press freedom as an ideal reveals him to be an indolent dreamer
who, refusing to do the serious work of scrutinizing legal opinions
and other such matters, will never be able to get down to the serious
work of offering clear direction to people in the real world who need
to make real decisions in resolving actual disputes involving press
freedom.

However, I submit that there is indeed something concrete and
practical about my thesis that journalists and their critics can and
must be encouraged to reflect upon the fact that the ideal of press
freedom is significant only within the context of an adequately broad
and deep framework of specifically moral conceptions and principles. I receive some support here from Stephen Klaidman and Tom
L. Beauchamp, who, recognizing that current media controversies
need to be approached from the broad perspective of moral analysis
as well as the more limited perspectives of legal and political analysis, have actually gone so far as to take the trouble to analyze concrete cases.[46] They regret the tendency of recent writers to emphasize the legal aspects of media controversies at the expense of the
moral aspects. With an eye on the American scene, and particularly
on the fascination of commentators with the First Amendment to
the United States Constitution, Klaidman and Beauchamp observe
that, "Journalists often write as if the First Amendment justifies
unrestrained freedom rather than a freedom that must be balanced
against other values, because . . . they worry that public concern

over competing values such as the need to avoid harm and to keep information confidential can be fashioned into a club by government to intimidate the press."[47] However, they add, "The defenses of unrestrained press freedom found in contemporary journalism seldom explicitly consider the range of moral rights and responsibilities that confront the press, and these defenses often amount to a demand for privileged treatment that moral analysis will not support. Journalists need not be moral philosophers, of course, but they should be aware that competing values may have moral weight equal to or greater than press freedom."[48] They also state, "Legal protections that permit irresponsible journalism do not imply that journalists have no moral responsibility. Quite the reverse is true: freedom from legal constraints is a special privilege that demands increased awareness of moral obligation."[49] Klaidman and Beauchamp are rightly troubled by how it has become almost habitual in the United States to treat issues of journalistic ethics (and related issues of social and political ethics) as if they were nothing more than issues concerning the interpretation and application of the First Amendment. A physician or lawyer, after all, does not routinely look upon questions of medical or legal ethics as problems involving medical or legal freedom; yet many journalists and even their critics almost instinctively approach questions of journalistic integrity by plunging into rhetoric, and later semi-scholastic polemic, about how we are to understand their society's constitutional tradition of press freedom. Unfortunately, not even Klaidman and Beauchamp seem to be consistently aware of the fact that ethical conceptions and principles are precisely the factors that animate the ideal of a free press; they are often quite prepared to treat freedom of the press as an essentially constitutional institution that is best considered as something quite independent of the ethical matters to which they properly attach so much importance.[50]

As a general rule, systems of constitutional law are based on ethical conceptions and principles. (Of course, there are bad laws, bad constitutions, and even, in a sense, bad ethical systems.) Consider the First Amendment itself: it did not appear out of the blue, by some mysterious process, and then invent the wonderful American institution of a free press. The First Amendment enshrines certain ideas and attitudes that were formed (and to some extent *realized*) even by some rare birds in the ancient world. The American tradition of press freedom did not simply begin with a lifeless formula, nor did it even begin with the deep ruminations of Thomas Jefferson and his fellow constitution builders. Jefferson and many of his colleagues were inspired by the vision of such seventeenth-century

European sages as John Locke, who, interestingly enough, was neither a journalist nor a constitutional lawyer but a philosopher given to rather abstract reflection on the human condition. And even Locke himself, for all his wisdom and ingenuity, cannot reasonably be given credit for having invented the concept or institution of fundamental freedoms. (The U.S. Constitution more plausibly gives most of the credit to the Supreme Being, who is seen as having "endowed" all men with "certain unalienable Rights.") In fact, Locke's own ethico-political system is certainly not beyond criticism, and is actually rather inferior in certain ways to versions of liberalism that succeeded it and even preceded it. Neither is the ethico-political foundation of American law beyond criticism, despite the millions of pages that have been written to clarify, defend, or refine it.

In an editorial note in a recent number of *Nieman Reports*, the editor, Tenney Barbara K. Lehman, exhibiting a patriotic fervor of which she perhaps never dreamed herself capable, writes that the First Amendment is the key to the glory and splendor of the American free press:

> This year [1987] marks the 200th anniversary of the Constitution of the United States. Festivities are appropriate, of course, but the most fitting exercises will be quiet ones, as thoughtful men and women choose to read, or re-read, the articles and amendments that are the fabric of the Constitution.
>
> The First Amendment warrants the particular regard of journalists. Without it, the tasks of newsgathering and dissemination would resemble the media in countries where the flow of information is controlled or wholly suppressed.[51]

When we read such words, we must remind ourselves that the free press—in this editor's sense, at least—is alive and well in societies that do not even possess a written constitution. One could also entertain the possibility that a constitutional amendment was not the only possible device that could have sustained American-style press freedom for all these years. Nor should it be forgotten that the First Amendment has frequently been ignored, distorted, trivialized, misused, overridden, and subordinated to other laws, principles, and concerns. And perhaps most important to remember is, that the kinds of "newsgathering and dissemination" that the First Amendment—along with vast amounts of legal and political machinery and documentation—has allowed and encouraged have not only failed to save America from many of its greatest evils and injustices but have actually contributed to and promoted some of them. (A few that come to mind are black slavery, imperialism, and the exploitation of the working poor by the idle rich.)

The tendency to confuse the ideal of a free press with a juridical formula is also apparent in an anthology recently published by the American Library Association with the title, *The First Freedom Today: Critical Issues Relating to Censorship and to Intellectual Freedom.*[52] The editors of this volume are librarians, not journalists, judges, lawyers, or celebrities from the world of broadcasting. That in itself should be something of an encouragement to the scholar, for though librarians are primarily technicians rather than scholars themselves, they are accustomed to working with and for people with an intellectual inclination and generally they have a romantic attachment to great books. They do not characteristically idolize the man or woman of action at the expense of the man or woman of thought. Yet, of the forty-five contributors to the collection, more than two-thirds are from the fields of journalism and law, not one is a theologian, and only one is a philosopher, albeit a very fine one.[53] Can our librarian friends have forgotten that freedom is so very much more than just a journalistic and legal conception? Even if they could rightly protest that philosophers have had relatively little to say about the legal and constitutional aspects of American press freedom, it remains that philosophers have always had many profound and provocative things to say about freedom itself, and particularly intellectual freedom. This has been as true in recent years as it was in the ages of Aristotle, Saint Augustine, Spinoza, and Mill. One need only to consider, for example, the existential philosophy of Sartre and Camus.

The title of the anthology is itself revealing. In justifying the title of their collection, the editors approvingly quote Franklin D. Roosevelt and also a resolution of the United Nations General Assembly; but their primary inspiration is the First Amendment:

> Notable historical precedents inspired the title *The First Freedom Today* for the present work, the first edition of which was published in 1960. When the Bill of Rights was added to the U.S. Constitution in December 1791, after being ratified by the required three-fourths of the states, the First Amendment specifically stated, in part, "Congress shall make no law . . . abridging the freedom of speech or of the press."[54]

As someone who has spent many years reflecting on religious liberty, I cannot help being awed by the misleading historical interpretation that these librarians have foisted upon us. The precise formulation of the First Amendment is this: "Congress shall make no law respecting an establishment of religion, or prohibiting the free exercise thereof; or abridging the freedom of speech, or of the press; or the right of the people peaceably to assemble, and to petition the Government for a redress of grievances." My reading of the text indicates that the eighteenth-century constitution builders did not regard freedom of the press, of speech, or even of expression as the first freedom; rather, they sagely regarded freedom of religion—and by implication, freedom of thought and conscience—as the true foundation of human liberty. This is not simply an interesting historical point but is a matter of great philosophical import.

It is the thought that underlies expression that makes the latter significant and valuable. It is the expression of thought, not the mere utterance of sounds, that concerns the guardian of the ideal of free expression. The most important thoughts are not the narrow or merely technical ones but those that grow out of our most profound and most personal convictions, our commitment to a world view or *Weltanschauung*, a vision that is at once religious, spiritual, philosophical, ethical, and metaphysical. Freedom of thought—and particularly of the most profound, personal, and spiritual thought—is ultimately the foundation and justification of freedom of expression of any kind. Thus, even those who are mesmerized by the elegance of the First Amendment should take note of the fact that it makes freedom of speech or the press the second freedom. In doing so, it follows the tradition of people such as Spinoza, who in his capital work reminds us that freedom of speech is essentially an extension of freedom of thought.[55] This point was not even lost during the somewhat graceless creation of Canada's new (1982) constitutional Charter of Rights and Freedoms:

Everyone has the following fundamental freedoms:
    (a) freedom of conscience and religion;
    (b) freedom of thought, belief, opinion and expression, including freedom of the press and other media of communication;
    (c) freedom of peaceful assembly; and
    (d) freedom of association.

Such a formula, of course, has not invented the fundamental freedoms of Canadians. It has acknowledged and reaffirmed their importance on the basis of an understanding derived from many centuries of deep contemplation upon the human condition. Without a tradition of such contemplation, one would have to conclude with the cynic that talk is cheap, as is any other form of human expression.

Thus it will not do for anyone who sincerely seeks to understand

press freedom to focus exclusively on niceties of constitutional law
and to slight the ethical conceptions that—rooted in a metaphysical
conception of human freedom including autonomy, creativity, and
responsibility—have inspired, have animated, and must always be
seen as outranking purely legal or political conceptions.

Turning then to the actual media controversies in the news in our
own society, we find an interesting assortment of items on this partial list offered by Lester A. Sobel:

> Conflicts of media rights with other rights. Examples include an accused
> person's right to a fair trial as opposed to the media's asserted right to
> print or broadcast material that may prejudice potential jurors.
>
> The demand for a "newsman's privilege," or "shield," that would permit
> reporters to refuse to reveal their sources of information to grand juries
> or other judicial or police inquisitors.
>
> The media's dissemination of military, diplomatic or intelligence secrets
> whose disclosure, according to government complaints, would jeopar-
> dize security, hamper foreign relations or endanger the lives of intelli-
> gence personnel.
>
> Censorship and alleged government attempts to control, coerce, intimi-
> date or manipulate the media.
>
> Political use of the media.
>
> The use of news personnel by the intelligence agencies.
>
> The growth of the media and media power and their increasing concen-
> tration in the hands of fewer owners.
>
> The apparent lack of effective restraint on the misuse of media power.
>
> The emergence of television as the dominant news medium.
>
> Self-regulation of the media.
>
> Unfair or inaccurate presentation of material by the media, including
> charges of staging news events.
>
> The declining effect of libel law.
>
> The emergence of the "new journalism," characterized by newsmen's
> "advocacy" as opposed to objectivity.
>
> The purported preponderance of sex and violence on television.
>
> Deceptive advertising of products ranging from automobiles and gaso-
> line to breakfast foods and pharmaceuticals.
>
> Methods used by the media in the competition for viewers and readers.[56]

Sobel's caveat that his list is only partial can be unsettling to the nerves of anyone who longs for the resolution of media controversies. Countless pages have already been written, and many more will be written, about almost every item on this list. "In probably no instance will a reader have much trouble in determining how a 'freedom of the press' issue is involved," Sobel states.[57] Not only is there enough subject matter to suit the needs of loquacious journalists, jurists, politicians, and media critics, but there is virtually no limit to the opportunity offered to the practitioner of "applied ethics" to do a properly moral analysis of the relevant concrete cases.

In setting aside the narrowly legal and political matters and getting down to the business of moralizing about media controversies, where is one to begin? One thing to do is to weigh alternative policies so as to determine which among them is morally best. Having assessed the alternatives by reference to such criteria as utility and universalizability, one would then be in a position to make or endorse such policy statements as: An accused person's right to a fair trial takes precedence over the media's right to print or broadcast material that may prejudice potential jurors. However, as new concrete cases emerged, one might well be tempted to modify such policy statements so that they allowed for special exceptions: *As a general rule*, an accused person's right to a fair trial takes precedence over the media's right to print or broadcast material that may prejudice potential jurors. Of course, there would always be some diehard absolutists who would insist on sticking to the original policies, regardless of their consequences in particular cases or even in the long run. I cannot see any compelling reason for regarding any such policies as being the kinds of rules that qualify as inviolable ethical principles. But once the moral analyst starts chipping away at the original policies, he will find that the analyst's chisel is not easy to put down, and that even if he is prepared to put it back in his tool chest, lots of other analysts are prepared to carry on where he left off. And the task of resolving the moral aspect of media controversies is not facilitated by the ambiguity of key terms and phrases in policy statements, such as *fair trial* and *prejudice* in this example.

Instead of concentrating on policies, then, the moralist would perhaps be more prudent to focus his attention on the concrete cases themselves. In considering a particular case, the moralist may find any number of policies relevant, and he can weigh all sorts of conflicting values, rights, responsibilities, and potential consequences.

Klaidman and Beauchamp are among those moralists who are interested in the analysis of concrete cases. They describe what they take to be the primary virtues to be cultivated by a journalist, dispositions to reach for truth, avoid bias, avoid harm, serve the public, maintain trust, escape manipulation, and invite criticism and be accountable.[58] They then use the principles developed in this framework to analyze concrete cases. They thereby provide the reader with numerous illustrations of how particular journalists in recent years have in fact failed to act in accordance with appropriate journalistic virtues. They also provide the reader with examples of how a rational ethical methodology can be applied in the assessment (and ultimately, the determination) of controversial forms of journalistic activity. Klaidman and Beauchamp are undoubtedly aware that few if any publishers, editors, journalists, or government officials are prepared to put a moral philosopher on the payroll to help them deal with the concrete cases that arise every day. Klaidman and Beauchamp are trying to give the journalist and others an idea of how to go about moralizing in the concrete.

As I perused the contents of their volume, I frequently found Klaidman and Beauchamp passing judgment on individual journalists and their actions. Perhaps that should not have bothered me as much as it did. Their aim, after all, was to show that their type of moral analysis can lead us to sound conclusions about concrete cases and can actually resolve specific instances of media controversy by enabling us to see what is right and what is wrong in specific situations in which journalists find themselves. They want to show that moral analysis does not necessarily leave one confused and paralyzed in a state of suspense as complex arguments fly from opposite directions. People who have taken the trouble to scrutinize concrete cases in a careful, disciplined, and fair way have at least as much right to pass judgment on particular journalists and their actions as do the sort of people whose judgments on journalistic behavior are usually aired in the mass media.

However, I am not convinced that philosophers in their role as philosophers should be passing judgment in the way that Klaidman and Beauchamp routinely have. Philosophers are on a perilous course when, in their role as philosophers, they slide from theoretical discussion of ideals and principles to quasi-authoritative pronouncements on concrete and very complex controversies. Friends and relatives sometimes ask me what I, as a moral philosopher, think about the behavior of this or that mutual friend, or the way in which they should handle a certain domestic squabble. I am usually happy to raise points for consideration, and even to offer my own opinion, but I know that they are sometimes a bit disappointed when I add that the study of moral philosophy does not make one an expert on morality at this level. A moral philosopher can teach, enlighten, and guide, but when he moves to the discussion of very specific situations, he must be mindful of the limitations of the kind of moral expertise that his education and reflection have afforded him. It does not follow, of course, that the moral philosopher's insights are useless or irrelevant. For example, it does not follow from the fact that Immanuel Kant's views on self-abuse are rather silly that his profound thoughts on the categorical imperative do not merit our respectful consideration, or that we cannot put his loftiest ideas to better use than he himself did.[59] Nor in retrospect is it surprising that I have found myself disagreeing with so many of the concluding judgments that Klaidman and Beauchamp append to their detailed discussions of concrete cases, even when I have shared their ideals and principles, and even when I have found most of their specific arguments to be reasonable enough.

Consider the case of Milton Coleman, a reporter who was partly responsible for bringing it to public attention that a prominent American politician had made certain anti-Semitic comments that the politician had signaled to Coleman and other reporters were "on background" and not for direct attribution. Klaidman and Beauchamp admit that in this particular case the two of them "agree on the principles but disagree on the decision."[60] Nevertheless, I consider them very severe when they suggest that, "Coleman's decision still casts some doubt on his trustworthiness as a reporter in reporter-source relationships, and it is difficult to estimate the consequences of the skepticism that naturally arises as a result."[61] I do not know much about Milton Coleman or his values, ambitions, and aspirations, and I do not know what sort of professional ethic he follows. Nor do I feel as competent as Klaidman and Beauchamp do to discourse about what sort of professional ethic someone like Milton Coleman should follow. But I do not at all find it inconceivable that Milton Coleman, reflecting on his own troubles as a black man in racist America, and on the situation of his Jewish acquaintances, and on the Inquisition and the Holocaust, decided, after careful deliberation, to do what he earnestly considered to be the right thing to do not only for a journalist but for a free and responsible human being. And from what I know about this case, I have no reason not to have the utmost trust and confidence in this man as a journalist and as a moral agent.

Reflecting further on the limited value of the treatment by Klaidman and Beauchamp of such cases as Coleman's, one is brought still closer to appreciating the most significant contribution that moral theory can make toward the realization—both in particular cases and in general—of the ideal of a free press. The framework within which Klaidman and Beauchamp chose to do their analysis is not a general framework of moral theory—philosophical, theological, or even social-scientific—but rather a relatively narrow framework that they designed to fit the kinds of media controversies that they sought to illuminate. Although much that they wrote indicates that they have been to some extent inspired by the philosophical tradition, the actual virtues that they stress, such as moderate skepticism and trustworthiness, indicate that what they ultimately offered is much closer to the kind of professional ethic that even some of the most unphilosophical of journalists claim to follow than to the genuinely philosophical kind of conception of morality that we associate with such thinkers as Plato, Aristotle, Spinoza, Kant, and Bentham. Early in their study, Klaidman and Beauchamp briefly discuss the concept of morality: when they indicate their special interest in the concept of virtue, the reader is momentarily led to expect a treatment of journalistic ethics within the framework of the classical self-realization ethic of Plato, Aristotle, and the medievals.[62] But they go on to imply that a virtue-based ethic is not superior to the major alternatives, and indeed they give us little reason to believe that it is.[63] Despite their commitment to the view that the insights of moral philosophy can enable journalists and others to resolve the media controversies of the day in concrete cases and can help journalists and others to understand both press freedom and journalistic integrity in their proper context, Klaidman and Beauchamp avoid sustained discussion of all the main issues, ideas, principles, models, systems, disputes, and methods that have emerged in twenty-four centuries of moral philosophy. As a result, they leave the reader with a vision of morality that is at best a pale copy of the sort of theory that one ordinarily expects to get from someone who takes traditional moral philosophy seriously. The moral theory we get has been skewed and diluted to accommodate the kinds of concrete cases that the authors are so eager to analyze. I am not very troubled by the failure of Klaidman and Beauchamp to refer to Plato, Aristotle, Spinoza, Kant, Marx, Kierkegaard, or Camus. Nor am I scandalized by their decision to avoid reference to deontologism, utilitarianism, relativism, and existentialism. I cannot blame them for declining to philosophize in the grand manner of the great sages of the past, and I can sincerely acknowledge that their type of moral analysis is valuable and raises the level of discussion of media controversies and of journalistic activity in general.

But the aim of moral philosophy is to make people better human beings, not simply to make them better journalists or lawyers or farmers. It is to promote understanding of the human virtues, not just journalistic virtues.

In point of fact, American journalists and editors have appreciated the value of professional codes of ethics for many years. In a recent study in the *Journalism Quarterly*, Douglas Anderson writes that, "The roots of the heightened concern about media ethics can be traced to the 1920s when the American Society of Newspaper Editors and the Society of Professional Journalists, Sigma Delta Chi, drafted codes."[64] Such codes have been valuable, and they will become even more valuable when they have come to reflect the sophisticated insights of writers like Klaidman and Beauchamp. But professional codes are not enough, especially when they are "merely broad statements of principle" and "are not brought to the attention of staffers."[65] And if Anderson's mail questionnaire to 165 managing editors of American daily newspapers elicited honest and accurate responses, then at least some managing editors do see the light, if only from a distance: "Managing editors also seem to be taking steps to help themselves deal with ethical issues: about four-fifths said they had attended convention sessions that dealt with media ethics and a little more than one-third said they had taken a college course in ethics."[66]

I have been looking over a slim monograph issued by the Skills Development Division of the Ministry of Colleges and Universities in my home province of Ontario. *Print Journalism: A Training Profile* has been designed for "use by program developers and trainers in the development of training courses and programs," and it "provides the minimum provincial performance standards for training to the competencies identified for this occupation by qualified representatives of business, industry, or profession."[67] As I peruse the descriptions of the various "training modules" on assembling information, writing copy, and so forth, I am struck by a reference here and there to the apprentice journalist's need to develop a "sense of ethics."[68] I am heartened by this prescription, even though it is swamped in a sea of hundreds of technical prescriptions, even though I know that a small fragment of a "training module" will not be enough to produce the free men and women whose writing will make other men and women freer and better and wiser.

I have not forgotten that free and responsible journalists do not alone make for a free and responsible press. The process of civilization requires the free and responsible self-realization of all citizens, and especially—as Plato often states in the *Republic*—of our society's Guardians. Ideally, freedom of the press is not freedom from government, but freedom promoted by government. I leave Spinoza to have the last word:

> The ultimate aim of government is not to rule, or restrain, by fear, nor to exact obedience,but contrariwise, to free every man from fear, that he may live in all possible security; in other words, to strengthen his natural right to exist and work without injury to himself or others.
>
> No, the object of government is not to change men from rational beings into beasts or puppets, but to enable them to develop their minds and bodies in security, and to employ their reason unshackled; neither showing hatred, anger, or deceit, nor watched with the eyes of jealousy and injustice. In fact, *the true aim of government is liberty.*[69]

6
Journalism and Philosophy

That the attitude of the philosopher toward the journalist should so often involve resentment can no longer be regarded as anomalous. As a rational moralist who works to promote virtue in himself and others, the philosopher can often transcend the pettiness, hedonism, hostility, and weakness of will that he so often eloquently denounces. Yet even the noblest of philosophers is only a human being, and if his humanity is a source of dignity, it also prevents him from completely avoiding all the negative aims, desires, and dispositions that he has himself detected in poets and journalists, physicians and carpenters, politicians and priests. The title of philosopher is often partly honorific, as when used to praise those who manifest the most inspiring qualities of the classical Stoics. But real philosophers, even the greatest among them, have always had their share of vices, and their capacity for peevish, unproductive resentment is particularly noteworthy. Simultaneously conscious of their intellectual gifts and of society's general neglect of what they have to offer, they find it easy to follow Plato in being disdainful.

Resentment, a powerful natural force in the human mind on both conscious and unconscious levels, can have a positive as well as a negative dimension. Even when not an impetus to creativity, it can help people to cope with unwarranted feelings of self-contempt; and if not the ideal device for overcoming feelings of inferiority that breed self-destructive and socially destructive attitudes—since it can itself breed these attitudes—it can sometimes be put to good use.

I have discussed ways in which it is appropriate for the philosopher to perceive the journalist as a rival—much as Plato appropriately viewed poets and sophists as rivals—and also how the philosopher's resentment of journalists is not necessarily a mere matter of jealousy or querulousness. If the philosopher looks down at the journalist, it can be partly because he sees himself as an agent of civilization who is obliged to cast a more critical eye on journalism than the typical consumer does. Consider these paragraphs that come near the end of José Ortega y Gasset's *Mission of the University*:

163

In the collective life of society today there is no other "spiritual power" than the press. The corporate life, which is the real life of history, needs always to be directed, whether we like the idea or not. Of itself it has no form, no eyes to see with, no guiding sense of direction. Now then, in our times, the ancient "spiritual powers" have disappeared: the Church because it has abandoned the present (whereas the life of the people is ever a decidedly current affair); and the state because with the triumph of democracy, it has given up governing the life of the people to be governed instead by their opinion. In this situation, the public life has devolved into the hands of the only spiritual force which necessarily concerns itself with current affairs—the press.

I should not wish to throw too many stones at the journalists; among other motives, there is the consideration that I may be nothing more than a journalist myself. But it is futile to shut our eyes to the obvious fact that spiritual realities differ in worth. They compose a hierarchy of values, and in this hierarchy, journalism occupies an inferior place. It has come to pass that today no pressure and no authority make themselves felt in the public consciousness, save on the very low spiritual plane adopted by the emanations of the press. So low a plane it is that not infrequently the press falls quite short of being a spiritual power, and is rather the opposite force. By the default of other powers, the responsibility for nourishing and guiding the public soul has fallen to the journalist, who not only is one of the least cultured types in contemporary society but who moreover—for reasons I hope may prove to have been merely transitory—admits into his profession the frustrated pseudo-intellectuals, full of resentment and hatred toward what is truly spiritual. Furthermore the journalist's profession leads him to understand by the reality of the times that which creates a passing sensation, regardless of what it is, without any heed for perspective or architecture. Real life is, certainly, purely of the present; but the journalist deforms this truism when he reduces the present to the momentary, and the momentary to the sensational. The result is that, in the public consciousness today, the image of the world appears exactly upside down. The space devoted to people and affairs in the press is inversely proportionate to their substantial and enduring importance; what stands out in the columns of the newspapers and magazines is what will be a "success" and bring notoriety. Were the periodicals to be freed from motives that are often unspeakable; were the dailies kept chastely aloof from any influence of money in their opinions—the press would still, of itself, forsake its proper mission and paint the world inside out. Not a little of the grotesque and general upset of our age—(for Europe has been going along for some time now with her head on the ground and her plebeian feet waving in the air)—is the result of this unchallenged sway of the press as sole "spiritual power."[1]

One cannot entirely blame those journalists, or their defenders, who would interpret these remarks as the careless generalizations of a bitter, self-serving, elitist, undemocratic crank; indeed, such an interpretation of Ortega's resentment would not be wholly inaccurate. And yet scrutinizing Ortega's grandiloquent indictment closely, I find that his resentment is rooted partly in a sincere concern about the future of civilization, and partly in a keen insight into the dark side of journalism and of a society that derives its wisdom primarily from journalists rather than philosophers and other reflective, spiritual types.

Ortega is concerned with the typical journalist's concern with success, notoriety, and the momentary. He recognizes the dangers of the journalist's tendencies to propagandize and pander. He worries about the lack of high culture among journalists and about their own resentment toward what is truly spiritual. And perhaps of greatest importance, he recognizes that journalists have been allowed to step into a vacuum that they are not suited to fill properly. Even so, his overgeneralizations reflect an unduly cynical appraisal of the potential of journalists, and he does not pay adequate attention to the failings of intellectuals and other spiritual types that have contributed to the development of the vacuum that journalists have had to fill.

At the risk of being repetitious, I would return to the philosopher's complaint, for now a wider view can be taken than was available earlier. As a general rule, the philosopher will allow that something resembling journalism will always be with us. No philosopher of stature has ever been prepared to argue that the outright elimination of journalism as such is possible or desirable. Whether as cynical puppeteer or participant in the liberating process, the journalist has found a niche in modern society; he is an accepted element in the scene of human affairs, and he could be no more easily disposed of than poet, politician, or priest. Even the philosopher is not prepared to give up his regular reading of newspapers and news magazines. Like the less intellectual plebs, he has gotten into the habit, and though he might justify that habit on oblique grounds—say, "I need to understand how other people think"—he can never successfully hide the fact that the kinds of pleasure and value he derives from reading a public journal are not categorically different from the kinds that less reflective people derive. Moreover, as the typical philosopher is not prepared to become a journalist himself, he cannot fairly or reasonably expect the typical journalist to be a philosopher. And again, he can appreciate the fact that a journalist is capable of doing his job relatively well or relatively badly, and he may even be prepared to grant that a journalist, being something of a professional, may understand certain aspects of journalistic communication that he himself is unable to understand.

What the philosopher might want then is for the journalist himself to become more philosophical: if it is too much to expect journalists to become full-fledged philosophers, they can at least be wiser, mroe virtuous individuals. As Ortega would say, they should be more cultured and liberated from any antipathy toward what is truly spiritual. The journalist needs to take a hard look at himself and realize that he needs to be liberated by those wiser than himself; he needs to put his mind in the hands of the great humanistic teachers so that it can be shaped into an instrument for promoting true self-realization and true social progress. Only then will he be able to transcend the narrow vision of the venal publishers for whom he works, the crooked politicians on whom he reports, the glamorous but empty-headed celebrities with whom he mixes socially, the purely technical-minded journalism professors under whom he was trained, and the Great Sophist itself, the general public for which he performs his show. Give this person a liberal education: make the budding journalist read some anthropology and some theology; feed him some Sophocles, Calderón, and Brecht; require him to get inside the head of a Thucydides or Gibbon. Above all, straighten out his *Weltanschauung* with liberal doses of philosophy: Aristotle, Spinoza, a soupçon of Nietzsche, Bertrand Russell, and lots of Plato, and more Plato. At the same time, weed out the corrupting influences that impose on him an unhealthy concern for what "the many" care for. "The virtuous journalist," Merrill tells us, "is one who has respect for, and tries to live by, the cardinal virtues which Plato discusses in *The Republic*."[2] Only such a journalist can be in the vanguard of the forces of civilization and light; other journalists are just so much dead wood, products of cultural determinism in the worst possible sense, confused and aimless souls, operators, mountebanks, unwitting agents of reaction and barbarism, and tools of special interest groups and crackbrained schemers.

But perhaps all this is just too, too much. The journalist will reflect, "Am I really the shallow sophist that these 'humanists' make me out to be? Did I not read some Shakespeare and Camus in my university days? Am I not a complex individual, indeed an intellectual of sorts? Am I not in the position to distinguish between good and evil and to know how to promote the former rather than the latter?" "Journalists," Merrill informs us, "are extremely complex persons and it is difficult to generalize about certain orientations which they may have. Affecting their work is a wide variety of interest, ideologies, educational levels and cultural backgrounds, special talents, and so on."[3] Servan-Schreiber adds that ". . .every journalist considers himself almost an intellectual. He is a worker whose tools are in his head. . . ."[4] But perhaps this is to miss the point. That the sophist is a complex person and something of an intellectual is undeniable, but if his moral vision is narrow, he is shallow nonetheless. So if the journalist is the child of the sophist, his complexity and intellectuality will help neither him nor those he serves.

This is only part of the philosopher's complaint, for he also wants us to note the limits and dangers of the journalistic enterprise itself. In Ortega's words, "the journalist's profession leads him to understand by the reality of the times that which creates a passing sensation, regardless of what it is, without any heed for perspective or architecture. Real life is, certainly, purely of the present; but the journalist deforms this truism when he reduces the present to the momentary, and the momentary to the sensational." A humanistic education can provide the journalist with something in the way of perspective or architecture, but in the last analysis, the journalist and his readers are limited by exigencies of time. When the journalist is to be distinguished from the philosopher, historian, social scientist, and belletrist, it is perhaps the factor of the deadline more than anything else that commands our attention. The journalist cannot afford the luxury of viewing things *sub specie aeternitatis*; the periodicity of the public journal led almost inevitably to its association with news, and, "The one quality of the report which is necessary in order to make it 'news' is timeliness."[5] Even if he were prepared to stand on the shoulders of the Platos, Gibbons, and Brechts, the journalist would still be compelled to sacrifice time for reflection in order to get his story out so as to provide his readers with up-to-date information. So it is not just ill will toward the classic liberator types that leads the journalist to sever the present from the past and devalue the architecture that counts for so much to the most cultured, spiritual types.

Following William James, who had already lamented that the leadership of American thought was "passing away from the universities to the ten-cent magazines,"[6] Harold Innis observed that, "The steadying influence of the book as a product of sustained intellectual effort was destroyed by new developments in periodicals and newspapers."[7] McLuhan endeavors to be somewhat less judgmental than his master when he emphasizes the ontological and functional differences between a book and a public journal: "The book is a private confessional form that provides a 'point of view.' The press is a group confessional form that provides communal participation."[8] Indeed, "Those who deplore the frivolity of the press and its natural form of group exposure and communal cleansing simply

ignore the nature of the medium and demand that it be a book, as it
tends to be in Europe."[9] Now, certainly a news periodical, regardless of how lofty the motives of its creators, is a creature of a very
different kind than a book. Nevertheless, what they have in
common—as forms of written communication, as influences on public opinion—should not be undervalued, and the conditions of
rivalry between journalists and authors are always present, even if
an Ortega, James, or Innis is a bit extravagant in indicating their
importance.

Even the journalist who does not fancy himself an author, and is
mindful of the serious limitations of his work as a civilizing force,
can appreciate the extent to which, willingly or unwillingly, he has
emerged as the rival or perceived successor to those involved in sustained intellectual effort. He knows that he can reach a readership
vastly greater (numerically, at least) than that to which the true sage
can normally aspire, and no matter how humble he strives to be, he
cannot help taking pride in the fact that he has a certain kind of
influence that deeper thinkers can only envy. In any case, he could
sincerely protest that the intellectual seems to be sending him conflicting messages and making contradictory demands on him. On
one hand, the intellectual wants him to be more of an intellectual
and to learn from intellectuals how to think and write more in the
way that they do; yet the intellectual also wants the journalist to
stop usurping the intellectual's own proper role and to work harder
at avoiding playing the part of the sage. Can the journalist's capi-
tulation to both demands be reconciled or balanced in a way that
will bring philosophers to overcome their resentment? Perhaps not.

Here, however, the philosopher may well protest that in his
coverage of the news, the journalist seems to go out of his way to
undervalue the humanistic intellectual's work. As Fulford observed,
"In the 1950's the Canadian newspaper reader was told just what
happened every time a government fell in France—because that was
politics, and obviously important; but in the same period he was not
told what Jean-Paul Sartre was saying and doing—because that was
philosophy, and not interesting. Yet in the long run, or maybe even
the short, the ramifications of Sartre's activities might be more important than those of a cabinet shuffle."[10] If the journalist were to
reply that he writes only about matters that are of interest to his
readers, he would not only be open to the charge of pandering but
would perhaps also be open to the charge of hiding his own resentment against the truly spiritual behind a questionable judgment
about reader interests.

But it is precisely at this point that the journalist should go on the offensive and articulate his own complaint against the philosophers, a complaint that will more than incidentally reflect the complaint against philosophers and other intellectuals that many of his readers, were they given the opportunity, would themselves voice. First he would suggest to philosophers the possibility that their failure to interest and influence the wide readership that the journalist reaches is partly, if not largely, a function of their own incompetence. It is not enough for the journalist to observe that he clearly offers the Great Sophist what it wants, while the philosopher does not. If he left his argument at that, the journalist would be vulnerable to attack from intellectuals on several fronts. But the journalist should be more aggressive and raise some hard questions for the philosophers. Does the contemporary philosopher really have something important to say? Is he capable of communicating it properly? Do the great philosophers of the past still have a message for modern humanity? Is their contemporary descendant communicating their message properly?

It will not do for the philosopher simply to shrug his shoulders and whine that people will not listen to him and that he lacks the access to mass media of communication that he deserves. In every generation, intellectuals must earn their audience, both by having something important to say and by being able to say it clearly, effectively, and passionately. Regardless of what people like Ortega would sometimes have us believe, the Great Sophist is not completely blind and deaf. This is especially obvious in a society like our own, one in which so many people have done university studies in the humanities and social sciences, and instead of being enlightened and inspired, have been disgusted by the wisdom to which they have been exposed. Granted, as Plato observed, people require time and effort (that of competent educators as well as their own) so that their eyes can become accustomed to a brighter order of objects of apprehension. But Plato also taught us well about the reprehensible passivity of the sage, the navigator on the ship of state who refuses to make a vigorous effort to communicate with his fellow seamen, the liberated individual who is comfortable in the ivory tower and disinclined to return to the world of the cave to play his proper social role.

A generation ago, Lippmann, philosopher and journalist, lamented that "the citadel is vacant because the public philosophy is gone, and all that the defenders of freedom have to defend in common is a public neutrality and a public agnosticism."[11] This observation may be interpreted in part as an indictment of Lippmann's fellow journalists, for it was they, after all, who stepped into the

vacuum that Ortega has described. But how did the vacuum develop, and how did the citadel become vacant? Does not Ortega
himself imply that intellectuals themselves share much of the blame
for having created the vacuum by abdicating their responsibility to
promote the public philosophy and the classical ideals of civilization? How much philosophical wisdom have journalists hidden from
the public, and how much of it have philosophers *themselves*
hidden?

When intellectuals bitterly complain about the quality of journalism in their society, they join a chorus of critics that includes politicians, businessmen, and carpenters in addition to philosophers, social theorists, and belletrists. And if criticism of the periodical press
is rarely if ever out of fashion, the same holds true in some measure
for criticism of intellectuals. Cultured, spiritual types, with their
airs, their self-importance, and their refusal to bake bread or otherwise contribute directly to the gross national product, are easy tar-
gets for most of the very people who also want to take the periodical press to task. Journalists, whether out of resentment or from
one of a dozen other motives, will sometimes find it as appropriate
to join the chorus of critics as intellectuals do. And perhaps the first
criticism that detractors of contemporary intellectuals will be inclined to make is that the philosophical and humanistic endeavors of
their own age and society appear to be in a particularly degraded
state. Concentrating on philosophy itself, one finds that such a criticism quite often hits the mark.

It has been routine for critics of high culture, both insiders and
outsiders, to complain that no one in the present generation of intellectual and artistic leaders has the stature of the giants of the past.
And even if there were a modern Plato or Spinoza in our midst,
chances are that he or she would go unrecognized for many generations anyway. Still, certain specific features of contemporary Western philosophical culture are genuinely lamentable. The modern
university, descendant of Plato's Academy and the institution on
which a professor such as Ortega thinks society should pin its highest hopes, is truly a wonderful place in which all sorts of valuable
thinking and research and dialogue go on, and where countless people have been exposed to both a noble tradition and vital methods of
rational inquiry. Yet it has also become institutionalized and
bureaucratized in ways that have led to a certain stagnation and lack
of adventurousness on the frontiers of speculation and theory. This
is especially evident these days in the philosophical department of
the academy. If the contemporary philosopher does not have to take
hemlock or go into exile, as some of his revered predecessors did, he

is still a martyr in various small ways: however, the typical contemporary philosopher has become too comfortable in the cloistered academic environment and the split-level suburban home. A budding philosopher typically enrolls himself in a university doctoral program in which, protected by scholarship money and the assorted compensations of a university setting, he carries on narrow research into fashionable epistemological or phenomenological issues. He serves up a dry-as-dust dissertation, and with the aid of shrewd academic politicians, finds himself a position at a place where, working toward tenure, he will find it expedient to turn out a bunch of short, technical, hastily crafted pieces for the learned journals. Desirous of professional respectability, security, and advancement, he is willing to compromise, temporarily, his integrity and human aspirations so that he can at some future time be free to do the exciting and inspiring work that he dreamed about doing as a wide-eyed intellectual recruit. But more often than not, he is simply absorbed into the system, and instead of coming to radiate wisdom and inspiration, he ends up stumbling through shallow lectures for increasingly uninterested students, retreating to narrower and less adventurous research projects, and strutting about hotel lobbies at national academic conferences.

Moreover, with respect to content, contemporary philosophy has become infected with certain regrettable tendencies, such as the fascination with unnecessary logical symbolism and increasingly opaque jargon, the refusal to take a genuinely broad and comprehensive view of the history of ideas, a puerile relativism, a misguided obsession with making the humanities more like the positive sciences, a cultivated avoidance of large issues, and a mode of false sophistication that disinclines the philosophical writer to be passionate, compassionate, and hortatory at the appropriate moments. Though he likes to think of himself as the heir to the tradition of Aristotle, Descartes, and Nietzsche, the typical contemporary academic philosopher, for all of his disdain for the philistines and operators of the "real" world, has come to be far too dependent on what "the many" care for; he has found it more comfortable, perhaps, to be puppeteer rather than liberator.

The increasing interest among academic philosophers in issues of "applied ethics" would seem to be a healthy development in recent philosophical discussion. Philosophers increasingly are convinced that they have something valuable to contribute to their society's understanding of such matters as nuclear energy policy, world hunger, abortion, and criminal punishment, among other issues. Philosophers indeed have something valuable to contribute here, but much recent work of this kind has been insufficiently philosophical. Too often, budding philosophers who specialize in issues of medical or legal ethics fail to do the historical spadework necessary for becoming true philosophers. Their work usually tends to be more social-scientific than philosophical, though it is sprinkled with the obligatory references to the ethical systems of Kant and Mill. Whatever his failings as a thinker—and he bears much of the responsibility for the degradation of recent English-language philosophy—G. E. Moore was at least right to warn of the dangers of allowing moral philosophy to degenerate into mere casuistry.[12] What is needed in contemporary moral philosophy, however, is the opposite of what Moore prescribed; the contemporary reflective moralist needs to widen his horizon, not restrict it further, and he needs to articulate the vision of a synoptic thinker, not that of a narrow specialist.

We often find now that the ambitious academic philosopher has allowed the imposition upon him of some of the very limitations for which he disdains the journalist. He may have an increasing fascination with cultivating the acquaintance of celebrities and influential people, he may be concerned with the fashionableness and marketability of his work, he may assess the work of his peers more by quantitative than qualitative standards, and he may be concerned with getting his work out quickly so that he can meet the deadlines imposed by tenure and promotion committees as he climbs up the academic ladder. Indeed, throughout much of the world of academic philosophy, the journal (learned rather than public, of course) has replaced the book as the preferred locus of publication.

Universities themselves have become increasingly infected with an obsession with publicity and public relations. This obsession has been justified, not altogether insincerely, on the grounds that the university needs to let the general public know what it has been doing to improve the quality of communal life. Innis insisted in the previous generation that, "The universities should subject their views about their role in civilization to systematic overhauling and revise the machinery by which they can take a leading part in the problems of Western culture. . . . The universities must concern themselves with the living rather than with the dead."[13] Yet Innis was also keen to observe that even in his own day, university curricula and methods were already coming more and more to mirror the emphases of *journalists*.[14]

When moved to reflect on the extent to which the philosophy, high culture, and higher educational system of his own society have become especially corrupted and degraded, the critic should be careful not to glorify the past uncritically. The good old days were rarely as good as reactionary, elitist traditionalists would have us believe. A survey of the history of higher education reveals that there are many levels on which the modern North American or Western European university is superior to its forerunners. One may consider, for example, the growth of academic freedom, the increased availability of higher education to the economically disadvantaged and to ethnic minorities and women, and the expansion of academic libraries. With respect to philosophy, one must remember that the background against which the greatest of the great philosophers stand out is rather starker than the one against which contemporary philosophers must stand out. For every Averroes, Leibniz, Hume, or William James that has emerged, there has always been a score of well placed, uninspired mediocrities serving as the semi-official voice of the intellectual community. Again, the hallowed names of philosophy were not consistently above uttering a good deal of obscure and maleficent rubbish. There are teachings of Hegel and Nietzsche, and of Plato and Aristotle for that matter, that ought to be a source of embarrassment to sympathetic professorial expositors of their works. Thus a journalist on the defensive would do well to say to the Ortegas of his society that there are a great many classical philosophical notions of the cultured and spiritual types that the journalist has performed a service by hiding or ignoring.

But when the journalist gets around to responding to the Ortegas, he will almost surely want to concentrate the main part of his analysis on the proverbial unworldliness of the philosopher. Marx scoffed at the philosophers for failing to change the world.[15] However, he overstated his point, for philosophers have changed the world, and in their weighty discussions of moral and political subjects, they have repeatedly indicated that they are not solely concerned with the personal satisfactions to be derived from living a contemplative life. Still, their critics have succeeded in establishing that philosophers, for all their talk about reality, do not consistently understand the real world of flesh-and-blood human beings. Several factors have contributed to the philosopher's difficulties in coming to grips with concrete human realities, but in the final analysis, we may simply say that unlike the Hebrew prophets or Socrates or Marx, the typical philosophical humanist has been temperamentally disinclined to return completely to the cave and participate wholeheartedly in the living scene of things in which ordinary human beings carry on the ordinary business of living. The Hebrew prophets, Socrates, and Marx saw that one cannot reasonably hope to reform the world if one has not observed closely enough the activity in the marketplace, law court, temple, and theater. But the typical philosopher has to some extent avoided the cave. He has not quite felt at home in the real world, perhaps partly because he has feared becoming corrupted by it. He prefers his armchair in his little corner of the academy, where he can construct his own consoling metaphysical interpretation of reality. Unfortunately, when one views things *sub specie aeternitatis*, they only become clearer in one sense, and so like Father Thales, the typical philosopher finds that his propensity to look at the heavens above causes him to stumble over the things in his path. Here the journalist-critic speaks for the multitude: the philosopher, for all his wisdom, has largely divorced himself from the living scene of things; he is not out there in the field, in the cave, where all the real action of real human life is taking place.

I cannot endorse the view of those such as Alexander Herzberg who have argued that the typical philosopher is an intellectually gifted but mentally disturbed person who uses his creative powers to escape from reality.[16] I have argued elsewhere against such a thesis, and have noted how the philosopher is, among other things, not as unworldly as his critics would have us believe.[17] Still, it is clear that the overwhelming majority of philosophers have had an ambivalent attitude toward life in the cave. No one understood this ambivalence better than Plato himself. When the liberated individual has escaped the cave, he will be more or less convinced that his new life is better than that enjoyed by even the most successful and respected people still down there, and so why should he return? The philosopher must be compelled, Plato suggests, to go back to the world of prisoners and puppeteers to play his proper role in the affairs of his fellow human beings. It is not enough to be convinced that one now enjoys a nobler, more satisfying life than do those in the cave; one must go down into the cave and help others to lead a nobler, more satisfying life. And helping those in the cave is not merely a just or charitable endeavor; there is a certain self-justification in it. The person who refuses to return to the cave may come to be haunted by the thought that his estimation of his new and old lives is based partly on resentment, and so he needs to return to the cave so that he can prove to lesser people (and to himself) that his new life is superior to his old one. When he returns to the cave, he may be ridiculed and hated, as Socrates was, so he needs to allow his eyes to become accustomed to the darkness, and he needs to participate in the affairs of the cave dwellers, however much or little those affairs may be worth. Only then can he be a liberator, and only then can he be sure that his new life is indeed a nobler one. But the cowardly intellectual, fearful of being robbed of what may be an illusion about the superiority of his new life, will be afraid to return to the cave.

If the *Seventh Letter* gives us an authentic insight into the life and mind of Plato, then Plato himself perfectly illustrates the plight of the alienated intellectual. As a young man, he tasted the fruits of political power and influence, but when he was deprived of them, he managed to convince himself that the life of the philosopher is a superior life. One of his attempts to return to the cave took the form of excursions to Sicily, where he hoped to create political leaders in his own image. These endeavors failed, and ultimately he confined himself to his Academy, an institution wherein he would be able to achieve social reforms through the training of philosophical leaders. Generations of intellectuals have followed Plato in this remarkable compromise, one which enables the intellectual simultaneously to divorce himself from the "real" world while indirectly participating in and influencing the events that will eventually take place in it. For from his perch atop the ivory tower, the intellectual can both look down at the plebs and yet still feel that he is helping to sort out their affairs for them. But a tough-minded journalist who refuses to be bullied by the Ortegas of his society will see through this scheme. He, after all, is more likely to have been the observer on the scene. What he lacks in distance, wide perspective, and architecture, he may compensate for with close acquaintance and empathy with those on whom he reports, those he serves. Even if he is not himself a researcher in the field, he is accustomed to handling information regarding concrete matters. He is able to summon up, if only with great effort, a sense of the drama of ordinary people's lives. Ordinary people—and their aspirations, disappointments, personal tragedies, and triumphs over adversity—have to matter to him more than they do to a lofty thinker whose primary concern is with general principles, timeless truths, the realm of the transcendent, and the realization of utopian ideals. The philosopher will fairly contend that his broad, synoptic vision has given him a richer insight into concrete particulars, but the price he must pay for his breadth of vision is that of losing the journalist's microscopic perspective.

What particularly galls the journalist is the philosopher's claim that his metaphysical vision gives him insight into the ultimate nature of reality, while the journalist and other unliberated types must settle for mere appearance. This contention is elaborately articulated by Plato, who treats concrete particulars as mere instantiations or copies of the true or highest realities that can only be grasped by the reflective mind and not by the senses. Since the journalist and his ilk do not have an insight into timeless, transcendent essences, such people are not in a position to recognize concrete particulars for what they are. And here the journalist must counter with the criticism that the philosopher's wide perspective has inevitably led him to depreciate concrete particulars, and particularly human individuals. It is bad enough that the philosopher appropriates for himself (and himself alone) the ordinary language term and category *reality*. What is equally irritating is that he depreciates not only the activity of journalists but the individuals on whom the journalist reports and for whom the journalist writes.

The journalist would be overstating a sound point if he joined the chorus of anti-intellectual scoffers and dismissed outright the philosopher's claims as having nothing to do with the real world. To dismiss a grand metaphysical construction as nothing more than a complex escapist device is to embrace sophistry at its most shallow. It is enough for the journalist to observe that a sound and useful approach to understanding reality is one that allows for the importance of all objects of apprehension, no matter how concrete. The philosopher's general principles and timeless truths do matter a great deal, but so also do the concrete affairs of the concrete human beings who inhabit the world at the present moment. Even Plato was himself prepared to grant that there cannot be philosophical wisdom without an antecedent apprehension of concrete particulars. But familiarity with the living scene of things is not just a ladder to be thrown away once one has been able to view things *sub specie aeternitatis*. Rather, it is a source of information that continuously enriches a loftier vision that is perpetually in need of further clarification and refinement. Were the journalist inclined to play the part of metaphysician for a moment, he might dare to suggest that the Platonist's general principles, timeless truths, transcendent essences, and the like derive their ontological importance from the concrete particulars through which they are derived by abstraction. Many a philosophical critic of Platonism would be prepared to endorse such a view, but in any case, a journalist need not go so far in order to get his primary point across.

Certainly even the finest public journals contain a great deal of information that is, even in the short term, trivial, misleading, and sensationalistic. When the philosopher makes this point, he will find that there is no dearth of ordinary, non-intellectual souls who are prepared to agree with him whole-heartedly. Still, when a newspaper or news magazine reports on corruption in local government, racist persecution, and even the revival of naturalism in the theater, it is talking about matters that have a great deal to do with justice, truth, and civilization. When Plato discoursed about justice and other high matters, he based his grandiose speculations on reflections about the living scene of things in the Greek world of his day. He was not wrong in believing that such reflection can yield insights into the human condition as such and even into the nature of reality, but a modern reader of Plato's dialogues can see that the limitations of Plato's vision are partly a function of the limited range of concrete realities to which Plato was exposed. It is really not all that remarkable that so much of what Plato said about, say, democracy still holds true today; neither is it remarkable that so much of what he said is largely irrelevant to modern democratic systems of which he could hardly have dreamed. The classical tradition of philosophy, for all its grandeur, must constantly renew itself if it is to come to grips with a world that is constantly changing on many levels. Any elementary school student can, from reading a serious newspaper on a fairly regular basis, learn certain things about justice that Plato at his most profound could never have grasped.

So if the journalist can learn from the philosopher, so too can the philosopher learn from the journalist. The journalist can draw on philosophical wisdom to understand and interpret better the concrete particulars on which he is called upon to report. In turn, the philosopher should view the journalist's reports as providing him not merely with information about the instantiation of higher realities or general principles, but with information that will be more valuable to him on two levels: first, in increasing his understanding of a certain order of reality that, as a human agent participating in and effected by the living scene of things, he needs to know about; and second, in helping him to clarify and refine his philosophical insights. A philosopher who reads in the newspaper about corruption at home or oppression abroad may be satisfied simply with noting that the particular occurrences about which he is reading can be understood by being subsumed under some general philosophical principle upon which he has already reflected many times. He may be moved to lament that the journalist whose work he is reading does not adequately understand the occurrences in question, and he may also feel that, when considered *sub specie aeternitatis*, the people directly involved in the events being described do not really matter very much. However, a sense of justice may lead him to act in some concrete way in response to the evils that have now been exposed to his view. For what, he may reflect, is the value of sound theory without sound practice? If the unexamined life is not worth living, it hardly follows that living a life involves little more than the examining of life. And again, in light of the concrete circumstances of the cases about which he is reading, the philosopher may be moved to revise some of his most basic ideas about justice, politics, human nature, and other high matters. For even if the ideals of civilization have a certain permanence or timelessness about them, a mortal being's apprehension of them can never be absolutely complete or perfect.

With the exception of a few extremely contemplative or mystical types, philosophers have felt a strong impulse to contribute to the advancement of civilization and the amelioration of the existential plight of their fellow human beings. Philosophers are rarely just thinkers; they are typically talkers, preachers, and writers too, and a large part of their discussion is taken up with moral and political subjects. In the case of a Marx or Sartre, we see how the concern with relating philosophical insights to concrete social problems can even be an impetus to the philosopher's taking upon himself the additional role of journalist. At the same time, to be a philosopher is to be a perpetual inquirer and not merely to be committed to a fixed, static, inflexible vision. When an individual becomes convinced that he has penetrated to the unchanging core of philosophical truth to the point where there is little of importance left for him to learn about, such a person has ceased to be a philosophical inquirer, though he may effectively promote a particular philosophical dogma, perspective, or insight. At his worst, Plato leaves us with the impression that he believes he has discovered all the answers to all of the important questions that perplexed his revered teacher. Yet even in the *Laws*, there are places where he indicates that future inquirers and reformers will have to build upon his work rather than take it as the last word. Indeed, there are places in some of his later dialogues where Plato seems to be poking fun at an earlier, more dogmatic, more self-confident self who had strayed too far from the Socratic principle that the wisdom of mortals is worth little or nothing.[18]

In his famous defense of freedom of the press, John Milton reminds us that mortal beings were not blessed with the gift of being able to grasp the supreme truths in their perfection or entirety. "For such is the order of God's enlightening his Church, to dispense and deal out by degrees his beam, so as our earthly eyes may best sustain it."[19] No matter how sincere we are in the confidence we have in our religious or philosophical vision, we would be imprudent and immoral to deny freedom of expression to dedicated, high-minded thinkers who have taken a path to the truth that we have preferred to avoid. It also follows, I think, that we should always be on our guard against being too hasty in dismissing as irrelevant, trivial, dangerous, or sophistical those attempts at enlightening us that initially strike us as uncongenial. "Who is wise?" Ben Zoma mused, concluding, "He who learns from every man."[20]

Willingness to learn must be tempered, of course, by the critical spirit, a healthy critical spirit as opposed to a rank skepticism, cynicism, or nihilism. Familiarity with a broad range of classical theories and methods will, when combined with logical rigor, save the journalist from the occasional temptation to genuflect before the shallow though fashionably opaque pronouncements of well-placed intellectual and cultural authorities. If the journalist were merely to enter the cult of guru-worship as a substitute for his present form of idol-worship (of the powerful, the beautiful, the celebrated, the dissident), he would not be able to attain the degree of intellectual and spiritual autonomy necessary for making productive use of classical wisdom. In turn, the philosopher, while making use of the information and interpretation that the journalist provides him, should never lose sight of the journalist's limitations.

Besides making use of the journalist's information, the philosopher would do well to recognize the value that the journalist could have as a promoter of philosophers and philosophy. Plato hoped that in time philosophers would come to master the complex skills involved in public relations. Whether or not the truly cultured and spiritual type could ever master such skills is an open question: the philosopher's ability to capture the journalist's respectful attention is perhaps more realistically to be hoped for than his ability to capture the attention of most other cave dwellers. For despite the many factors that alienate the journalist and intellectual from one another, there are also, as we have seen, points at which their interests and aspirations converge. They are both, for example, people of words. This is particularly important just now, for as a result of the ever increasing influence of the electronic media, people of words may be brought to appreciate the necessity of joining forces against a rival that does not share their respect for (and dependence upon) communal literacy. Whatever prudential considerations or sentiments of good will have contributed to journalists embracing television and radio newspeople as colleagues, it will become increasingly apparent to journalists, I believe, that electronic journalism is as much a threat to pure journalism as an extension of it. After noting William James's fear that the leadership of American thought was "passing away from the universities to the ten-cent magazines," Innis added that, "Today he might have argued that it had passed to the radio and television."[21] But more than professional or economic competition is involved here. Leadership is passing away from those who prize literacy to those who believe that the written word is not nearly as important as the classical humanistic tradition has taken it to be. Perhaps the time has come for the men and women of words to set aside internecine resentments and concentrate on a potent threat to a shared element in their professional ideologies.

In the presentation of news and ideas, as in many other spheres, radio and television have many advantages over the media of communication that depend on the written word. The electronic media allow for measures of timeliness, spontaneity, dialogue, and imagery that no book or journal can match. Writers and teachers have come to the defense of the written word, but their arguments have often been platitudinous, self-serving, and generally hollow. It has already dawned on many intellectuals that the rapid growth of the electronic media has inaugurated a new phase of the oral-aural tradition in communications, a tradition that is older and in some ways deeper if not more dignified than the tradition of manuscripts, books, and journals. Writers and publishers have decried the philistinism of forms of mass communication that do not promote or depend on the skills of the literate mind, yet they have simultaneously scrambled to make use of the technology of the electronic age. Academics have heaped scorn on the television set, but have concurrently looked with envy upon the rare intellectual who is in a position to lecture via the electronic media to the classroom of the world.

Written communication will survive, even if its influence is further diminished or transmuted. Meanwhile, whatever philistinism for which the electronic media may fairly be condemned, their ascendancy has had the salutary effect of providing writers of books and journal articles with an occasion for renewed reflection on the value of reading and writing. When they consider their relation to one another in this particular context, the philosopher and the journalist will inevitably be reminded of how much they have in common, especially insofar as they both communicate directly with an audience of literate persons.

Even here it would seem, however, that the philosopher has the upper hand over the journalist, for not only is high-powered reflection his natural business, but he has a freedom to apply his theories in his writing that is denied to the ordinary journalist and even to the powerful publisher or editor who must bend the knee to the cruder forces in the marketplace. When the journalist wishes to reform his work in the light of newly acquired insights into the value of reading and writing, he finds himself faced with certain largely fixed expectations of certain readers, publishers, and editors who are apt to be turned off by anything too calculatedly creative in the pages of their friendly, familiar newspaper. The philosopher has considerably more freedom, for even despite the constraint represented by the classical humanistic tradition to which he owes some allegiance, the philosopher knows that he writes for readers who are often prepared to tolerate (and at times even admire) something radically original with respect to methodology, subject matter, or perspective, provided that it is the work of an obviously gifted thinker who has previously demonstrated his ability to play one of the ordinary intellectual games that have been fashionable among his colleagues. We should not underestimate the conservative tendencies that determine much of what appears in scholarly books and journals, particularly in the academic world. The character of philosophical discussion in university press books and learned journals is very much influenced by the intellectual fashions of the day, which are in turn shaped partly by well-placed academic politicians. Still, I believe that the vision needed for transforming journalism is far more likely to emerge from the ranks of philosophers than from the ranks of the journalists themselves.

Journalism and philosophy could never interact with one another in a vacuum, since both are inevitably influenced by a wide range of cultural (and natural) forces, and the effect upon them of those forces will always play a large role in determining their relationship with each other. For example, political crises with pronounced ideological overtones tend to stimulate interest among journalists in what political philosophers have been saying, while at the same time stimulating philosophers to consider journalistic abuses and other practical problems and to put more abstract metaphysical and aesthetic concerns on the back burners. In turn, journalistic and philosophical activity both influence the forces acting upon them. If philosophical activity is freer and less determined than journalistic activity, it still is never purely the result of autonomous reason or an unbridled will to power, so that when the philosopher and journalist communicate with each other, it is always in a voice that has been modulated to some extent by third parties.

If the puppeteer is influenced far more than he realizes by the attitudes and values of the Great Sophist, perhaps so too is the liberator, who comes from the world of the cave and is further influenced by its denizens upon his return. The most powerful influences of the Great Sophist are those that are least visible to the elite of judgment shapers. But reporters, manipulators, and intellectuals also struggle in the light against Bacon's famous idols of the tribe, cave, marketplace, and theater. At the same time, many of them are prepared to learn whatever they can from those outside their elite.

Two particular forces in society, the state and religion, deserve special consideration here, for both explicitly contend that they are entitled to a unique form of priority over journalism and philosophy alike, and it is no coincidence that these two forces, acting together or on their own, have boldly defended their presumed right to impose limits on freedoms of thought, expression, and the press. Underlying the various metaphysical and political arguments that statesmen offer to establish their priority is the theme of order: avoidance of anarchy is proposed by them to be the single primary condition of civilization. Liberals have generally not found the various arguments compelling, partly because they have not been convinced that there is indeed a single primary condition of civilization. Religion contends that it derives its priority from spiritual forces that are in some sense transcendent. Religion, however, is as much a field for highly personal reflection and commitment as philosophy is—philosophy and religion are intertwined in a very complex way—so that religion can only be an official public source of values if one of its countless forms is enabled, through worldly force, to dominate or suppress the others available in a particular society. Although there were adumbrations of it even in the ancient world, the general type of religious liberty that is now taken more or less for granted in most Western democracies developed largely in the last few centuries, and its gradual ascendancy has been accompanied by profound debates about its long-term viability as an instrument for social progress. Even so, in the modern Western democracies, most people strongly believe that religionists should press their claims to spiritual and moral wisdom with due regard to the ideals of peace, freedom, and tolerance.[22]

Historically there has been no dearth of journalists prepared to promote the agenda laid down for them by authoritarian statesmen and religionists. Even in modern democracies, there are many journalists who look to particular political or religious leaders for a guidance that they feel the apolitical, ecclesiastically independent humanist is unable to provide. Philosophers too have often been prepared to put their sometimes imposing rhetorical and argumentative skills at the service of powerful politicians and religious leaders. I am not thinking here of sophists but of some of the most justly respected of philosophers, such as Thomas Aquinas. Of course, some of the most courageous and potent critics of the political or religious Establishment have also come from the journalistic and philosophical ranks.

Though their own special creativity can hardly be denied, charismatic statesmen have rarely been primary sources of moral insight; whatever moral wisdom the great statesman seems to embody is largely derivative, and much of his greatness stems from his ability to draw on the insights of intellectuals and apply them through concrete social policies. This holds true also for certain religious leaders, particularly for powerful ecclesiastical politicians, but some religious leaders have been great moral thinkers in their own right and have possessed a kind of moral insight that seems to transcend philosophical understanding itself. The teachings attributed to Moses, Gautama Buddha, or Jesus of Nazareth have a mystical profundity about them that even some of the most secularist of philosophers find hard to deny, and sometimes so too do the teachings of lesser figures. If philosophy has influenced religious thought, so too has it been influenced by religion, a form of experience that contributed to its coming into being and to which it has never been able to shake off completely its filial loyalty. Though relatively few philosophers and journalists in modern democracies are prepared to devote their careers to working for a great religious reawakening, the historic connection between religion and the ideals of civilization is something that no potential liberator can afford to ignore. It is perhaps worth noting in passing that Lippmann devoted some of his loftiest reflection to the subject of the relation of religion to the ideals of civilization, as is particularly noticeable in his *Preface to Morals*.[23]

The philosopher and the journalist may be particularly interested in the way their distant ancestors in ancient and medieval priesthoods made use of the powers that come with literacy to promote desirable forms of social stability and change, as well as to reinforce or increase their own personal influence. While not underestimating the centrality of the oral-aural tradition in even the most advanced natural religions, one can hardly ignore the importance of the sacred book not only in the Jewish-Christian-Islamic tradition but in the Middle Eastern religions that antedate Jewish monotheism. To be able to read the revealed word of God was obviously a great boon to the believer, but the wise man who had the additional gift of being able to express himself fluently in writing was in an especially high position. Such a person could not only perform a variety of cultural services but could leave a concrete legacy to future generations in the form of a public record of codes, beliefs, and historical events that might otherwise be forgotten. Thus, the ability to write not only allowed the priestly figure to be a more influential teacher but enabled him to increase the importance of his fellow religionists by capturing aspects of their being in words that could be conveyed to their descendants and to outsiders long after they had quit this world. The modern philosopher and journalist are heirs to the priestly tradition inasmuch as they possess not only a special power to teach but powers to record and immortalize. Herbert Spencer gives us a sense of how the master of the written word must have awed the lowly and the powerful alike in ancient and medieval times: "Beyond the wonder excited among the common people by the ability to convey ideas in hieroglyphics, ideographs, etc., there is the immense aid to cooperation throughout the ecclesiastical hierarchy which an exclusive means of communicating intelligence gives; and the history of medieval Europe shows how power to read and write, possessed by priests but rarely by others, made their assistance indispensable in various civil transactions and secured great advantages to the Church."[24] In a modern democratic society, the writer cannot inspire such awe, but if he does what he does particularly well, the philosophical writer or journalist may perhaps inspire something akin to it. For even when there is nothing particularly religious or spiritual about his communication, he is still perceived as performing the quasi-sacerdotal social roles of public scribe and spokesman for the age.

Historically, much philosophy and much journalism have been carried on within a rigidly authoritarian or otherwise highly institutionalized religious framework. Even today, much philosophy is unabashedly apologetical, and some periodicals are classified as religious journalism. However, with the rise of political and religious liberalism, both philosophers and journalists have come to feel more and more that to be regarded as truly free and responsible inquirers and communicators, it is necessary for them to distance themselves from the official teaching and preaching establishments of particular organized religions. Hence, in the modern Western democracies, most university humanities programs and most public journals appear to have a secular cast, even if they deal with religious subjects regularly and respectfully. Educators at, say, Roman Catholic or Baptist universities, and editors and journalists on the staffs of Roman Catholic and Baptist periodicals, have often been moved to justify the existence of their own institutions by decrying what they view as the dogmatic "secular humanism" being promoted by rival institutions. This complaint is usually unfair, I believe, for few universities and public journals are ideologically antireligious. In fact, I would tend to believe there is far too little criticism of organized religious institutions in Western universities and news periodicals. The problem here is that in the eyes of the devout religionist, an independent academic or publishing institution simply cannot take religion seriously enough.

Because of its deep-rooted role in the general shaping of Western culture, the Christian religion can be presumed to exercise still an indirect but pervasive influence on all major Western social institutions, so that however religiously neutral modern Western journalists strive to be, they carry on their work in a society guided by a vaguely Christian world view. An observer unsympathetic to Christian doctrine and practice, such as a Nietzsche or Marx, would not have much difficulty in showing how even the most secularized Western newspaper takes certain aspects of the Christian world view to be matters simply of natural or intuitive morality. Also, in areas where, say, Roman Catholicism is the dominant ecclesiastical presence, the Christian inspiration of the leading public journals may normally be expected to have something of a Roman Catholic cast, even though editors and publishers might sincerely protest that they have endeavored to produce periodicals with no such bias. Such Roman Catholic influence on the local public journals would mirror that upon the ostensibly secular public schools and universities of the area. Of course, there is a substantial convergence of the teachings of all great religions, semi-religious philosophies, and even avowedly secularist ideologies; such ideals of civilization as justice, peace, and prosperity are not in the special preserve of any particular religious or ideological tradition. It must thus be acknowledged that a large part of the Christian influence on the public journals has been a matter of promoting values and attitudes that are not exclusively Christian.

Those who look to religion as the main hope for social, moral, and cultural renewal and progress may well feel that the public journals would be more effective instruments of civilization if they were more consciously religious. In its golden age under the editorship of Erwin Canham, the *Christian Science Monitor* seemed to represent to a wide diversity of readers, including some atheists, a somewhat more spiritual approach to the whole journalistic enterprise. Canham's achievement should not be underestimated, for it is no easy task to go about consciously making journalism more religious without reducing periodicals to instruments for the dissemination of religious dogma.

Plato, as he set about publicizing his navigational skills on a ship of state being rocked by waves of political, moral, economic, and military misfortune, could never quite determine precisely how to fit traditional religion into his utopian schemes. In his defense, he did not have the freedom to criticize the religious establishment that many contemporary social theorists enjoy. His revered teacher was poisoned with hemlock for alleged impiety, but despite Plato's resentment about that whole sorry business, he learned some useful

lessons from it. In remarkable lines in the *Republic*, Plato cere-
moniously announces that he has no intention of undercutting the
influence of the religious authorities of his society,[25] and book 10 of
the *Laws* is written in the narrowest tones of religious conservatism.
There was, of course, much for Plato to admire in traditional Greek
religion, particularly its efficacy as an instrument of social control
and its anti-materialistic teaching. And of course, Plato's own
metaphysical and moral vision was partly shaped by the cultural religious values and attitudes with which he had grown up. Still, it is
hard to believe that Plato could have regarded himself as working
wholly within the parameters of religious orthodoxy.[26] In any case,
the countless philosophers who have produced footnotes to Plato's
work have simply been unable to agree as to precisely where priest
and prophet are situated within (or beyond) the cave.

Having duly noted that religion is inevitably a variable in any
equation by which the actual or proper relations of philosophy and
journalism are to be determined, I return now to what has been the
main practical question of my inquiry, the question of what light
philosophical reflection on journalism sheds on how journalism
could be made a more effective instrument for the advancement of
civilization. I have observed that despite the characteristic detach-
ment that is partly a function of their temperament, partly a matter
of their choice, and partly a condition that has been imposed upon
them by the Great Sophist, philosophers usually do feel that it is
their business to prescribe remedies for communal ills, and few of
them have been so cynical as to conclude that there is no point in
offering advice to their fellow creatures. Lippmann wrote that, "It
will help us to cherish Plato's ideal, without sharing his hasty conclusion about the perversity of those who do not listen to reason."[27]
Yet we have seen that despite his frustration and resentment, even
Plato believed that philosophers can, through their teaching, make
this world a better place.

If the practitioners of the now fashionable "applied ethics" had
their way, then when the discipline *philosophy of journalism* finally
emerged and began to take shape, it would look something like the
currently fashionable disciplines of philosophy of medicine and philosophy of law. Thus, philosophers closely familiar with the details
of the journalistic enterprise—and preferably philosophers with
professional journalistic training and experience—would concentrate on such specific issues as when (if ever) a journalist should
reveal his sources of information, or when (if ever) a journalist
should publicize a politician's addiction to alcohol or drugs. Whatever value such "philosophy of journalism" would have, it would be

only marginally *philosophical*, for a sine qua non of genuine philosophy is broad, synoptic vision. Moreover, a true philosophy of journalism would probably be more closely akin to the classical disciplines of political philosophy, philosophy of education, and aesthetics than to philosophy of medicine and philosophy of law, if only because it would have to be largely preoccupied with determining what journalism is and what practical functions it serves.

I have before me now, spread out on the coffee table in my living room, the Sunday edition of a major metropolitan newspaper. It contains all sorts of stories, but it is not an anthology of contemporary fiction; rather, its stories ostensibly provide me with information about the real world. This information is supposed to be valuable to me on several levels. There are stories about political problems in faraway lands, the manufacturing industry in the neighboring province, last night's hockey games and concerts, and a big high society party of the kind to which I am never invited. There are also short essays that interpret recent events for me, there are crossword puzzles and comics, and there are columns in which regular contributors pass judgment on all sorts of people and institutions, policies and fashions. As I move from section to section, page to page, and article to article, I am alternately amused, enraged, enlightened, surprised, diverted, bored, narcotized, or stimulated to further reflection. Sometimes I am simultaneously affected by two or more of these states. I may clip out an article or two for future reference or to pass on to a friend. Later I shall deposit the rest of the newspaper in the garbage can. Unlike many other people, I feel obliged to read a major public journal from time to time, but unlike many others, I do not feel obliged to read one every day. The time I spend reading through the paper could easily be spent on more worthwhile endeavors, but I feel that I can and ought to spare some time for newspaper reading.

As far as I can tell, most of the people with whom I am acquainted are affected by newspapers in roughly the same ways as I am, although I know that some people are affected rather more or rather less than I am. Almost everyone I know is given to complaining regularly that the newspapers and news magazines they read are not particularly good. As I do, these people often find that some matters have been covered by the papers in too much detail, others in too little, and that the papers have neglected completely certain important issues and events. As I am, these people are offended by the newspaper's handling of this or that matter, or by a particular commentator's perception, description, or estimation of a certain event or figure in the news. When people complain that newspapers are not good enough, they are invariably indicating that newspapers do not do an adequate job of saying the sorts of things that they themselves want the newspapers to say. Sometimes they are justified in wanting something different; sometimes they are not. Obviously, all sorts of considerations can enter into their judgment.

However, a person given to concentrated moral reflection of a philosophical order would be less inclined than other people to focus his criticism on the newspapers' handling (or neglect) of particular events or issues of the day, and would be more concerned with how public journals fail generally to improve the quality of the polis and the quality of life of individuals within and beyond the polis. He would also be different from the increasingly prominent type of professional media critic who stresses the presence of particular political-ideological biases in his society's major mass media. The question writ large in his consciousness would be a big one: what journalistic reforms would make news periodicals more effective instruments for the promotion of the joyous self-realization of individuals and societies?

A Platonic theme that rarely receives adequate attention even from dedicated Platonists is that social institutions are reformed primarily through the improvement of the individuals who participate in them. So much attention has traditionally been given to Plato's radical political theories that Plato's emphasis on the "republic of the soul" is usually left in the background. The social institution of journalism primarily is to be reformed through the intellectual advancement and the moral advancement of the individuals who participate in it; these are journalists, editors, publishers, readers, and those professionally outside of the journalistic process who exploit it as a means of influencing public opinion. Because there is already a vast body of literature on methods of educating individuals *qua individuals*, I would concentrate here on the advancement of journalists.

The fastest way to advance the journalistic profession would be to recruit into the journalistic ranks some of our society's most gifted and enlightened teachers, or at least classically educated young people with the potential to develop into such teachers. For any number of reasons, several of which I have already considered, our greatest moral teachers have generally not considered journalism an appropriate outlet for their skills. I am reminded here of a powerful passage in *Only in America* where the wise and witty journalist, Harry Golden, criticizes Albert Schweitzer for exiling himself in Lambaréné and ministering there to the needs of the obscure natives instead of employing his prodigious gifts as an educator to confront directly the enormous barbarism of Nazism and fascism.[28] Though Golden's criticism is a powerful one, Schweitzer clearly believed, in the noblest tradition of Socrates, that he had gone where he sincerely believed he could personally do the most good for himself and for his fellow creatures.[29] We simply cannot know whether the world would be a better place if Schweitzer had become a crusading journalist, Socrates a politician, Dietrich Bonhoeffer a civil liberties lawyer, or Jane Addams a banker. In any case, for many years now I have urged my brightest philosophy students to consider journalism as a profession in which their humanistic training could be put to use. I have almost invariably been met with coolness and surprise; I can see in these students a reflection of my own disinclination to enter the journalistic ranks. It must be granted that few journalists reach a position in their profession to discourse directly about high matters, and it would take remarkable imagination to disseminate the loftiest moral truths gracefully in articles on postal strikes, the local footwear industry, and the amateur hockey championship. I still wonder, however, at the reluctance of our most gifted moral teachers even to contribute to public journals, and at the failure of our most high-minded periodical editors to encourage submissions from such individuals.

An alternative would be for interested parties to induce future and apprentice journalists to draw more consistently, more knowledgeably, and more imaginatively on the moral teachings of the classical humanistic and religious traditions. Merrill has harsh words for the journalism schools, which he sees as turning out too many narrowly trained, unreflective, unimaginative products.[30] Journalism schools cannot reasonably be expected to devote a large part of their curriculum to general humanities courses, but in their admissions policies, they could attach more importance than they now do to the moral and intellectual qualities of their applicants, and particularly to the humanistic training of those applicants. One of the most lamentable effects of the growing preoccupation of journalism schools with the electronic media, and particularly television, has been an exaggerated emphasis on such superficial qualities of the successful journalist as calculated cleverness in impromptu conversation, prettiness, charm, jocularity, eagerness to please, willingness to serve as a token representative of a highly particularized ethnic or ideological constituency, and mastery of the art of dramatic posturing. If the gravity of a Lippmann, Childs, Martin, or Fulford is perhaps sometimes too much for plain folks to endure, it hardly follows that surface slickness is an appropriate substitute for intelligence, wisdom, courage, compassion, and kindred virtues.

One would not have to rely here exclusively on the good judgment of journalism school teachers and administrators. Because publishers, editors, and journalists are highly susceptible—as they have to be, given the nature of their enterprise—it is crucial they receive a steady flow of constructive advice, criticism, and feedback from reflective readers who regard public journals as potentially more than vehicles of diversion, entertainment, and manipulation. One form of feedback that a Western publisher gets is in terms of sales: if readers do not like changes that have been introduced into a periodical, they may well stop buying it, and when sales increase, it is often presumed that the journal has somehow been improved. Moreover, market research can save publishers the trouble of having to take economic risks. However, journalists who associate journalistic excellence primarily with profit and circulation figures have ceased to be craftsmen and become businessmen. Being a true craftsman requires that one be prepared to do for one's clients what one has sound reason to believe is good for them, and not merely what one rightly or wrongly feels that they want one to do for them. Even if the journalist were in a position to interpret sales figures correctly, and even if market research were more reliable than it is, journalists and publishers would still have to be prepared to make sacrifices, economic or otherwise, in order to achieve excellence in journalism as such. Pressured by publishers, small-minded readers, and special interest groups to set his quest for professional excellence aside, the high-minded journalist must have the courage to affirm in public and in his own mind that writing is for him a craft and a profession and not simply a way of putting bread on the table and getting on in the world. It will thus be a great boon to him if he and his publishers and editors receive direct communication from those readers who have a genuine concern about excellence in journalism, and particularly from professional writers and teachers.

I cannot stress enough that the journalist is primarily, if not essentially, a writer. Although one should not confuse the meaning of a term with its etymology or primary use, and although one must grant that the title of journalist is bestowed more and more on people who do little if any writing for the public, one need not stand by idly as language is deprived of descriptive precision. One should at the very least make it clear that substantial categorial and qualitative differences must be recognized between classical journalism and other things now widely characterized as journalism. If journalism is primarily writing, then journalistic excellence is primarily excellence in writing. What makes a writer a fine writer is that he has something worth saying and can say it well via the written word. If the journalist is to work within the framework of the classical humanistic tradition, he must be concerned about more than digging out facts, interviewing celebrities, and creating a sensation; he must constantly put questions of value before his mind. Why is it important for people to read about such-and-such? How can I relate the subject matter of this article to the concrete needs of individuals and society itself? What approach to presenting this information will give readers practical insights that can be fruitfully applied in their lives as citizens and seekers of spiritual fulfillment? A journalist is not a scientist whose work is to be assessed in terms of his discoveries; he is a literary artist whose work is to be assessed in terms of the force and imagination with which he uses descriptions of concrete human experience as vehicles for transmitting non-technical information and ideas to people who will be able to make constructive use of them in their lives. Unlike the writer of fiction, the news journalist has advertised himself as someone who reports, and so it may often be appropriate for him to do his own research in the field rather than relying exclusively on testimony or on the input he receives from research associates. But it is only when he fills the pages of news periodicals with words of value that he becomes part of the classical journalistic and humanistic traditions.

When publishers and editors come to believe that they have a substantial number of people in their journalistic corps who are more than mere technicians and have moral vision, humanistic knowledge, and creative powers of expression, they will recognize the prudential and moral value of allowing those individuals to manifest their professional virtues more freely. Earlier I suggested that the uniformity of style that marks individual periodicals is partly necessitated by the regular reader's preference for a journal with a familiar identity, and partly by other factors. But a serious newspaper or news magazine must also allow talented journalists the freedom to depart from ritualized patterns of writing that have indurated into an official house style. Neither change nor variegation necessarily deprives an object of its essential identity; indeed, change and variegation are often needed to sustain an object. The finest journals are those that are able to accommodate the finest writers, but a writer cannot cultivate his craft if he is constantly obliged to turn out work that is essentially indistinguishable from that of his colleagues. Although most news periodicals allow for some journalistic individuality in editorial page columns, special essays, and other signed correspondence, they tend to encourage a rather impersonal style of reporting basic news. The result is often a waste of journalistic talent and a pretense of objectivity. But the time is now particularly ripe for creative journalism, for just as the birth of photography forced painters in an earlier generation to reconsider the uses to which their craft can be put, the advent of the electronic news media will increasingly force journalists to reflect on what they can do better than those who have appropriated some of their traditional functions.

My frequent references to a classical humanistic tradition may vex some who believe, not altogether unfairly, that they are both vague and haughty enough to qualify as platitudinous. I have not given many concrete examples of how journalists can apply classical moral teachings in their discussions of specific events, and I have even intentionally avoided the citation, critical analysis, and correction of specific pieces of journalistic writing. I am neither a journalist nor a professional media critic: my skills—and interests—lie elsewhere. Throughout this inquiry, I have been concerned primarily with the motives, self-images, and assessments of their potential that do, might, and should figure in the minds of journalists. There would be little point in my trying to show that Journalist X, when he prepared his report on yesterday's industrial accident, should or could or might have incorporated into his analysis some of the spirit that animated Voltaire's response to the Lisbon earthquake or the existentialist critique of the dehumanization that technology breeds. Such a suggestion might well sound preposterous: in any case, I leave journalists to find their own way.

But those who would argue that there is no such thing as a classical humanistic tradition, or that this tradition is an incoherent hodgepodge of arbitrary, inconsistent, and unjustified opinions, are poor historians of ideas who, by obfuscating the agenda of civilization, help barbarians with their work. Certainly there have been genuine and profound disagreements among reflective moralists, and certainly some of the great moral teachers have mistaken their useful perspective for a definitive and ultimate solution to all of the eternal problems of moral philosophy. But one should not be too tolerant of those self-proclaimed intellectuals who mischievously obscure that significant body of insights grasped in raw form almost intuitively by all decent people and clarified and refined by generation upon generation of wisdom lovers. As R. G. Collingwood has eloquently observed,

> The bickerings of philosophical sects are an amusement for the foolish; above these jarrings and creakings of the machine of thought there is a melody sung in unison by the spirits of the spheres, which are the great philosophers. This melody, *philosophia quaedam perennis*, is not a body

of truth revealed once and for all, but a living thought whose content, never discovered for the first time, is progressively determined and clarified by every genuine thinker.[31]

While we may be moved to regret the particular way in which Plato hypostatized moral ideals as transcendent, unchanging Forms, I would never undervalue the vigor, clarity, and integrity with which he warned his successors of the lifelessness, murkiness, and corruptness of the relativism of the cynical sophistic mind.

It is perhaps cynicism itself, so often a byproduct of a false sophistication, that the journalist and philosopher alike must guard against above all things. If a cynical frame of mind is a rung on the ladder of enlightenment, it is one on which we must be careful not to linger. Cynicism, when it hardens into a fixed perspective on the human condition, is the king of vices, because it is so easily put to the service of our justifying the maintenance of all the others. The shrill voice of cynics emanates from many quarters, and often from the precincts of the press and the academy: This is the way of the world. This is the best we can do. Our fellow human beings do not want anything better, and they will not tolerate anything better. Indeed they do not deserve anything better. The world is cruel, and life is hard, and we are frail creatures on the foundering ship of state, in the darkness of the cave. We cannot afford the luxury of indulging in vain hopes and aspirations. It is hard enough for us just to get by.

I find it rather touching, very touching indeed, that Walter Lippmann, who was prepared to indict even Plato himself for cynicism, chose to close *Public Opinion* with a mighty warning to a generation of readers that, like our own, had good reason to be bitterly disillusioned by recent events and worried about the declining prospects for civilization: "And if amidst all the evils of this decade, you have not seen men and women, known moments that you would like to multiply, the Lord himself cannot help you."[32]

Notes

Chapter 1. Journalist and Philosopher on the Ship of State

1. Walter Lippmann, *Public Opinion* (New York: Macmillan, 1922), p. 320.

2. Walter Lippmann, *Essays in the Public Philosophy*, An Atlantic Monthly Press Book (Boston and Toronto: Little, Brown, 1955), pp. 96–102.

3. Plato *Republic* 474B–480A.

4. Robert R. McCormick, *What is a Newspaper?* (Chicago: Public Service Bureau of *The Chicago Tribune*, 1924), p. 21.

5. John Hohenberg, *The Professional Journalist*, A Holt-Dryden Book (New York: Henry Holt, 1960), p. 11.

6. John Calhoun Merrill, *The Imperative of Freedom: A Philosophy of Journalistic Autonomy*, Communications Arts Books (New York: Hastings House, 1974), p. 8.

7. Frank Luther Mott, *The News in America* (Cambridge: Harvard University Press, 1962), p. 29.

8. Ibid.

9. Margaret A. Blanchard, "The Hutchins Commission, The Press and the Responsibility Concept," *Journalism Monographs* 49 (May 1977), pp. 29–51, esp. 36, 47, 51.

10. Robert Fulford, "The Press in the Community," in *The Press and the Public: 8th Winter Conference*, ed. D. L. B. Hamlin (Toronto: University of Toronto Press [for the Canadian Institute on Public Affairs], 1962), pp. 29–30.

11. Lippmann, *Public Opinion*, p. 411.

12. Plato *Republic* 487E–489D.

13. Lippmann, *Public Opinion*, p. 412.

14. Ibid., p. 414.

15. Plato *Republic* 499E–500A.

16. Lippmann, *Public Opinion*, p. 416.

17. Plato *Republic* 489D–495C.

18. Plato *Apology* 31C–32A.

19. Plato *Republic* 519C–520D.

20. Merrill, *Imperative of Freedom*, p. 8.

21. Ibid., p. 4.

22. Ibid., p. 143.

23. Bernard C. Hennessey, *Public Opinion*, 3d ed. (North Scituate, Mass.: Duxbury Press, 1975), p. 273.

24. Merrill, *Imperative of Freedom*, p. 18.

25. Jean-Louis Servan-Schreiber, *The Power to Inform*, trans. with the cooperation of Paris Research Associates (New York: McGraw-Hill, 1974), p. 112.

26. Ibid., p. 136.

27. Plato *Apology* 21A–24A, 30C–31C, 40E.

Chapter 2. The Essential Nature of Journalism

1. Plato *Apology* 18E–24A. A good example of Socrates at his mission is Plato's *Euthyphro*.

2. Plato *Republic* 345B–E.

3. Lippmann, *Public Opinion*, p. 358.

4. Servan-Schreiber, *Power to Inform*, p. 145.

5. Ibid., p. 114.

6. For interesting discussions of open-mindedness, see William Hare, *Open-mindedness and Education* (Montreal: McGill-Queen's University Press, 1979), and *In Defence of Open-mindedness* (Montreal: McGill-Queen's University Press, 1985).

7. Fred S. Siebert et al., *Four Theories of the Press* (Urbana, Ill.: University of Illinois Press, 1956), p. 1.

8. Plato *Republic* 475E–476E, 595A–598D.

9. Hennessey, *Public Opinion*, pp. 250–51.

10. Harold A. Innis, *The Bias of Communication* (Toronto: University of Toronto Press, 1951), p. 32.

11. McCormick, *What is a Newspaper?*, pp. 14–15.

12. Innis, *Bias of Communication*, p. 59.

13. Mott, *News in America*, p. 22.

14. Ibid.

15. Warren Breed, *The Newspaperman, News and Society* (New York: Arno Press, 1980), p. 252. This work was Breed's doctoral dissertation in sociology at Columbia University.

16. Ibid., pp. 253–54.

17. Mott, *News in America*, p. 1.

18. Ibid., p. 4.

19. Breed, *Newspaperman*, p. 423.

20. Mott, *News in America*, p. 4.

21. Servan-Schreiber, *Power to Inform*, p. 243.

22. Marshall McLuhan, *Understanding Media* (New York: McGraw-Hill, 1964), p. 216.

23. Ibid., p. 207.

24. Breed, *Newspaperman*, pp. 286–99.

25. Charles H. Brown, *Informing the Public* (New York: Holt, Rinehart and Winston, 1957), pp. 169–288.

26. Mott, *News in America*, p. 27.

27. William Ernest Hocking, *Freedom of the Press: A Framework of Principle* (Chicago: University of Chicago Press, 1947), p. 88.

28. See, for example, Alfred Adler, *Understanding Human Nature*, trans. W. Béran Wolfe (London: George Allen and Unwin, 1928).

29. McCormick, *What is a Newspaper?*, p. 32.

Chapter 3. The Journalist and the World of Plato's Cave

1. Lippmann, *Public Opinion*, p. vii.

2. Plato *Republic* 514A–517A.

3. Ibid., 517A–521B.

4. Francis MacDonald Cornford, in Plato *Republic*, trans. with introduction and notes by Francis MacDonald Cornford (London: Oxford University Press, 1941), p. 228.

5. Lippmann, *Public Opinion*, p. 320.

6. Cf., for example, Hennessey, *Public Opinion*, pp. 247, 273.

7. Lippmann, *Public Opinion*, p. 334.

8. Hennessey, *Public Opinion*, p. 247.

9. Ibid., p. 277.

10. Ibid., p. 245.

11. Ibid., p. 246.

12. McCormick, *What is a Newspaper?*, p. 15.

13. Fulford, "Press in the Community," pp. 24–25.

14. Ibid., pp. 27–28.

15. Fred S. Siebert, in Siebert et al., *Four Theories*, p. 9.

16. Ibid., p. 18.

17. Lippmann, *Essays*, p. 26.

18. Kingsley Martin, *The Press The Public Wants* (London: Hogarth Press, 1947), p. 116.

19. The Commission on Freedom of the Press, *A Free and Responsible Press* (Chicago: University of Chicago Press, 1947), p. 77.

20. Hennessey, *Public Opinion*, p. 245.

21. Peter Hood, *Ourselves and the Press* (London: John Lane the Bodley Head, 1939), p. 218.

22. Martin, *The Press*, p. 93.

23. Ibid., p. 67.

24. McCormick, *What is a Newspaper?*, p. 19.

25. Mott, *News in America*, p. 32.

26. Breed, *Newspaperman*, p. 423.

27. McCormick, *What is a Newspaper?*, p. 21.

28. Fulford, "Press in the Community," p. 26.

29. Hennessey, *Public Opinion*, pp. 249–52.

30. Cf. R. G. Collingwood, *The Idea of History* (Oxford: Clarendon Press, 1946), pp. 257–61.

31. McCormick, *What is a Newspaper?*, p. 26.

32. Ibid.

33. Cf. Hohenberg, *The Professional Journalist*, chap. 6.

34. McCormick, *What is a Newspaper?*, p. 21.

35. Cf., for example, Herbert J. Gans, *Deciding What's News: A Study of* CBS Evening News, NBC Nightly News, Newsweek, *and* Time (New York: Pantheon Books, 1979), p. 314.

36. Breed, *Newspaperman*, p. 423.

37. Ibid.

38. Lippmann, *Public Opinion*, p. 362.

39. Ibid.

40. Siebert et al., *Four Theories*, p. 1.

41. Baruch Spinoza, *A Theologico-Political Treatise* (1670), trans. (with *A Political Treatise*) R. H. M. Elwes (New York: Dover, 1951), p. 216.

Chapter 4. The Journalist as Educator

1. Arthur Schopenhauer, *Essays and Aphorisms*, selected and translated with an introduction by R. J. Hollingdale (Harmondsworth, England: Penguin Books, 1970), pp. 222–23. This passage, and the other quotations from Schopenhauer that follow, are from the *Parerga und Paralipomena* (1851).

2. Hennessey, *Public Opinion*, p. 277.

3. Martin, *The Press*, p. 67.

4. Schopenhauer, *Essays*, p. 222.

5. Ibid., p. 221.

6. Ibid., p. 222.

7. The Commission on Freedom of the Press, *A Free and Responsible Press*, pp. 27–28.

8. Blanchard, "Hutchins Commission," p. 12.

9. Marshall McLuhan, *The Gutenberg Galaxy* (Toronto: University of Toronto Press, 1962), p. 246.

10. McLuhan, *Understanding Media*, p. 206.

11. Lippmann, *Public Opinion*, pp. 321–23.

12. Martin, *The Press*, p. 115.

13. John Dewey, *Reconstruction in Philosophy* (New York: Henry Holt, 1920), chap. 7.

14. Arthur M. Schlesinger Jr., "Walter Lippmann: The Intellectual v. Politics," in *Walter Lippmann and His Times*, ed. Marquis Childs and James Reston (New York: Harcourt, Brace, 1959), pp. 202–3.

15. Walter Lippmann, *Public Opinion*, chap. 6–10, 20. Cf. Lippmann's later book, *The Phantom Public* (New York: Harcourt, Brace, 1925).

16. Cf. Walter Lippmann, *Liberty and the News* (New York: Macmillan, 1920).

17. Lippmann, *Public Opinion*, pp. 364–65.

18. Schlesinger, "Walter Lippmann," pp. 219–20.

19. Ibid., p. 220.

20. Ibid., pp. 221–22. Cf. Reinhold Niebuhr, "The Democratic Elite and American Foreign Policy," in *Walter Lippmann and His Times*, ed. Childs and Reston.

21. Cf. Jay Newman, *Foundations of Religious Tolerance* (Toronto: University of Toronto Press, 1982), chap. 4.

22. Gans, *Deciding What's News*.

23. Ibid., p. 313.

24. Ibid., p. 332.

25. Ibid.

26. Ibid., p. 305.

27. Ibid., p. 310.

28. Ibid., p. 306.

29. Ibid., p. 207.

30. Ibid., pp. 208–12.

31. Plato *Republic* 369D–370A, 374B–D.

32. Newman, *Foundations of Religious Tolerance*, pp. 28–29.

33. Gans, *Deciding What's News*, p. 334.

34. Cf. Newman, *Foundations of Religious Tolerance*, chap. 5.

35. William Gass, "The Case of the Obliging Stranger," *Philosophical Review* 66 (1957), 204.

36. John Milton, *Areopagitica* (1644), in *John Milton*, Paradise Lost *and Selected Poetry and Prose*, ed. Northrop Frye (New York: Holt, Rinehart and Winston, 1965), pp. 473–74.

Chapter 5. The Ideal of a Free Press

1. Plato *Republic* 557A–558C.

2. Ibid., 575B–580C.

3. Martin, *The Press*, p. 22.

4. The Commission on Freedom of the Press, *A Free and Responsible Press*, p. 6.

5. Hocking, *Freedom of the Press*, p. 89.

6. Innis, *Bias of Communication*, pp. 80–81.

7. Ibid., pp. 28–29, 32, 80.

8. Servan-Schreiber, *Power to Inform*, p. 241.

9. Ibid.

10. Innis, *Bias of Communication*, pp. 28–29.

11. Servan-Schreiber, *Power to Inform*, p. 275.

12. Martin, *The Press*, p. 140.

13. The Commission on Freedom of the Press, *A Free and Responsible Press*, p. 119.

14. Ibid., p. 129.

15. Ibid., pp.37–51.

16. Ibid., p. 94.

17. Ibid., p. 83.

18. Ibid., p. 18.

19. Ibid., p. 10.

20. Ibid., p. 18.

21. Hocking, *Freedom of the Press*, p. 69.

22. Lippmann, *Essays*, p. 126.

23. The Commission on Freedom of the Press, *A Free and Responsible Press*, pp. 20–21.

24. Lippmann, *Essays*, p. 127.

25. Ibid., pp. 127–29.

26. Theodore Peterson, in Siebert *et al.*, *Four Theories*, p. 24.

27. Ibid.

28. It is widely held that this expression first appeared in Thomas Babington Macauley's 1828 essay on Hallam's *Constitutional History*. Cf., for example, Mott, *News in America*, p. 6.

29. Merrill, *Imperative of Freedom*, p. 3.

30. Ibid., pp. 3–4.

31. Ibid., p. 78. Cf. pp. 78–84.

32. Ibid., p. 27.

33. Ibid., p. 93.

34. Ibid., p. 95.

35. Ibid., p. 5.

36. Ibid., pp. 17–18.

37. Ibid., pp. 170–82.

38. The Commission on Freedom of the Press, *A Free and Responsible Press*, p. 132.

39. Siebert et al., pp. 1–2.

40. Plato *Republic* 592A–B.

41. Servan-Schreiber, *Power to Inform*, p. 242.

42. Hood, *Ourselves and the Press*, p. 55.

43. Ibid., pp. 264–65.

44. Lippmann, *Public Opinion*, p. 362.

45. Plato *Republic* 592A–B.

46. Stephen Klaidman and Tom L. Beauchamp, *The Virtuous Journalist* (New York: Oxford University Press, 1987), p. vii.

47. Ibid., p. 9.

48. Ibid., p. 10.

49. Ibid., p. 12.

50. Ibid., pp. 5–14.

51. T. B. K. L. [Tenney Barbara K. Lehman], "Three Cheers and a Fanfare," *Nieman Reports* 41, no. 3 (1987): 2.

52. Robert B. Downs and Ralph E. McCoy, ed., *The First Freedom Today: Critical Issues Relating to Censorship and to Intellectual Freedom* (Chicago: American Library Association, 1984).

53. Paul Kurtz.

54. Downs and McCoy, "Introduction" to *The First Freedom Today*, p. xiii.

55. Spinoza, *Theologico-Political Treatise*, ch. 20.

56. Lester A. Sobel, "Introduction" to Lester A. Sobel, ed., *Media Controversies* (New York: Facts on File Inc., 1981), pp. 2–3.

57. Ibid., p. 2.

58. Klaidman and Beauchamp, *The Virtuous Journalist*, pp. ix–x.

59. Immanuel Kant, *The Doctrine of Virtue* (pt. 2 of *The Metaphysic of Morals*), trans. Mary J. Gregor (New York: Harper and Row, 1964), pp. 87–90.

60. Klaidman and Beauchamp, *The Virtuous Journalist*, p. 170.

61. Ibid.

62. Ibid., pp. 17–19.

63. Ibid., p. 20.

64. Douglas Anderson, "How Managing Editors View and Deal with Ethical Issues," *Journalism Quarterly* 64 (1987): 341.

65. Ibid., p. 345.

66. Ibid.

67. *Print Journalism: A Training Profile* (N.p.: [Ontario] Ministry of Colleges and Universities, 1984), p. 5.

68. Ibid., pp. 16, 24, 37.

69. Spinoza, *Theologico-Political Treatise*, pp. 258–59. I have modified the spelling of one word and italicized the last sentence.

Chapter 6. Journalism and Philosophy

1. José Ortega y Gasset, *Mission of the University*, trans. Howard L. Nostrand (New York: W. W. Norton, 1966), pp. 89–91. Cf. Merrill, *Imperative of Freedom*, p. 10.

2. Merrill, *Imperative of Freedom*, p. 165.

3. Ibid., p. 143.

4. Servan-Schreiber, *Power to Inform*, p. 124.

5. Mott, *News in America*, p. 22.

6. William James, quoted by Norman Hapgood in *The Changing Years: Reminiscences* (New York, 1930).

7. Innis, *Bias of Communication*, p. 79.

8. McLuhan, *Understanding Media*, p. 204.

9. Ibid., p. 207.

10. Fulford, "Press in the Community," pp. 29–30.

11. Lippmann, *Essays*, p. 113.

12. G. E. Moore, *Principia Ethica* (Cambridge: Cambridge University Press, 1903), chap. 1.

13. Innis, *Bias of Communication*, p. 195.

14. Ibid., pp. 83–84.

15. Karl Marx, *Theses on Feuerbach*, no. 11.

16. Cf., for example, Alexander Herzberg, *The Psychology of Philosophers*, trans. E. B. F. Wareing (London: Kegan Paul, Trench, Trubner, 1929).

17. Jay Newman, "The Unconscious Origins of Philosophical Inquiry," *Philosophical Forum* 9 (1978): 409–28.

18. Plato *Apology* 23A.

19. Milton, *Areopagitica*, p. 503.

20. Mishnah Aboth 4.1.

21. Innis, *Bias of Communication*, p. 83.

22. Cf. Newman, *Foundations of Religious Tolerance*.

23. Walter Lippmann, *A Preface to Morals* (New York: Macmillan, 1929).

24. Herbert Spencer, *The Principles of Sociology*, 3 vols. (New York: D. Appleton, 1899), 3: 129.

25. Plato *Republic* 427B–C.

26. A recent discussion of Plato's views on religion is Michel Despland, *The Education of Desire: Plato and the Philosophy of Religion* (Toronto: University of Toronto Press, 1985).

27. Lippmann, *Public Opinion*, p. 416.

28. Harry Golden, *Only in America* (Cleveland, Ohio: World Publishing, 1958).

29. Plato *Apology* 31C–32A.

30. Merrill, *Imperative of Freedom*, pp. 138–42.

31. R. G. Collingwood, *Speculum Mentis* (Oxford: Clarendon Press, 1924), p. 13.

32. Lippmann, *Public Opinion*, p. 418.

Bibliography

Adams, Larry L. *Walter Lippmann*. Boston: Twayne, 1977.

Adler, Alfred. *Understanding Human Nature*. Translated by W. Béran Wolfe. London: George Allen and Unwin, 1928.

Anderson, Douglas. "How Managing Editors View and Deal with Ethical Issues." *Journalism Quarterly* 64 (1987): 341–45.

Annas, Julia. *An Introduction to Plato's* Republic. Oxford: Clarendon Press, 1981.

Aristophanes. *The Clouds*.

Aristotle. *Metaphysics*.

———. *Nicomachean Ethics*.

———. *Poetics*.

———. *Politics*.

———. *Rhetoric*.

Armour, Leslie, and Elizabeth Trott. *The Faces of Reason: An Essay on Philosophy and Culture in English Canada, 1850–1950*. Waterloo, Ont.: Wilfrid Laurier University Press, 1981.

Blanchard, Margaret A. "The Hutchins Commission, The Press and the Responsibility Concept." *Journalism Monographs* 49 (May 1977).

Blum, D. Stephen. *Walter Lippmann: Cosmopolitanism in the Century of Total War*. Ithaca: Cornell University Press, 1984.

Breed, Warren. *The Newspaperman, News and Society*. New York: Arno Press, 1980. This work was Breed's doctoral dissertation in sociology at Columbia University.

Brown, Charles H. *Informing the Public*. New York: Holt, Rinehart and Winston, 1957.

Brucker, Herbert. *Freedom of Information*. New York: Macmillan, 1949.

Calvert, Brian. "Plato and the Equality of Women." *Phoenix* 29 (1975): 231–43.

Childs, Marquis, and James Reston, eds. *Walter Lippmann and His Times*. New York: Harcourt, Brace, 1959.

Collingwood, R. G. *The New Leviathan*. Oxford: Clarendon Press, 1942.

———. *Speculum Mentis*. Oxford: Clarendon Press, 1924.

Commission on Freedom of the Press, The. *A Free and Responsible Press*. Chicago: University of Chicago Press, 1947.

Crombie, I. M. *An Examination of Plato's Doctrines*. 2 vols. London: Routledge and Kegan Paul; New York: Humanities Press, 1962.

Cross, R. C., and A. D. Woozley. *Plato's Republic: A Philosophical Commentary*. London: Macmillan; New York: St. Martin's Press, 1964.

Dam, Hari N. *The Intellectual Odyssey of Walter Lippmann*. New York: Gordon Press, 1973.

Despland, Michel. *The Education of Desire: Plato and the Philosophy of Religion*. Toronto: University of Toronto Press, 1985.

201

Dewey, John. *Democracy and Education*. New York: Macmillan, 1916.

————. *Reconstruction in Philosophy*. New York: Henry Holt, 1920.

Downs, Robert B., and Ralph E. McCoy, eds. *The First Freedom Today: Critical Issues Relating to Censorship and to Intellectual Freedom*. Chicago: American Library Association, 1984.

Efron, Edith. *The News Twisters*. Los Angeles: Nash, 1971.

Ellul, Jacques. *Propaganda: The Formation of Men's Attitudes*. Translated by Konrad Kellen and Jean Lerner. New York: Alfred A. Knopf, 1968.

Epictetus. *Manual*.

Fraser, Lindley. *Propaganda*. London: Oxford University Press, 1957.

Fulford, Robert. "The Press in the Community." *The Press and the Public: 8th Winter Conference*. Edited by D. L. B. Hamlin. Toronto: University of Toronto Press (for the Canadian Institute on Public Affairs), 1962.

Gans, Herbert J. *Deciding What's News: A Study of* CBS Evening News, NBC Nightly News, Newsweek, *and* Time. New York: Pantheon Books, 1979.

Gouldner, Alvin W. *Enter Plato: Classical Greece and the Origins of Social Theory*. New York: Basic Books, 1965.

Guthrie, W. K. C. *A History of Greek Philosophy*. 5 vols. Cambridge: Cambridge University Press, 1962–78.

Hall, Robert W. *Plato*. London: George Allen and Unwin, 1981.

Hare, William. *In Defence of Open-mindedness*. Montreal: McGill-Queen's University Press, 1985.

————. *Open-mindedness and Education*. Montreal: McGill-Queen's University Press, 1979.

Hennessey, Bernard C. *Public Opinion*. 3d ed. North Scituate, Mass.: Duxbury Press, 1975.

Herzberg, Alexander. *The Psychology of Philosophers*. Translated by E. B. F. Wareing. London: Kegan Paul, Trench, Trubner, 1929.

Hocking, William Ernest. *Freedom of the Press: A Framework of Principle*. Chicago: University of Chicago Press, 1947.

Hofstadter, Richard. *Anti-intellectualism in American Life*. New York: Alfred A. Knopf, 1963.

Hohenberg, John. *The Professional Journalist*. A Holt-Dryden Book. New York: Henry Holt, 1960.

Hood, Peter. *Ourselves and the Press*. London: John Lane the Bodley Head, 1939.

Hornby, Robert. *The Press in Modern Society*. London: Frederick Muller, 1965.

Hynds, Ernest C. *American Newspapers in the 1970s*. New York: Hastings House, 1975.

Ickes, Harold L. *America's House of Lords: An Inquiry Into the Freedom of the Press*. New York: Harcourt, Brace, 1939.

Innis, Harold A. *The Bias of Communication*. Toronto: University of Toronto Press, 1951.

————. *Empire and Communications*. Oxford: Clarendon Press, 1950.

Kerferd, G. B. "Plato's Account of the Relativism of Protagoras." *Durham University Journal* 42 (1949): 20–26.

————. *The Sophistic Movement*. Cambridge: Cambridge University Press, 1981.

Klaidman, Stephen, and Beauchamp, Tom L. *The Virtuous Journalist*. New York: Oxford University Press, 1987.

Klosko, George. *The Development of Plato's Political Theory*. New York and London: Methuen, 1986.

Krieghbaum, Hillier. *Pressures on the Press*. New York: Thomas Y. Crowell, 1972.

Levinson, Ronald B. *In Defense of Plato*. Cambridge: Harvard University Press, 1953.

Liebling, A. J. *The Press*. New York: Ballantine Books, 1964.

Lippmann, Walter. *Essays in the Public Philosophy*. An Atlantic Monthly Press Book. Boston and Toronto: Little, Brown, 1955.

———. *An Inquiry Into the Principles of the Good Society*. Boston: Little, Brown, 1938.

———. *Liberty and the News*. New York: Harcourt, Brace, and Howe, 1920.

———. *The Phantom Public*. New York: Macmillan, 1927.

———. *A Preface to Morals*. New York: Macmillan, 1929.

———. *Public Opinion*. New York: Macmillan, 1922.

Lodge, Rupert C. *The Philosophy of Plato*. London: Routledge and Kegan Paul, 1956.

Lucas, Christopher J., ed. *What is Philosophy of Education?* New York: Macmillan, 1969.

Luskin, John. *Lippmann, Liberty, and the Press*. University, Ala.: University of Alabama Press, 1972.

McCormick, Robert R. *What is a Newspaper?* Chicago: Public Service Bureau of *The Chicago Tribune*, 1924.

Machiavelli, Niccolò. *The Prince* (1515).

McLuhan, Marshall. *The Gutenberg Galaxy*. Toronto: University of Toronto Press, 1962.

———. *Understanding Media*. New York: McGraw-Hill, 1964.

Martin, Kingsley. *The Press the Public Wants*. London: Hogarth Press, 1947.

Merrill, John C. *The Elite Press: Great Newspapers of the World*. New York: Pitman, 1968.

———. *The Imperative of Freedom: A Philosophy of Journalistic Autonomy*. Communications Arts Books. New York: Hastings House, 1974.

Mill, John Stuart. *On Liberty* (1859).

Milton, John. *Areopagitica* (1644).

Mott, Frank Luther. *American Journalism, A History: 1690–1960*. 3d ed. New York: Macmillan, 1962.

———. *The News in America*. Cambridge: Harvard University Press, 1962.

Nettleship, Richard Lewis. *Lectures on the* Republic *of Plato*. 2nd ed. London: Macmillan, 1901.

Newman, Jay. *Fanatics and Hypocrites*. Buffalo: Prometheus Books, 1986.

———. *Foundations of Religious Tolerance*. Toronto: University of Toronto Press, 1982.

Nietzsche, Friedrich. *Beyond Good and Evil: A Prelude to a Philosophy of the Future* (1886).

Ortega y Gasset, José. *Mission of the University*. Translated by Howard L. Nostrand. New York: W. W. Norton, 1966.

———. *The Origin of Philosophy*. Translated by Toby Talbot. New York: W. W. Norton, 1967.

Plato. *Apology*.

——. *The Collected Dialogues*. Edited by Edith Hamilton and Huntington Cairns. Bollingen Series. Princeton: Princeton University Press, 1961.

——. *Euthyphro*.

——. *Gorgias*.

——. *Ion*.

——. *Protagoras*.

——. *Republic*.

——. *Theaetetus*.

Popper, K. R. *The Open Society and Its Enemies*. Vol. I, *The Spell of Plato*. 4th ed. Princeton: Princeton University Press, 1963.

Print Journalism: A Training Profile. N.p.: [Ontario] Ministry of Colleges and Universities, 1984.

Raven, J. E. *Plato's Thought in the Making*. Cambridge: Cambridge University Press, 1965.

Robinson, T. M. *Plato's Psychology*. Toronto: University of Toronto Press, 1970.

Ross, Sir David. *Plato's Theory of Ideas*. Oxford: Clarendon Press, 1951.

Schapsmeier, Edward L., and Frederick H. Schapsmeier. *Walter Lippmann: Philosopher-Journalist*. Washington, D.C.: Public Affairs Press, 1969.

Schlesinger, Arthur M. Jr. "Walter Lippmann: The Intellectual v. Politics." *Walter Lippmann and His Times*. Edited by Marquis Childs and James Reston. New York: Harcourt, Brace, 1959.

Servan-Schreiber, Jean-Louis. *The Power to Inform*. Translated with the cooperation of Paris Research Associates. New York: McGraw-Hill, 1974.

Shorey, Paul. *What Plato Said*. Chicago: University of Chicago Press, 1933.

Siebert, Fred S., Theodore Peterson, and Wilbur Schramm. *Four Theories of the Press*. Urbana, Ill.: University of Illinois Press, 1956.

Smith, Anthony. *Goodbye Gutenberg: The Newspaper Revolution of the 1980's*. New York and Oxford: Oxford University Press, 1980.

——. *The Newspaper: An International History*. London: Thames and Hudson, 1979.

Sobel, Lester A., ed. *Media Controversies*. New York: Facts on File Inc., 1981.

Spinoza, Baruch. *A Theologico-Political Treatise* (1670).

Taylor, A. E. *Plato: The Man and His Work*. London: Methuen, 1926.

Untersteiner, Mario. *The Sophists*. Translated by Kathleen Freeman. Oxford: Basil Blackwell, 1962.

Wellborn, Charles. *Twentieth Century Pilgrimage: Walter Lippmann and the Public Philosophy*. Baton Rouge, La.: Louisiana State University Press, 1969.

White, Nicholas P. *A Companion to Plato's* Republic. Indianapolis, Ind.: Hackett, 1979.

Winspear, Alban Dewes. *The Genesis of Plato's Thought*. 2d ed. New York: S. A. Russell, 1956.

Index

205